THE TANNADICE ENCYCLOPEDIA

THE TANNADICE ENCYCLOPEDIA

An A–Z of Dundee United

MIKE WATSON
with Matthew Watson

MAINSTREAM
PUBLISHING

EDINBURGH AND LONDON

Author's Note

An asterisk* in the text indicates that the entry is cross-referenced. To avoid over-use, this does not apply to current Scottish League clubs.

First published in Great Britain in 1997 by
MAINSTREAM PUBLISHING COMPANY (EDINBURGH) LTD
7 Albany Street
Edinburgh EH1 3UG

ISBN 1 85158 996 1

A catalogue record for this book is available from the British Library

Typeset in Janson
Printed and bound in Great Britain by Butler and Tanner Ltd, Frome

This book is dedicated to the memory of
Patrick Reilly (1874-1937)

Illustrations

The cover illustrations are (*left to right*): Peter McKay; (*centre top*) Maurice Malpas lifts the Scottish Cup in 1994; (*centre bottom*) Dundee Hibs v Forfar 1911; Duncan Hutchison; (*back*) 1994 Scottish Cup final - the goal.

The majority of the photographs featured are the copyright of publishers DC Thomson. They supplied all those featured on the cover, plus those on the following pages: 13, 33, 37, 46, 56, 94, 147, 157, 158, 172, 178/9, 182, 189 and 220.

With the exception of that on page 169 (courtesy of *The Catholic Herald*) the remainder of the illustrations were supplied from the personal collections of Peter Rundo and Mike Watson.

Acknowledgements

My intention was to ensure that *The Tannadice Encyclopedia* was not overburdened by statistics. On the other hand, any serious football history is, by definition, a statistical record. I hope I have succeeded in striking a balance between words and figures which will serve to make the book an interesting and entertaining read as well as a valuable reference source.

In pursuit of that aim, a useful constraint was the amount of time needed for the preparation of accurate figures; even then, had it not been for the unstinting effort of Matthew Watston (no relation) the detail associated with the playing records against the other League clubs would not have been possible and I am extremely grateful for his assistance. Matthew's father, Dave, also spent hours at the laborious arithmetic involved in ensuring that these records are as accurate as possible. That said, any errors or omissions in these sections remain my responsibility.

As editor of the club programme and monthly magazine, Peter Rundo is the recognised statistical authority on Dundee United and the finished article would have been much diminished without his assistance, particularly in respect of players' appearances.

Fraser McLean has also assembled a vast amount of detailed records on various aspects of the club and he it was who, with deadlines fast approaching, come to my aid with missing pieces of information which had proved unobtainable from any other source.

Much of the information relating to under-21 and youth caps is available only from the Scottish Football Association. Thanks are due in no small measure to the SFA's press and public relations officer, Andy Mitchell, not simply for welcoming me within the hallowed portals of 6 Park Gardens, but for providing the information available in a form which made my task much more straightforward than it would otherwise have been.

This book would not have been possible without access to the vast files of cuttings and photographs held by the publishers D.C. Thomson in Dundee. As in the past when I have requested access, it was willingly granted, for which I am most appreciative. However, further assistance was readily provided by Joyce Lorimer, head of the photo-files department, who spent considerable time preparing for my visits, thus simplifying and curtailing my research. I would also like to record my thanks to Ron Caird for his help in facilitating the provision of the photographs which were eventually chosen for inclusion.

Assistance was also provided in various ways by Ken Gallacher, Neil Glen, Malcolm Hartley, George Hill, Norrie Price and John Reilly for which I am most grateful.

Proof-reading the text for inaccuracies, omissions or gaffes is a thankless and wearing task, yet it was willingly undertaken by John McGregor, Fraser McLean and Derek Robertson, three lifelong Arabs to whom I am most grateful. Thanks are also due to John for researching the information relating to Clepington Park.

Finally, I pay tribute to the support and forbearance of my wife Lorraine, who for months saw much less of me than did my keyboard and screen. She commented that '. . it had better be worth it!' Hope it is.

Introduction

No matter the club, for most supporters, discussion, dissent and disputation on the ghosts of football past are as much a part of the game as the most recent match action – and rightly so. The people who support their club – often at considerable expense – are the most important part of it and their involvement and commitment extends far beyond 90 minutes each week . For them it is not just an integral part of their life, but a life sentence – unlike the players, manager and, increasingly, directors who are simply passing through. That is not intended as a criticism, simply a statement of fact.

The dilemma with a book such as this is not what to include, rather what to exclude. Doubtless, on both scores, my decisions will stimulate argument. It may settle some disagreements about aspects of the fascinating history of Dundee United, a great club which has consistently defied the various stereotypes which fit most others in Scottish football; I trust it will also provoke a few.

There was no limit imposed on the number of players to be featured in *The Tannadice Encyclopedia*; qualification was achieved by meeting at least one of the following criteria :

* to have won a medal in one of the club's four trophy successes between 1979 and 1994;

* to have won full international recognition while at the club;

* or – a bit of a catch-all this, and necessarily subjective – to have made a
particularly noteworthy contribution as a player with Dundee Hibs/United.

To Arabs who find their favourite hasn't made it then I can only say, sorry, but he must have had talents of which I was unaware !

Where reference is made to a club drawn against Dundee Hibs/United in one of the domestic trophies, the year used signifies when the match actually took place. Thus, for example, the year 1985 would signify season

1984/85 for the Scottish Cup, given that that competition is played in the second half of the season. The same year would signify 1985/86 for the League Cup, because it is played at the beginning of the season. In the very few cases where there have been exceptions to this, these are indicated.

The percentage appearing in brackets following the League record against other clubs represents United's success rate.

Unless otherwise stated, informaton has been collated and statistics calculated up to the end of season 1996/97.

ABANDONED MATCHES

Throughout the club's history, only four matches involving Dundee Hibs/United have been abandoned. All of them happened at Tannadice.

The first occurred during the club's inaugural season, a meeting between Dundee Hibs and their then chief local rivals, Dundee Wanderers, on 25 April 1910. The match was being staged for the benefit of a Wanderers player, but was brought to a premature end due to bad light. Being a testimonial, it was not replayed.

The same problem also caused the abandonment of the Division Two fixture with Brechin City on 14 December 1935 and United were very much the losers as a result. They were leading 5–1 when darkness descended, but when the match was replayed, on 2 January, it ended in a 2–2 draw.

Almost 40 years elapsed before the next occurrence. On 3 November 1973, United were leading Falkirk 2–0 in a Division One fixture with only seven minutes remaining when the referee decided that the fog which had been present for much of the afternoon made further play impossible. The match was replayed 18 days later, on a Wednesday afternoon due to restrictions on the use of floodlights during the National Union of Mineworkers strike then under way. For that reason, the match attracted an attendance of only 1,250, the lowest ever at Tannadice for a League match in the top division. Although the re-match was rather closer than the original, at least United did not suffer a loss of points, winning it 2–1.

The most recent abandonment came in a Premier Division match on 6 October 1990 in which Dunfermline Athletic were the visitors. Torrential rain throughout had left pools of water across the pitch and shortly after half-time the referee decided play could not continue. With United 2–1 ahead, it was not a decision welcomed by many Arabs, but they need not have worried, the margin of victory was extended to 3–0 when the match was replayed four days later.

ABERCORN FC

Abercorn were one of the original members of the Scottish League in

1890. Based in Paisley, they were for many years the premier club in that town. They were the second visitors to Tannadice in Dundee Hibs' inaugural season as a Scottish League club, the Hibs winning 4–1 on 17 September 1910. That result was to set the pattern for meetings between the clubs over the next five seasons, home advantage usually proving decisive. Hibs were undefeated at Tannadice, but won only once at Ralston Park.

The clubs last met in season 1914/15. Abercorn did not return to the Scottish League after World War One and the club disbanded in 1921.

The full Scottish League record against Abercorn was:
P 10 W 5 D 1 L 4 F 16 A 14

ABERDEEN FC

The club's first meetings with Aberdeen were at reserve-team level – at least, as far as Aberdeen were concerned. Dundee Hibs met Aberdeen 'A' in their first season in the Northern League* and also encountered them in local north-eastern cup competitions.

The clubs did not meet at first-team level until Dundee United reached the First Division in 1925, and had three further seasons in that division between then and 1932. Thereafter they did not meet at League level until 1960, but since then the only season missed was the one following United's relegation in 1995.

In 1967, the clubs met in Washington DC as part of the North American Soccer League* and nine years later were drawn together in the Anglo-Scottish Cup*.

During the 1980s, the success enjoyed by Aberdeen and United at the expense of Celtic and Rangers led to the North East clubs being dubbed 'the New Firm'. Between 1979 and 1989, United won the Premier Division championship and two League Cups*, while Aberdeen won the championship three times, the Scottish Cup on four occasions and the League Cup twice. They also famously won the European Cup Winners' Cup* in 1983 and surpassed even that by adding the European Super Cup a few months later. The rivalry of the two managers, Jim McLean* and Alex Ferguson, as well as that of the fans, fired the two clubs to a level of achievement which was largely responsible for Celtic and Rangers responding with the massive investment which these clubs have made in the 1990s. The unfortunate result is that it is difficult to envisage the New Firm - or any other Scottish club for that matter - again achieving that level of supremacy over the Glasgow clubs.

It's a fact: Aberdeen hold the record for the biggest victory by a visiting team at Tannadice. The Dons' 9–1 win came in a wartime North Eastern League* fixture on 10 February 1945.

The playing record against Aberdeen in major competitions is:
Scottish League (total): P 122 W 36 D 37 L 49 F 146 A 181 (45%)

Premier Division: P 84 W 26 D 25 L 32 F 96 A 110 (46%)

Scottish Cup: the clubs were drawn together in 1952, 1966, 1967 (semi-final), 1971, 1972, 1975, 1984, 1985 (semi-final), 1988 (semi-final), 1989, 1990 (semi-final), 1993 and 1994 (semi-final).
Record: P 22 W 4 D 9 L 9 F 14 A 31

League Cup: the clubs were drawn together in 1961, 1963, 1966, 1967, 1968, 1973, 1981 (semi-final), 1982, 1985 and 1988 (semi-final). They also met in the 1979 final.
Record: P 21 W 8 D 5 L 8 F 32 A 28

Summer Cup: the clubs met in sectional ties in both 1964 and 1965.
Record: P 4 W 3 D 0 L 1 F 9 A 7

Notable transfers to: Francis Munro (1966), Mixu Paatelainen* (1992)

Notable transfers from: Bobby Temple (1938), Ray McKinnon (1995)

It's another fact: United have played more Scottish Cup ties against Aberdeen than against any other club.

AFRICA

United have visited Africa on two occasions. In June and July of 1963, the club ventured abroad for the first time, and in doing so did not indulge in half-measures. In a sojourn lasting a month, a total of nine matches were played in Nyasaland (now Malawi), Northern Rhodesia (now Zambia), South Africa and Southern Rhodesia (now Zimbabwe). The unfamiliar conditions may have had something to do with the fact that the players did not have things all their own way: five matches were

United's Donald Mackay with a local dignitary prior to a match in Bulawayo during the club's visit to Southern Rhodesia in 1963. To Mackay's right is manager Jerry Kerr, to his left, team-mates Benny Rooney and Tommy Millar

won, two drawn and two lost, with a goals total of 29–16. It must have been the trip of a lifetime for the players, though it deprived them of a close-season break, the party arriving back in Dundee on 17 July, a mere three weeks before the new season got under way.

In 1963, a visit to these apartheid regimes raised scarcely an eyebrow, though it would have been politically impossible nine years later when United returned to that continent. Some lessons had been learned, not least that the visit should be both earlier and shorter. On this occasion the destination was Nigeria, where five games were played during the tour, which lasted for two and a half weeks. United won only one of their matches, losing two and drawing the same number. With a goal tally of 5–9, it can be seen that the first signs of Nigeria emerging as a footballing nation were in evidence.

AIRDRIEONIANS FC

The clubs first met in a Scottish Cup tie in 1914, in which Airdrie beat Dundee Hibs 5–0 at Broomfield Park.

The second time they came into contact was an embarrassing experience for the Hibs. It occurred in 1922/23 in what was the club's worst ever season, bar none. Having lost their Scottish League place they played in the Scottish Alliance*, a league which comprised the reserve teams of Division One clubs. Despite that, the Hibs could do no better than finish third from bottom, and their heaviest defeat, in April 1923, was 0–7 at Airdrie – yes, it was that bad!

The next meeting – the first time the clubs had met in the Scottish League – took place in Division One and provided a stark example of the swift turnaround in the club's fortunes brought about by Jimmy Brownlie*. It was in April 1923 when Dundee Hibs lost by seven goals to Airdrie reserves at Broomfield Park, yet in December 1925 Dundee United won 1–0 at Broomfield Park against Airdrie who that season finished runners-up in Division One for the fourth consecutive season.

United's three further seasons in Division One and Airdrie's three in Division Two saw their only other meetings at League level between the wars; though they were joint members of Southern League* B Division in 1945/46. They shared a total of four seasons in B Division before United won promotion in 1960, and they then met regularly until the inception of the Premier Division, of which Airdrie have been members on only four occasions. **It's a fact:** Airdrie were the only club United failed to beat in their brief sojourn in the First Division in 1995/96; they won once, at Tannadice, and the remaining matches were drawn.

The playing record against Airdrieonians in major competitions is:
Scottish League (total): P 68 W 24 D 17 L 27 F 134 A 132 (49%)
Premier Division: P 16 W 10 D 3 L 3 F 32 A 10 (78%)
Scottish Cup:　the clubs were drawn together in 1914, 1927, 1937, 1974, 1987, 1988, 1991 and 1994.
　　　　　　　Record: P 9 W 5 D 2 L 2 F 14 A 11
League Cup:　the clubs were drawn together in 1949 and 1979.
　　　　　　　Record : P 4 W 2 D 0 L 2 F 11 A 7
Notable transfers to: Gordon McLeod (1993), Paddy Connolly (1996)
Notable transfers from: Gibby Ormond (1960)

ALBION ROVERS FC

Albion Rovers were already members of Division Two when Dundee Hibs were elected to it in 1910. They remained together in that division until its suspension in 1915, but met less frequently in the inter-war period due to each club having a total of four seasons in Division One, though never concurrently. They did, however, meet in Southern League* B Division in 1945/46.

After the war, with the exception of the one season which Rovers managed in A Division, life in the lower regions was the order of the day for both clubs until 1960. United then won promotion, consolidated their position in Division One, and the clubs have not met since in the League.

The clubs met in the final of the Qualifying Cup* in 1913. The first match, watched by a crowd of 11,000, was held at Tynecastle Park, as was the replay. Both finished level at 1–1, but Rovers ran out 3–0 winners in the third match at Easter Road.

The playing record against Albion Rovers in major competitions is:
Scottish League: P 52 W 21 D 7 L 24 F 104 A 95 (47%)
Scottish Cup: the clubs have been drawn together just once, in 1963 when United won 3–0 at Tannadice.
League Cup: the clubs were drawn together in 1947, 1955 and 1977. Record: P 6 W 3 D 1 L 2 F16 A 11
Notable transfers to: Bill Monteith (1911)
Notable transfers from: Tommy Campbell (1960), Tommy Dunne (1967)
It's a fact: United last met Albion Rovers in a League match at Cliftonhill Park in February 1960. Despite his team's 4–1 victory, manager Jerry Kerr* was so impressed with the Rovers centre forward that he signed him three days later. Tommy Campbell scored nine times in the final seven matches of the season to help United secure promotion.

Jimmy ALLAN   (born 1897; died 1982)

He was appointed United manager following the termination of Bobby McKay's* contract on the outbreak of the Second World War.

Allan took the club to its first major cup final, in the Emergency War Cup*, against Rangers at Hampden Park in May 1940, but resigned in July of that year when the club decided not to compete in season 1940/41. He agreed to manage the surrogate club, United Juniors*, and remained with them even though United returned to senior competition for season 1941/42.

He lived for much of his life in the Lochee district of the city and ran a barber's shop there for more than 40 years. He had a brief senior career playing for Cowdenbeath and Falkirk before becoming trainer at Tannadice.

ALLOA ATHLETIC FC

Dundee Hibs' first contact with Alloa came in the Central League* of 1920/21 and both clubs were among those accepted into Division Two the following season.

Apart from the four seasons which Dundee United spent in Division One between 1925 and 1932, they and Alloa were inseparable from 1923 until 1960, sharing League status each season. This does not include wartime, although the clubs did meet in the Southern League* of 1945/46. In contrast, the clubs have not played a League match since United were promoted in 1960, nor is there much likelihood of them doing so again.

It's a fact: When Alloa visited Tannadice for a Division Two match in April 1958, they triumphed 7–1 in one of United's heaviest-ever home defeats. Three of the goals were scored by Dennis Gillespie* and the Alloa manager was Jerry Kerr*; a year later both began careers at Tannadice which lasted well into the 1970s.

The playing record against Alloa Athletic in major competitions is:

Scottish League: P 54 W 25 D 11 L 18 F 122 A 100 (56%)

Scottish Cup: the clubs have been drawn together only twice, in 1934 and 1936.
  Record: P 4 W 1 D 2 L 1 F 7 A 8

League Cup: the clubs were drawn together in 1983, 1985 and 1990.
  Record: P 4 W 4 D 0 L 0 F 14 A 2

Notable transfers from: Dennis Gillespie* (1959)

ANGLO-SCOTTISH CUP

This trophy was competed for between 1975 and 1981 and the Scottish entrants were the top four clubs in the Premier Division the previous season which had not qualified for one of the European competitions. As a result, United took part only once – and very briefly at that. In season 1976/77 they played Aberdeen, winning the home leg 1–0 but going down 1–3 in the return at Pittodrie.

APPEARANCES

Between 1910 and 1922 (six seasons), a total of 103 signed players appeared for Dundee Hibs in Scottish League matches. With 105 appearances, Willie Linn was the only one to reach three figures, the nearest being Tom Boland (75) and George Forbes (67).

Since 1923 (67 seasons), a total of 584 players have represented Dundee United in the Scottish League (including substitute appearances, but excluding trialists). Thirty-four made but a single appearance, while the following comprise the top ten:

1	Dave Narey	612	(1973–93)
2	Maurice Malpas+	543	(1981–97)

3	Paul Hegarty	493	(1974–89)
4	Hamish McAlpine	477	(1969–85)
5	Doug Smith	456	(1959–76)
6	Paul Sturrock	386	(1974–89)
7	Dennis Gillespie	346	(1959–71)
8	Andy Rolland	328	(1967–78)
9	Dave Bowman+	317	(1986–97)
10	Jim McInally	302	(1986–97)

+ still with the club at the start of season 1997/98

The greatest number of signed players to be used by the club during a League season is 34 in the promotion year of 1959/60. Two trialists were also used that season, bringing the total to 36, but this falls well short of the record, which was set two years earlier. Amazingly, during 1957/58, a total of 57 players appeared for United in their 36 Division Two matches, of whom 26 were signed players and 31 trialists.

The fewest players fielded by the club during a League season is 16 in 1934/35 (14 signed, plus two trialists).

ARABS

The collective noun applicable to supporters of Dundee United. It is now fairly common currency among tabloid sports journalists, though some remain confused as to whom it actually refers, sometimes mistakenly using it to describe the team (as in headlines such as 'Arabs grab late equaliser'). Just as Hibees are the team, while Hibbies are the fans, Jam Tarts are the team while Jambos are the fans, so Dundee United are the Terrors while their supporters are Arabs (the definite article is rarely used).

The origin of the term is guaranteed to spark debate among those to whom it applies; by its very nature, there is no definitive explanation. It is probably fair to say that the most commonly accepted version dates back to the mid-1960s. The winter of 1962/63 was particularly harsh and United had already been denied two matches due to Tannadice being icebound when the Scottish Cup third-round tie with Albion Rovers that January was also postponed. At this, the management decided on a radical – some would say desperate – measure to get the pitch playable, hiring a tar burner of the kind used by road-layers to melt the ice. That it did, though with the predictable after-effect of leaving the playing surface all but devoid of grass. Undaunted, the directors ordered several lorry-loads of sand, spread it around, painted some lines on it and, astonishingly, the referee pronounced the 'pitch' playable!

United won the tie handsomely, prompting some to comment that they had taken to the new surface 'like Arabs'. There is also dispute as to the source of this observation – was it United fans? a sports reporter? the Albion Rovers manager? or, least probable since they were most unlikely to have been there, supporters of rivals Dundee FC? Each – and no doubt several others – has their advocates, but what is not in dispute is that the term was originally applied to the *players*.

The supporters, however, quickly hijacked it for themselves, the next few matches witnessing some of the more extrovert and imaginative arriving at Tannadice with crude approximations of Arab headgear. The practice never became widespread, though gradually it came to be fairly common at derby matches. Around the late '70s and early '80s it was extended to cup semi-finals and finals, and by the early 1990s even the official club souvenir shops were selling replicas of Arab *keffiyehs* in tangerine and black.

By that time the term 'Arabs' had become more widely used, largely as the result of regular references to it by the popular United fanzine *The Final Hurdle* (see Fanzines), which first appeared in 1988.

ARBROATH FC

Being county rivals, Arbroath were regular opponents of Dundee Hibs in the club's early days. They first met in a local competition, the Carrie Cup*, at Gayfield Park in November 1909, and in the years which followed the Qualifying Cup* and, of course, the Forfarshire Cup*, provided many keenly fought and often well-attended encounters.

A League meeting had to await the reintroduction of Division Two in 1921, where they again met following the name change to Dundee United. The two clubs each had four seasons in Division One between 1925 and 1939, but never concurrently. With both Dundee clubs in Division Two during 1938/39, this left Arbroath as the county's only representative at the top level.

After sharing membership of the Southern League* B Division in 1945/46, United and Arbroath were together for the first 15 years after the war, although they continued to avoid each other in Division One, Arbroath gaining promotion in 1959, only to get themselves relegated a year later as United went up.

The only occasions on which the two clubs did meet in Division One were 1968/69, and between 1972 and 1975. Their last League meeting was at Tannadice in March 1975.

The playing record against Arbroath in major competitions is:
Scottish League: P 52 W 23 D 10 L 19 F 116 A 109 (54%)
Scottish Cup: the clubs were not drawn together until 1988, and met again in 1994.
                Record: P 2 W 2 D 0 L 0 F 10 A 2
League Cup: the clubs were drawn together in 1946, 1949, 1956, 1970 and 1977.
                Record: P 10 W 9 D 0 L 1 F 30 A 10
It's a fact: The highest scoring drawn match in which Dundee United has

been involved is 5–5. This has occurred on four occasions, two of them with Arbroath.

Notable transfers to: Frank Kopel* (1982), Graeme Payne* (1984)

ARGENTINA

Although United have never visited Argentina (nor anywhere else in South America) they have met clubs from that country on two occasions. In May 1979, they drew 2–2 with San Lorenzo in the invitation Japan Cup* tournament. Eight years later in another tournament, the Gold Cup played in Los Angeles, United fought out a 1–1 draw with Rosario Central.

The most notable connection with Argentina is of course Victor Ferreyra, the supremely talented striker who joined up at Tannadice from San Lorenzo in October 1991 for a fee which equalled United's then record of £350,000. Like many of his countrymen, his temperament got him into the odd spot of bother both with referees and opposing fans, but he was a huge favourite with Arabs, most of whom wished his stay could have been prolonged. As it was, after just 35 appearances in tangerine and black, he departed for the Mitsubishi club in Japan in 1993.

A rather less memorable Argentinian to arrive at Tannadice was Walter Rojas, who never made a first-team appearance. He had apparently been recommended to Jim McLean* by an agent in London and, having watched him perform only on video, the manager signed him for a fee of around £200,000 in the summer of 1991. It emerged that United had been the victim of duplicity; Rojas was well short of the required standard and his stay at Tannadice was a short one. The transfer fee was eventually refunded.

ARMADALE FC

Dundee Hibs first encountered Armadale in the Eastern League*, one of the regional leagues established during the First World War. The clubs met between 1915 and 1918, but Armadale then withdrew.

Contact was resumed during season 1920/21 in the Central League*, a breakaway competition set up by clubs excluded from the Scottish League, which had refused to reinstate a second division following the war. However, in 1921 Division Two was finally re-established and both Armadale and Dundee Hibs were included in it. The first League meeting took place at Volunteer Park in September 1921, Armadale winning 3–1.

League meetings continued sporadically throughout the next 11 years as Hibs/United popped in and out of Division Two, but the last League encounter took place in 1932, Armadale winning 5–3 at Volunteer Park. That result was subsequently struck from the record as Armadale were expelled from the League two months later for the non-payment of guarantees to visiting clubs. There was one final meeting, however: in the first round of the Scottish Cup that same season, United advanced by a 2–0 margin at Armadale.

The full Scottish League record against Armadale was:
P 13 W 7 D 2 L 4 F 36 A 19

ARMED FORCES

United have met teams representing the armed forces in various guises through the years. As is to be expected, the meetings occurred predominantly during wartime, though in the two decades following the Second World War, the number of young men on national service meant that the services could often field sides capable of giving League clubs a serious contest.

Professional footballers were not exempted national service and often clubs would attempt to have them stationed near to where the club was based, making them available on Saturdays. This was often possible, but even when stationed further afield, United thought nothing of bringing players 'home' for the weekend whenever commanding officers would allow it. A prime example of this was Ron Yeats*, a key member of United's 1959/60 promotion team, who regularly made the journey to and from Aldershot at the club's expense.

The following have provided United with opposition: 2/7th Argylls 1916; Royal Garrison Artillery 1917; Labour Centre Garrison XI 1918 (twice); Highland Light Infantry 1918; Army Pay Corps 1918; Canadian XI 1918; Naval XI 1933; Scottish Command XI 1941; Polish Army XI 1942; RAF XI 1942; Infantry Training Centre XI 1942; RAF Select 1943; Norwegian Forces XI 1944; Infantry Training Centre XI 1944; Polish Army XI 1946; United Services XI 1955; Scottish Command (Army) 1958; Combined Services 1960; British Army 1961.

ARTHURLIE FC

Arthurlie played at Dunterlie Park, Barrhead in Renfrewshire and had been members of Division Two of the Scottish League for nine seasons before Dundee Hibs joined them in 1910. The first encounter ended in a 2–0 home win for the Hibs in October 1910 and the pair continued in Division Two until it was suspended on the outbreak of the First World War.

Contact was not resumed until season 1924/25, then again in 1927/28 and 1928/29, all in Division Two. The final meeting took place at Tannadice in March 1929, United winning 4–3 on their way to the championship. By the time that was achieved, Arthurlie had resigned from the Scottish League due to financial problems. They never returned, in 1931 adopting the junior status which they still hold, with some success, today.

The full Scottish League record against Arthurlie was:
P 16 W 8 D 3 L 5 F 38 A 28

ATTENDANCES

Largest ever

The largest crowd ever to watch Dundee United was in excess of 100,000 (considerably above the official capacity) for the formal opening of the Shah Alam Stadium in the Malaysian capital of Kuala Lumpur in July 1994.

The highest attendance at a competitive match involving United was the 90,000-plus who watched the Emergency War Cup* final against Rangers at Hampden Park on 4 May 1940. Due to wartime safety regulations, the crowd was officially restricted to 75,000, but the match was not all-ticket and newspaper reports refer to the numbers in attendance being obviously in excess of that limit.

Smallest ever

The smallest 'crowd' (though the term is scarcely justified in this instance) at a competitive match involving Dundee United was 85 for the Division Two visit to Edinburgh City* on 15 December 1934.

Largest at Tannadice

The record for any match at Tannadice Park was the 28,000 all-ticket crowd which watched the Fairs Cup* second round, second leg, victory over Barcelona on 16 November 1966. Given the recent ground reconstruction, this is a record which will stand in perpetuity.

The record for a domestic match is 26,407 for the visit of Aberdeen in the fourth round of the Scottish Cup on 23 February 1952.

The record attendance for a Scottish League match stands at 25,000, the official figure given for the city derby on 3 January 1927.

Smallest at Tannadice

The lowest recorded home attendance for a competitive first-team match is the reported figure of 200 for the Second Division visit of Edinburgh City on 18 November 1933. The few who did turn up that day certainly got their money's worth, though, United winning by 9–3!

The lowest attendance for a home Scottish League match in the top division was 1,250 for the visit of Falkirk on 21 November 1973. The National Union of Mineworkers was on strike at the time and the government had banned the use of floodlights, so the match took place on a Wednesday afternoon.

Average attendances

Prior to the First World War, newspapers rarely mentioned attendances, with the result that the size of the crowds at very few of Dundee Hibs' matches in Division Two between 1910 and 1915 is known.

From around 1920, newspapers adopted the habit of reporting an attendance figure, usually rounded to the nearest 500. These were often no more than the estimate of the match reporter, but given that the Scottish League do not retain any records of attendances prior to 1956, these are the only indication of the numbers attending League matches at Tannadice prior to that.

Using the figures available, the average seasonal attendance at Scottish League matches played at Tannadice Park since 1920/21 is 7,537. In the Premier Division (from 1975/76) it is 9,438.

The highest average League attendance at Tannadice was 12,830 (Premier Division) in season 1988/89. The lowest was 1,700 for season 1937/38 in Division Two.

The lowest average for a season in which United were in the top division of the League was 5,517 in 1973/74 (Division One).

The highest average during a season in which United were not in the top division of the League was 10,400 in B Division, 1946/47.

The city clubs

It is interesting to note that, averaged over the years, United and Dundee FC show an almost identical level of support. The facts are that in 34 seasons when the two clubs have been in the same division of the Scottish League, Dundee FC have had a higher average attendance on 17 occasions, United on 16 occasions, and once the average was exactly the same.

When the city's clubs first shared status in the League, 1925/26 in Division One, United averaged 11,100 to Dundee FC's 10,900. But it was not until season 1968/69 (8,300 to 7,900) that United again enjoyed the upper hand, and they repeated it in 1970/71 (8,200 to 7,400). Dundee FC then regained dominance until United turned the tables in 1979/80, a position of superiority they have never since relinquished.

Only twice have the two clubs been together outside the top division of the League. In Division Two in 1938/39 both had an average attendance of 4,600, while in the First Division of 1995/96 United had more than double Dundee FC's average (7,300 to 3,600).

Throughout a total of 34 seasons of shared League status, United's average of averages is 8,800, while Dundee FC's is 9,100.

AUSTRIA

United have twice met Austrian clubs in European competition, and triumphed on each occasion. The European Cup quarter-final of 1984 sent United to the capital city of Vienna. They produced a fine performance, taking an early lead through Derek Stark*, but the Austrians attacked relentlessly thereafter and had their reward with two late goals. The result left United's players disappointed, though not deflated, knowing a single-goal win at Tannadice would secure a place in the semi-final. That they duly achieved, courtesy of Dave Dodds*, proving themselves the better side over the two legs.

Later that year, United returned to Austria, on this occasion to face Linz ASK in the second round of the UEFA Cup. A 2–1 away win in the first leg made United firm favourites and they completed the job in some style, cruising home 5–1 at Tannadice.

AWARDS

Arguably the most prestigious honour bestowed on a Dundee United player was the MBE awarded in 1992 to Dave Narey*. In recognition of his (then) 19 years of service to the club and 35 Scottish caps, it was a richly deserved award from beyond the world of football to one of the club's all-time greats.

Although Jim McLean* did not receive the royal recognition many felt he merited, he was honoured by Dundee's municipal leaders, receiving the Freedom of the City of Dundee in 1993.

The following have been honoured either by their fellow players in the Scottish Professional Footballers Association or by the Scottish Football Writers Association:

SPFA Player of the Year
Paul Hegarty 1978/79
Richard Gough 1985/86

SPFA Young Player of the Year
Graeme Payne 1977/78
Ray Stewart 1978/79
Billy McKinlay 1988/89
Robbie Winters 1996/97

SFWA Player of the Year
Paul Sturrock 1981/82
Hamish McAlpine 1984/85
Maurice Malpas 1990/91

Following the club's exceptional achievement in reaching the final of both the UEFA and Scottish Cups in 1986/87, Jim McLean was named manager of the year and the players were named Team of the Year by BBC *Sportscene*.

Also in 1987, in recognition of the general good behaviour of United fans across Europe during the season and in particular the generous reception given by the crowd at Tannadice to IFK Gothenburg following the second leg of the UEFA Cup final, UEFA awarded them their Fair Play Award. This came with a sizeable cash donation to the club, to be spent on ground improvements; the board decided that it would match the award and spent it on building the Fair Play Award enclosure between the main stand and The Shed*, designating it a parent and child area.

Give that man an Oscar !

Although it did not involve an award to a United player, it should be recorded that a former player received the motion picture industry's greatest accolade in 1960. Neil Paterson, who had been club captain in season 1936/37, went on to become a screenplay writer in Hollywood and he received an Oscar for his work on *Room at the Top* – an apt title given that the award came just a few weeks before his old club gained promotion to Division One!

Neil Paterson

AWAY GOALS

This method of deciding a winner in European competitions was introduced during the 1960s.

It was a vast improvement on the previous methods of playing a third game, which was costly, and tossing a coin*, which was farcical.

United first benefited from the away goals rule in the UEFA Cup of 1979/80 when Frank Kopel* scored against Anderlecht in Brussels to tie the score at 1–1, after the first leg at Tannadice had ended goalless.

The following year, in the same competition, Belgium took its revenge. KSC Lokeren secured a 1–1 draw at Tannadice, but the return remained goalless.

The most important occasion came in the European Cup in 1984. Rapid Vienna won 2–1 in Austria but a single goal by Dave Dodds* at Tannadice was enough to send United into the semi-final.

The most recent incidence saw United lose, this time at Tannadice, in a thrilling encounter with Brondby. The Danes brought a 2–0 lead with them, but two second-half goals for United took the tie into extra-time. Each team scored during that period, and Brondby went through.

AYR UNITED FC

It's a fact: It was the formation of Ayr United which opened the door to the Scottish League for Dundee Hibs. Both Ayr FC and Ayr Parkhouse were members of Division Two when they decided in 1910 to amalgamate to form Ayr United, thus creating the League vacancy which the Hibs filled.

The clubs first met later that year in Division Two, and did so again in the two which followed. During the inter-war period they were together on only four occasions, two of them in Division One, but were more regular League opponents between 1946 and 1960, always in the lower division. Since Dundee United gained promotion in 1960 they have spent only eleven seasons together, three in the Premier Division, the most recent being 1977/78. The clubs were also joint members of Southern League* B Division in season 1945/46.

24

The playing record against Ayr United in major competitions is:

Scottish League (total): P 66 W 25 D 14 L 27 F 128 A 132 (48%)

Premier Division: P 12 W 8 D 2 L 2 F 27 A 11 (75%)

Scottish Cup: the clubs were drawn together in 1950, 1963, 1969, 1970 and 1984.

              Record: P 5 W 5 D 0 L 0 F 14 A 3

League Cup: the clubs were drawn together in 1950, 1952, 1954, 1956, 1974, 1981 and 1986.

              Record: P 13 W 7 D 1 L 5 F 28 A 26

Notable transfers to: Derek Frye (1979)

Notable transfers from: Herbert Dainty* (as player/manager, 1915)

B

Eamonn BANNON (born 1958)

Manager Jim McLean* established a new record for a transfer fee paid by a Scottish club when he signed Bannon from Chelsea in October 1979 for £165,000. Previously with Hearts*, the penetrative left-sided midfielder made an immediate impact; within two months of arriving at Tannadice he had achieved two 'firsts' – the League Cup with United and a full international cap for himself.

An essential ingredient in the great United team of the early 1980s, Bannon was a constant threat to opposing defences and scored regularly. He was particularly effective on the European stage where United played their counter-attacking game to greatest effect. Indeed, he scored what was one of the best goals ever by a United player in the never-to-be-forgotten rout of Borussia Moenchengladbach in 1981.

After nine excellent years' service, his last game for United was the 1988 Scottish Cup final, following which he returned to Hearts. He spent five seasons there before taking up a coaching post with Hibs, then had a further brief spell at Tynecastle in the same capacity. He also played on a non-contract basis with Stenhousemuir, famously adding to his medal tally at United's expense in the final of the 1995 League Challenge Cup*.

His first managerial appointment came at Falkirk in the close season of 1996, but lasted barely six months before he was sacked following a disagreement with the club chairman.

Dundee United playing record (1979–88)

	Appearances	Goals
Scottish League	290	72
Scottish Cup	41	10
League Cup	58	18
European competitions	51	8
Scotland	11	
Scotland U-21	3	

26

Scottish League champion 1982/83
League Cup winner 1979,1980
UEFA Cup finalist 1987
Scottish Cup finalist 1981,1985,1987,1988
League Cup finalist 1981,1984

BATHGATE FC

Bathgate played at Mill Park and held membership of the Scottish League between 1921 and 1929, the period when West Lothian boasted no fewer than four League clubs.

During that period Dundee Hibs/United shared Division Two status with Bathgate on five occasions, though the clubs had met previously. They were fellow members of the wartime Eastern League* in 1915/16 and 1916/17 as well as the Central League* during 1920/21. Their first Scottish League encounter came in September 1921, with Bathgate turning home advantage into a 4–2 win. The last two League meetings resulted in wins of 6–1 (home) and 4–0 for United, but these were subsequently expunged by the League, following Bathgate's resignation due to financial difficulties in March 1929.

The full Scottish League record against Bathgate (including season 1928/29) was:

P 10 W 6 D L 3 F 25 A 16

BELGIUM

Over six ties, United have shared the spoils with Belgian clubs in European competition.

The first meeting occurred in the UEFA Cup of season 1978/79. The opposition was provided by Standard Liege and the first leg is probably best remembered for an incident which occurred at Brussels airport. Frank Blunstone, assistant manager of Derby County, made an illegal approach to Dave Narey* in the terminal building with a view to discussing a possible transfer of United's star player. An incensed Jim McLean* reported the matter to the SFA, who in turn referred it to their English counterparts, as a result of which both Derby and Blunstone were fined. United lost the match 1–0, and the return leg at Tannadice remained goalless.

The following season the tables were turned when, following another goalless draw at Tannadice, United travelled to Brussels to meet Anderlecht. The Belgians took a first-half lead, but were stunned when Frank Kopel* scored with a thunderous volley from 30 yards to send United through on the away goals rule.

The UEFA draw sent a third Belgian club to Tannadice in 1980 and this time the pendulum swung back when United lost out in the same manner, KSC Lokeren drawing 1–1 at Tannadice and then denying United by holding on for another goalless draw.

In what was now becoming an annual event, United headed back across the channel in December 1981, again in the UEFA Cup, on this occasion to meet one of Belgium's lesser-known clubs, Winterslag, who had nevertheless eliminated Arsenal in the previous round. After a 0–0 draw in the first leg, United demolished their visitors 5–0 at Tannadice to progress to the quarter-finals in Europe for the first time.

The next visit by a Belgian team was in the European Cup of 1983/84, and it provided revenge for United's defeat at the hands of Standard Liege five years earlier. Yet again one of the legs finished goalless; this time it was the first leg in Liege, as United defended well and returned optimistic of progression to the quarter-finals. On a night set alight by the magic of Ralph Milne*, Standard were swept aside and the 4–0 margin of victory in no way flattered his team.

The tie which evened the 'score' at 3–3 came in 1989, when the UEFA Cup first round sent United to the diamond capital of the world to meet Royal Antwerp. It was the home side which sparkled, though, United suffering their heaviest-ever defeat in European competition by going down 0–4. This of course made the second leg academic, though United did salvage some pride with a 3–2 win.

The only Belgian to play for the club is Armand Benneker, a defender who joined from the Dutch League club MVV Maastricht in August 1996. No fee was involved, this being the first signing made by United which took advantage of the Bosman judgment.

BERWICK RANGERS FC

The first meeting with the Northumberland club came in 1946 in C Division*, although it was United's reserve team which participated in that league. They did meet at first-team level in 1953, when Berwick gave United a bloody nose, winning a Scottish Cup replay 3–2 at Tannadice. They remain the only non-League club to beat United in the competition. Two years later Berwick were admitted to the Scottish League and they shared status with United in Division Two over the following five seasons.

It's a fact: The last League meeting between the clubs was a momentous occasion. On 30 April 1960, Jerry Kerr's* team regained a Division One place after an absence of 28 years by beating Berwick Rangers 1–0 at Tannadice on the last day of the season in front of a crowd of 16,000.

The playing record against Berwick Rangers in major competitions is:
Scottish League: P 10 W 8 D 0 L 2 F 40 A 16 (80%)
Scottish Cup: the clubs were drawn together in 1953, 1975, 1992 and 1996.
                Record: P 6 W 3 D 2 L 1 F 15 A 8
The clubs have never met in the League Cup.
Notable transfers from: Stuart Markland (1968)

Gary BOLLAN (born 1973)

Dundee-born, he played in the Scotland team which reached the World Youth Cup final in 1989, following which he joined up at Tannadice from Fairfield Boys Club.

He was always regarded as a 'utility player' (the description usually given to one who cannot command a regular first-team place) although, in fairness, Gary suffered a number of injuries, which restricted his appearances. He was a member of the squad (an unused substitute) which achieved the long-awaited Cup final victory in 1994.

His latter days at Tannadice were dominated by a protracted contractual dispute with the club, and, with the backing of the Scottish PFA, he was set to test the matter in court when he was transferred to Rangers in January 1995; it was a joint deal with Alex Cleland* worth £750,000, of which Bollan was said to have accounted for one third.

Dundee United playing record (1990–95)

	Appearances	Goals
Scottish League	46	4
Scottish Cup	3	
League Cup	7	
European competitions	1	
Scotland U-21	17	
Scotland youth	28	2

Scottish Cup winner 1994
BP Youth Cup winner 1990, 1991

BO'NESS FC

Bo'ness were the most successful of West Lothian's League clubs, reaching Division One in season 1928/29. The club played at Newton Park, and first encountered Dundee Hibs in the Central League* of 1920/21. Acquaintance was renewed the following season in Division Two of the Scottish League, the first meeting at that level being the 2–2 draw at Tannadice in August 1921.

There were four further seasons when the clubs clashed as members of Division Two, and they last met in April 1931 when United, needing a win to clinch promotion, lost 0–1 at Tannadice (they got the points the following week!).

In November 1932, Bo'ness were expelled from the League for failing to pay match guarantees to visiting clubs. The club adopted junior status in the 1940s as Bo'ness United and have won the Scottish Junior Cup twice. They still play at Newton Park, and anyone interested in knowing what a minor Scottish League club ground looked like in the 1930s should pay a visit!

The full Scottish League record against Bo'ness was:
P 10 W 2 D 5 L 3 F 12 A 10

Dave BOWMAN (born 1964)

The son of a prominent Hearts player of the 1950s, Dave arrived at Tannadice from Coventry City in the summer of 1986 as part of a joint transfer with Jim McInally*. He quickly won the hearts of Arabs*, who dubbed him 'Psycho'; this was due less to his resemblance to actor Anthony Perkins than to that of the character which the actor played in the film of that name!

His tough-tackling, all-action style was certainly effective in United's midfield though it tended to obscure the fact that Bowman was a player with more to offer. He had won an Under-21 cap while with Hearts and his broader talents were deservedly recognised by Scotland coach Craig Brown at a time when it seemed a full international cap had passed him by.

In recognition of his service to the club, the board granted him a testimonial year (1995/96), by which time his leadership qualities had earned him the job of club captain, and he played an essential role in United's immediate return from the First Division.

Dundee United playing record (1986–97)

	Appearances	Goals
Scottish League	319	9
Scottish Cup	38	3
League Cup	21	
European competitions	25	
Scotland	6	

Scottish Cup winner 1994
Scottish Cup finalist 1987,1988,1991
UEFA Cup finalist 1987

BRAZIL

For many Arabs, the major association with Brazil is the most famous 'toe-poke' in the history of Scottish football, the wonder goal scored by Dave Narey* in the 1982 World Cup finals. That happened to be the only one Dave scored in 35 appearances for his country; sadly it was also the only one his country scored in that match, while the Brazilians responded with four of their own.

United have met Brazilian clubs on three occasions. The first came in 1967, in the North American Soccer League*; Bangu were representing Houston, while United represented Dallas*. The Brazilians were the only club which they met twice during that competition and United drew 0–0 at home, but lost 0–2 away.

In the summer of 1983, in the wake of their League championship triumph, United were invited to take part in the pre-season Costa Dorada tournament in Spain. Having defeated RCD Espanyol in the semi-final, they met Brazilians Americo de Rio in the final, but lost 1–2.

United's other connection with the country more immediately associated with football than any other is Sergio Gomes, the striker who spent six months at Tannadice in 1995 after his transfer from Portuguese club Amora. His skills quickly won over the Arab faithful, but his brief stay unfortunately coincided with the club's demise from the Premier Division. Ultimately, he became a victim of Home Office red tape when his work permit was not renewed, leading to his transfer to a Kuwaiti club, where he sought to win over a different sort of Arabs!

BRECHIN CITY FC

City were one of Dundee Hibs' earliest opponents in the Northern League* in 1909, and in the pre-1914 period the clubs also met in various local cup competitions. They were joint members of the Eastern League* in 1919/20, but did not meet in the Scottish League until 1930/31.

Having been regular League opponents throughout the 1930s, the clubs did not meet again at first-team level in a League match until 1954, although City played in C Division* along with United's reserves between 1946 and 1952. United's promotion season of 1959/60 was the last time the two met in the Scottish League.

It's a fact: United's record away League win (8–0) was achieved at Glebe Park in a Division Two match in October 1934. Nor did the players show any mercy when Brechin came to Tannadice two months later in the return fixture, which United won 9–2. This represents the highest number of goals scored by Dundee Hibs/United against opponents in any one League campaign.

The playing record against Brechin City in major competitions is:
Scottish League: P 28 W 11 D 7 L 10 F 69 A 48 (52%)
Scottish Cup: the clubs were drawn together in 1981, 1982 and 1987, each
                time at Glebe Park.
                Record: P 3 W 3 D 0 L 0 F 7 A 3
League Cup: the clubs were drawn together in 1954 and 1960.
                Record: P 4 W 1 D 0 L 3 F 3 A 6

Craig BREWSTER (born 1966)

The young Brewster came to the attention of manager Jim McLean* in the early 1980s when he was an S-form signing. Despite playing regularly for the youth team he was not offered a full-time contract, as a result of which he signed for Dundee junior club Stobswell. Eighteen months later he was given a second chance in the senior grade by Forfar Athletic and in 1991 was transferred to Raith Rovers where he won a First Division championship medal in season 1992/93.

Prior to joining Rovers he had been a midfielder, but manager Jimmy Nicholl moved him forward and it was only then that his potential was fully realised. He joined United in the close season of 1993 for £250,000 and was a regular scorer, although the goal which earned him cult status was the one which brought United their first Scottish Cup triumph.

A lifelong Arab, Brewster took as much pleasure from that event as any supporter and it was with a heavy heart that he left the club when his contract expired in 1996. The first United player to move without a fee under the Bosman judgment, he joined Greek League club Ionikos.

Dundee United playing record (1993–96)

	Appearances	Goals
Scottish League	92	40
Scottish Cup	13	6
League Cup	3	
League Challenge Cup	2	1
European competitions	2	
Scottish Cup winner 1994		
League Challenge Cup finalist 1995		

BROTHERS

The most famous brothers associated with Dundee United are, of course, Jim* and Tommy* McLean. It is rare indeed for brothers to manage the same club, though Tommy can claim to be part of a treble double-act because both he and his other brother, Willie, also managed Motherwell and Raith Rovers!

George* and Johnston* Grant were for 14 years together as directors of Dundee United. Both held the position of chairman, although George sadly died just two days after assuming the chairmanship in 1988.

Only five sets of brothers have played for the club.

Michael and Peter O'Rourke junior played five times in the same team for Dundee Hibs during the brief spell between December 1922 and March 1923 when their father, Peter senior*, managed the club.

Chic and Bert McIntosh both played for United during the 1930s, though they were not on the club's books at the same time. Goalkeeper Chic was a regular between 1931 and 1934, while season 1936/37 was left back Bert's only one at Tannadice.

As one of the club's all-time greats, the exploits of Duncan Hutchison* are well known; less so, though, is the fact that his younger brother Dan spent a season at Tannadice. The outside left made 14 League appearances during 1937/38, all but two in the company of his brother.

During the 1950s, another famous United player had a brother as a team-mate. Johnny Coyle* scored a club record 41 League goals during season 1955/56, during which he was regularly accompanied by brother

Jimmy on the right wing. The two also played together on fewer occasions the following season, at the end of which the partnership ended when Jimmy was given a free transfer.

Right back Tommy Millar was a United stalwart between 1962 and 1968. During his final two seasons he was joined by brother Jimmy, a centre forward who had won many honours in 12 years with Rangers.

Perhaps the least well known brothers were Joe and Sandy White, although they are unique in the annals of Dundee United as the only twins to play for the club. Right back Joe and outside left Sandy were together at Tannadice between 1971 and 1973 but only twice played together at first-team level.

Jimmy BROWNLIE (born 1885; died 1973)

It is beyond question that Jimmy Brownlie was one of the greatest servants Dundee United has ever had. Player/secretary/manager, secretary/manager, manager and director/manager are the various roles which this exceptional character undertook between 1923 and 1939. These were turbulent years for Dundee United and on more than one occasion the club's very future was in serious doubt. It is no exaggeration to assert that without Jimmy Brownlie's drive, determination and inspiration United could have perished during the inter-war years.

In fact, when Brownlie arrived at Tannadice Park in the summer of 1923, the club he joined as player/manager was Dundee Hibs, and the new board saw him as an essential part of the series of events which were transforming the club and creating a new image for it. Four months later it became Dundee United; less than two years later Brownlie had taken it from non-League status to a place in Division One. It was a stunning achievement and one which would almost certainly have been beyond anyone else.

Certainly, Brownlie brought first-class credentials with him to Tannadice. He had joined Third Lanark*, then one of the country's leading clubs, in 1906 and he spent his whole career with them, making over 500 appearances. He was for much of that time the top goalkeeper in Scotland and his haul of international caps would have exceeded 16 but for the First World War. He was also a real crowd-pleaser, often doffing his distinctive cap to spectators in response to applause for one of his saves.

He quickly made his presence felt at Tannadice, using his extensive knowledge of the Scottish football scene to sign

An enthralled young Arab collects Jimmy Brownlie's autograph in 1963

33

virtually a new squad of players, and in his second season he led his team to the championship of Division Two. Having convinced the board of the need to finance full-time football at Tannadice for the first time, he confounded the cynics who predicted United's fall would mirror their rise. They did go down after two seasons in the top flight, but were soon back and, most importantly, the club was at last established as a force.

In 1931, after eight years in charge – and in circumstances which were never adequately explained – he was dismissed following a disagreement with the board, but that was far from being the end of his connection with United. After the club was saved from bankruptcy in March 1934, for the second time a new board saw him as a saviour and, although lack of available finances precluded him building another promotion bid, he did give the club the onfield stability it had been lacking since his departure. In October 1936 he became the victim of another bout of boardroom manoeuvring and once more departed, but another chapter of his contribution remained to be written.

It is a mark of the precarious nature of Dundee United during the 1930s that yet another new board of directors took over in June 1938, one of them being none other than Jimmy Brownlie. He had begun to establish a business in the city, but could not turn down the opportunity of once more serving the club that was close to his heart. Rather than appoint a new manager he was joined by fellow director Sam Irving*, and between them they adopted the unprecedented role of joint manager/directors!

It took the outbreak of the Second World War finally to end Jimmy Brownlie's formal role with Dundee United, but he never did completely sever the connection, remaining a regular match-day attender at Tannadice, where a seat in the directors' box was always his for the asking.

He lived to the grand old age of 88 and took great delight in seeing the club securely established at the top level during the 1960s, always downplaying his own role in ensuring that the name of Dundee United was not erased from the face of Scottish football all those years ago.

Dundee Hibernian/United playing record (1923–26)

	Appearances
Scottish League	30
Scottish Cup	2

BROXBURN UNITED FC

Dundee Hibs had met Broxburn United in four different competitions before their first Scottish League meeting in 1921. The first came in the Qualifying Cup* in 1912, the Hibs winning 1–0 at the West Lothian club's Sports Park. During World War One they were members of the Eastern League* together (1915/16 and 1916/17) and met in that League's knock-out competition, the Eastern Cup, in the former season.

Their paths crossed again on the formation of the Central League* for season 1920/21 and continued the following season in Division Two of the Scottish League. The Hibs lost their League place at the end of that season, but were re-elected for 1923/24, that and the following season being their last along with Broxburn.

The full Scottish League record against Broxburn United was:
P 6 W 3 D 1 L 2 F 6 A 8

BURMA
Not known as a force in world football, but United met their national team in a tournament in Japan in May 1979, winning 4–0.

C

C DIVISION

When the Scottish League resumed after a seven-year absence in 1946, it involved A and B Divisions, comprising 16 and 14 clubs respectively. Several clubs which had been members of Division Two in 1939 were left out in the cold and they were accommodated in a new C Division, along with the reserve sides of Dundee FC, Dundee United and St Johnstone.

These clubs were not regarded as being members of the Scottish League; they were not allowed to compete in the League Cup and did not have a vote at meetings of the League. However, they could replace the bottom club in B Division if they won the C Division championship, although for obvious reasons reserve teams were not allowed to be promoted if they took the title (as happened on all but two occasions). In 1949, C Division was expanded and divided into North/East and South/West sections so that, in theory, the bottom two clubs in B Division could have lost their League status if the champion of each C Division section was one of the minor clubs. In practice this never happened although, as outlined below, it was Dundee United who tried hardest to put the theory to the test, coming far too close for comfort!

United's reserves participated in C Division from 1946 to 1952, but in 1954 they very nearly suffered the indignity of having their first team as members. The club avoided bottom place in B Division only on goal average, and were spared the indignity of C Division thanks to Rangers reserves pipping Stranraer for the championship of the South/West section.

C Division was scrapped in 1956, with the minor clubs being admitted to an expanded B Division and reserve leagues introduced (though United declined to join).

Kenny CAMERON (born 1943)

Signed from Kilmarnock in 1968, he holds the distinction of being the first United player to be the leading League scorer in the top division; he remains the only one to do so in his own right.

His senior career began with Dundee FC, for whom he scored in the

1964 Scottish Cup final. Without ever coming close to equalling his 27 League goals of 1968/69, he was a regular scorer during his six years at Tannadice, leaving in 1974 to join Montrose*, whom he later managed. Kenny returned to Tannadice as coach, then chief scout, until leaving in February 1996 (after fifteen years) to become full-time manager of junior club Dundee St Joseph's. He returned to Dens Park in June 1997 as assistant manager.

Kenny Cameron scoring against Dunfermline at East End Park in 1972

Dundee United playing record (1967–73)

	Appearances	Goals
Scottish League	132	63
Scottish Cup	7	5
League Cup	28	13
European competition	1	

CANADA

United's only visit to Canada was in May 1992 for the Guinness Challenge Cup, played in Vancouver. It was not one of their more successful overseas visits, resulting in a 1–1 draw with Vancouver 86ers, followed by defeats at the hands of Chelsea (0–3) and Vancouver Island All Stars (1–2).

More happily to recall, it was against Canada in June 1983 that Eamonn Bannon*, Richard Gough*, Dave Narey* and Paul Sturrock* represented their country, the only occasion on which four United players have been selected for a full international.

CARRIE CUP

This competition was also known as the Forfarshire League and was a subsidiary competition to the Northern League*, being open only to its members from Forfarshire. Dundee Hibs won it in 1910, the first trophy ever won by the club. There is no record of the competition being played in the following seasons.

CELTIC FC

The clubs met for the first time in September 1925 in United's first season in Division One. It attracted a then record crowd of 20,000 to Tannadice and United capped a great day by winning 1–0 with a goal by Jimmy Howieson. They had had three more seasons together by 1932, but did not meet again in the League until 1960. Since then, the only interruption was United's brief sojourn in the First Division in 1995/96. The clubs also met in the Drybrough Cup* in 1979.

United's first win at Celtic Park was delayed more than 40 years, ironically coming in May 1967 (see below) at the thirteenth attempt. United's biggest win over Celtic is 3–0, at Tannadice in April 1980 and May 1982 (both Premier Division), and at Parkhead in November 1980 (League Cup) and October 1985 (Premier Division). Their heaviest defeats have been 0–5 at Tannadice in December 1967 and 0–7 at Celtic Park in March 1930, both in Division One.

Without a doubt, United's most famous win over Celtic came in January 1949. At the time, United were a mid-table Division Two side and few expected the first-round tie to be more than a straightforward afternoon's work for the record holders of the trophy. But the romance of the Cup can have had few better illustrations as Willie MacFadyen's* team, roared on by most of the 25,000 all-ticket crowd, took a two-goal lead through a Peter McKay* penalty and Jimmy Dickson. Celtic pegged it back, only for McKay to strike again – after the referee had disallowed a United 'goal' for the *third* time in the match! Celtic quickly made it 3–3, but United were not to be denied and George Cruikshank strode through to score what proved the winner. It was almost certainly as a result of this match that United came to be known as The Terrors*, and small wonder!

It's a fact: In season 1966/67 Celtic won every competition they entered, including the European Cup. In retaining the Scottish League championship, they suffered only two defeats, both of which were inflicted by United, each by a margin of 3–2.

The full playing record against Celtic is:
Scottish League (total): P 122 W 31 D 32 L 59 F 142 A 213 (39%)
Premier Division: P 84 W 24 D 23 L 37 F 95 A 118 (42%)
Scottish Cup: the clubs were drawn together in 1931, 1949, 1970, 1981 (semi-final), 1992 and 1996. They also met in the finals of 1974, 1985 and 1988.
Record: P 10 W 2 D 1 L 7 F 13 A 23
League Cup: the clubs were drawn together in 1962, 1965, 1967, 1970, 1974, 1976, 1978, 1980 (semi-final), 1982 (semi-final), 1984, 1988, 1990 (semi-final) and 1994.
Record: P 22 W 5 D 5 L 12 F 19 A 30
Notable transfers to: Tom McAdam (1977), David Hannah* (1996)
Notable transfers from: Frank Quinn* (1948), Neil Mochan (1960), Jamie McQuilken (1995)

CENTRAL LEAGUE
When the Scottish League decided against re-establishing a Second Division following the First World War, the excluded clubs – which

included Dundee Hibs – played in regional leagues in season 1919/20.

However, they decided to establish a rival competition for the next season, resigning *en masse* from the Scottish League and establishing the Central League. Because this was an entirely separate organisation, Central League clubs were able to sign Scottish League players without paying a transfer fee. This tactic had the desired effect, and the Scottish League, fearing the loss of many of its players, capitulated and admitted virtually the entire Central League to form a new Division Two for season 1921/22.

The parlous financial state of Dundee Hibs prevented them from competing in the transfer market, but their involvement in the Central League for the single season of its existence ensured their place within the expanded Scottish League set-up.

CLACKMANNAN FC

This club played in the Central League* along with Dundee Hibs during season 1920/21; most members of that competition were admitted to Division Two of the Scottish League when it was reinstated in 1921. At the end of the following season the bottom two clubs dropped out to reduce the numbers to eighteen; Dundee Hibs finished second from last, with only Clackmannan below them. Hibs won the League encounter at Tannadice 7–1, with the return at Chapelhill Park ending 1–1.

The following season both clubs were members of the Eastern League. That competition was not played out to a conclusion and the Hibs only met Clackmannan away from home.

That was the last contact between the clubs. The Hibs returned to Division Two in 1923, at which time Clackmannan were admitted to the new Division Three. They remained there for the three years of that division's existence, but disbanded shortly thereafter.

Alex CLELAND (born 1970)

One of many fine products of the club's scouting system in the west of Scotland, Cleland was a schoolboy cap (U-15) when he joined in June 1987. He made his first-team debut at 17 but took a further three years to claim the right back place on a regular basis. A member of the Scottish Cup-winning team, he was transferred to Rangers in January 1995, in a joint deal with Gary Bollan* worth £750,000, within which Cleland was valued at £500,000.

Dundee United playing record (1988–95)

	Appearances	Goals
Scottish League	151	8
Scottish Cup	7	
League Cup	14	
European competitions	9	2

Scotland U-21   11
Scotland youth   5
Scottish Cup winner 1994

CLEPINGTON PARK
See also Tannadice Park
In 1875, the area of Dundee between Coldside and Maryfield was countryside, the only habitation being the farmhouses of West Clepington and East Clepington farms. Between these, Dens Road and Mains Road converged, but degenerated into a cart-track at what is now Provost Road, and this continued several hundred yards north to meet Clepington Road. The area immediately south of Clepington Road was simply open fields, some of which were cultivated, the remainder grassland which was not part of either farm. The only road leading into this area was Arklay Street, a mere hundred yards in length north from Dens Road.

Organised football was by then burgeoning throughout the city and it seems the grassy part of that area – basically covering what are now the allotments behind Tannadice Park – was first used in the late 1870s. Ironically, the first club to claim part of that area as its home ground – though in those days that meant nothing more than erecting goalposts – was called East End FC. They did so in 1882, giving it the name Clepington Park. The irony lies in the fact that, 11 years later, East End would be one of the two clubs which amalgamated to form Dundee FC. East End remained there until moving to a new ground in 1890, and Clepington Park was then taken over by Dundee Wanderers*.

By that time, Provost Road had come into being, and, like Arklay Street, had been built as far north as Clepington Road. The area to the left of Arklay Street remained open land, the bulk of it still East Clepington farm, but that to the right was being gradually developed. Proceeding north up Arklay Street in 1890, one of the new streets you would have passed on your right had been given the name Tannadice Street.

The following year Dundee Wanderers decided to enclose the ground they had taken over to enable them to charge for admission. But, in order to provide a better vantage point for spectators, it was decided to harness the natural slope roughly a hundred yards to the west (below what is now Sandeman Street). It was this area which they enclosed and the club built what was termed a 'grandstand', although this was a simple wooden structure of bench seats, probably no more than ten deep; it had no roof and would have accommodated 500 spectators at most.

By 1909, development of the area south of East Clepington farm – which remained a bastion against progress – had proceeded apace. The farm formed the northern side of Sandeman Street, which had been built between Arklay Street and Provost Road. Meanwhile, Tannadice Street had been extended across Arklay Street to meet Sandeman Street at an angle. At the point where these two streets met was Dens Park*, the new Dundee FC ground, opened in 1899. The triangular area immediately to its east, circumscribed by Sandeman, Arklay and Tannadice Streets, contained Clepington Park.

When Dundee Hibs were formed that year, their choice of a ground came as a surprise. Given the club's origins within the city's Irish community, it had been expected they would set up home in the Lochee district, where the bulk of that community had settled. However, rather than construct their own ground, the men who had formed the new club decided to seek ready-made accommodation at Clepington Park, home for the past 19 years of Dundee Wanderers, a club which would be the Hibs' main local rivals in the Northern League*. On behalf of his committee, the Hibs' secretary Pat Reilly* made an offer to the landlords which clearly exceeded what Wanderers were paying. The result was that the established tenants were informed that their lease would not be renewed for the coming season, and instead was to be transferred to the Hibs.

This caused quite a furore in the city, reflected in the letters column of the *Dundee Evening Telegraph*, which carried an acrimonious exchange between Pat Reilly and his Wanderers counterpart. The extent of the Wanderers' anger can be gauged from the fact that, before departing Clepington Park, the club dismantled the grandstand and wooden changing rooms along with the fencing which enclosed the ground; even the goal-posts were removed, leaving Hibs with what was, literally, an open space!

Immediately on taking over the lease, the Hibs committee decided to emphasise the arrival of the new club by changing the name of the ground. They settled on Tannadice Park, simply adopting the name of the street on which the main entrance to the ground was to be situated.

CLUB BADGES

The first known instance of the club having an official badge was in 1923, following the take-over which led to Dundee Hibs becoming a limited company for the first time – and changing the official colours from green and white to black and white.

In their first season, Dundee United also wore a badge, but that initial attempt to foster a club identity makes it all the more surprising that there is no evidence of a United jersey again carrying a badge for more than 30 years. It should be noted, however, that very few Scottish clubs during the '30s, '40s and '50s did so. In 1959, a new strip was introduced – all-white, with two black bands – incorporating a badge. It is not clear why the official club crest, which had been featured on the match programme since 1956, did not appear on the jersey.

The badge introduced in 1959 simply involved the placing of 'DUFC' within the shape of a shield, but it endured for ten years until the adoption of tangerine as the official club colours. A circular badge then appeared for

Dundee Hibs jersey badge,
1922–23

Dundee United jersey badge,
1923–25

Official club crest, 1946–69

Blazer badge, 1959–69

Jersey badge, 1969–73

Jersey badge, 1983–84

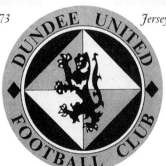

Official club crest and jersey badge since 1993

the first time, featuring a 1970s version of the lion rampant, and this continued until superceded by variations of 'DUFC' between 1974 and 1983 None of these constituted a badge as such, though this was very much the trend in Scotland throughout the period.

The Premier Division championship triumph was marked by a commemorative jersey badge which used the lion rampant design for the first time, and that basic design was retained for ten years. 1993 brought a radical change, introducing a modern corporate image for the club. This included a new logo, in circular form, which was used both as the official club crest as well as the jersey badge. Initially, Arabs were not exactly united in their enthusiasm for it, but within a year the club had won the Scottish Cup for the first time, according the new badge the status of a talisman

CLYDE FC

The clubs first met in 1924/25, during United's first championship season in Division Two, but their contact was restricted to just five more seasons (three in Division One) between then and 1960. Clyde were fellow members of Division One for most of the intervening period until the formation of the Premier Division, but the clubs have not met in a League match since then. United's last visit to Shawfield Stadium was in April 1975.

The playing record against Clyde in major competitions is:
Scottish League: P 36 W 16 D 6 L 14 F 68 A 74 (53%)
Scottish Cup: the clubs have been drawn together just once, in 1995. Following a goalless draw at Tannadice, United won 5–1 at Broadwood Stadium
League Cup: the clubs were drawn together in 1957, 1968 and 1970. Record: P 6 W 1 D 2 L 3 F 10 A 17
Notable transfers to: Johnny Coyle* (1957)
Notable transfers from: Jimmy Loney (1910)
It's a fact: Clyde inflicted United's heaviest defeat in the League Cup when they won 8–1 at Shawfield Stadium in August 1957. It was no fluke; five months earlier the Glasgow club had won a Division Two match 7–1 at the same venue.

CLYDEBANK FC (1914–1931)

Not to be confused with the present-day club of the same name, they played at Clydeholm Park and first confronted Dundee Hibs in Division Two in season 1914/15. It was to be a further ten seasons before their paths crossed again, though it was a joyful reunion, both clubs winning promotion to Division One in 1925, Dundee United as champions.

In addition to the following season in Division One, the clubs spent a further three together in Division Two and the last League meeting took place in April 1931. Due to financial problems, Clydebank resigned from

the Scottish League and went out of existence in July of that year.
  The full Scottish League record against Clydebank was:
  P 12 W 6 D 1 L 5 F 24 A 28

CLYDEBANK FC (1965–)

United first met the new Clydebank in the Scottish Cup of 1971, their first League meeting coming in the Premier Division six years later. The Dunbartonshire club lasted just one season on that occasion, but managed two when they returned in 1985. The only other League meetings between the clubs came in the First Division of 1995/96 although United also won a League Challenge Cup tie at Clydebank in the same season.
It's a fact: Clydebank's game against United at Kilbowie Park in May 1978 attracted an attendance of 430, the lowest in the history of the Premier Division.
  The playing record against Clydebank in major competitions is:
Scottish League (total): P 16 W 11 D 4 L 1 F 34 A 9 (81%)
Premier Division: P 12 W 8 D 3 L 1 F 22 A 7 (79%)
Scottish Cup: the clubs have been drawn together just once, in 1971. United won 5–1 at Tannadice following a goalless draw at Kilbowie Park.
League Cup: the clubs were drawn together in 1980 and 1985. Record: P 3 W 2 D 0 L 1 F 7 A 3
Notable transfers from: Tommy Coyne (1983)

COMBINED RESERVE LEAGUE

This was a competition established in 1958 to cater for those Division Two clubs which wanted to run a second team; it also included the Celtic and Rangers third XIs. United joined in 1959 at the insistence of new manager Jerry Kerr*, who believed it essential for his entire squad of players to play regularly if he was to achieve promotion after a gap of almost 30 years. The soundness of his judgement was evidenced by his success in reaching Division One at the first attempt. As a result, United were no longer eligible for membership of the Combined Reserve League.

CONSOLATION CUP

In 1895 the SFA had been forced to introduce a Qualifying Cup* due to the large number of clubs entering for the Scottish Cup. This meant that only 16 of the smaller clubs qualified for the major competition and over the years pressure grew for a further competition to be introduced to cater for the non-qualifiers. Eventually the SFA agreed and in 1908 the unimaginatively named Consolation Cup emerged.
  Dundee Hibs participated in this competition in their first season, 1909/10, having been dismissed from the Qualifying Cup by Brechin City.

Any hopes that the Consolation Cup might live up to its name were dispelled when they again drew Brechin – and again lost!

The Hibs also participated in 1910 and 1911, reaching the third round on each occasion, and would have made another appearance in 1914 had the competition not been abandoned following the outbreak of war. The Consolation Cup was never revived.

COWDENBEATH FC

Cowdenbeath were perennial opponents of Dundee Hibs, being fellow members of Division Two during the Hibs's first five seasons of Scottish League membership. They also shared membership of the Eastern League* during and after World War One, and the Central League* of 1920/21.

As the Central Park club spent most of the inter-war period in Division One, United encountered them much less frequently, but they did spend four seasons together at the top level. They were together in Southern League* B Division in 1945/46 and normal service was resumed in the League's lower division in the late 1940s and 1950s, since when Cowdenbeath have had just one season at the top level; the clubs last met in a League match at Tannadice in April 1971.

It's a fact: United suffered their heaviest defeat against Cowdenbeath in a Division Two match at Central Park in October 1925. The result was 7–0, though there were mitigating circumstances. After goalkeeper Bob Morrison failed to arrive for the match, full back Dave Collington had to deputise. *The Sunday Post* commented kindly that he '. . . played brilliantly in goal despite the heavy defeat', but, more tellingly, went on to say that '. . . perhaps, however, he would have been of greater service at right back'.

The playing record against Cowdenbeath in major competitions is:
Scottish League: P 62 W 14 D 19 L 29 F 98 A 155 (38%)
Scottish Cup: the clubs have been drawn together just once, Cowdenbeath winning 5–3 at Central Park in 1936.
League Cup: the clubs were drawn together in 1946, 1947, 1950, 1951, 1958, 1980 and 1995.
                 Record: P 13 W 5 D 2 L 6 F 24 A 23
Notable transfers from: Andy Rolland (1967)

It's another fact: United's Scottish League record against Cowdenbeath is their second poorest against another League club (after that against Rangers).

Johnny COYLE (born 1933)

Signed by manager Willie MacFadyen* from St Joseph's Juniors in 1950 at the age of 17, the Dundee-born youngster made his debut a year later. Although he did not manage a goal on that occasion, he more than made up for it by scoring four in his second appearance, a League Cup tie at Tannadice.

That served notice of his appetite for goals, though it would be some time before he blossomed into Dundee United's all-time record scorer. Until 1955, his appearances were restricted through a spell on loan to Brechin City* followed by national service, but on returning his form was sensational. The 41 goals he scored in Division Two in season 1955/56 established a record which has stood for more than 40 years, and it seems quite likely to last at least as long again.

Johnny Coyle, pictured in 1951

He had the misfortune to be a big fish in a small pond during the two and a half seasons in which he was a regular at Tannadice, and the status of the club at that time is well illustrated by the fact that United could not hold on to Coyle when Clyde (then in Division One) offered him the chance to play at a higher level. The sizeable fee of £8,000 which United received was scant consolation to the supporters, though the move worked out well for Coyle; a few months later he scored the goal which won the 1958 Scottish Cup for his new club, and he continued to score regularly in Division One.

Nonetheless, he remained a part-time player with the Glasgow club, and in 1961 he moved to England, joining Cambridge City of the Southern League. The rest of his career was spent in non-League football, following which he remained in Cambridge, working at his trade as a bricklayer.

Dundee United playing record (1951–57)

	Appearance	Goals
Scottish League	96	77
Scottish Cup	9	10
League Cup	27	25

Arthur CRAM (born 1894; died 1958)

An accountant by profession, he shares the distinction with Pat Reilly* of being the only men to hold the position of secretary/manager of Dundee Hibs/United who had not previously been professional players.

Cram was working with a firm of accountants in the city when he was invited to take over as club secretary of Dundee United shortly after the outbreak of World War Two. The previous manager, Bobby McKay*, had had his contract terminated following the abandonment of the Scottish League due to hostilities in Europe and, as the manager's job at Tannadice had always been (and would continue to be until 1967) bracketed with that of club secretary, the board were left in a position where they had no one in charge of the day-to-day administration.

Obviously, there would have been a lot less of such work to be handled during wartime, but Cram clearly had the knowledge of running an organisation and his accountancy qualification enabled him to oversee what limited financial matters there were. It seems most unlikely that his post would have been a paid one and most probably he accepted it as a favour to board members who were personal friends. He continued to act as secretary until the club closed down in the summer of 1940.

Had his service to Dundee United gone no further than that, it would scarcely have been worthy of mention. However, despite having no known connection with football as a player, even at amateur level, he was appointed secretary/manager at Tannadice when the club ended its brief respite and joined the newly formed North Eastern League* in 1941. For the following three seasons, Cram retained the dual title, although the exigencies of wartime meant that his administrative abilities were more exercised than any other, particularly in securing the release of former professional players who were stationed with the armed forces within travelling distance of Dundee (see Wartime Football). At a time when several clubs – including Dundee FC – closed down rather than make the kind of efforts that Cram did on United's behalf, the club and its supporters owed him a considerable debt for keeping the flag flying at Tannadice.

As the end of the conflict began to approach, the Tannadice board decided that a team manager should be introduced for the start of season 1944/45, and the job was allocated to one of their own number. At 34, former player Jimmy Littlejohn* took on the role while Arthur Cram reverted to being club secretary. At the same time, he was rewarded for his efforts by being made a director, a position he held until 1951.

CZECHOSLOVAKIA
See also Slovakia

United visited Czechoslovakia on three occasions on European business, and in all three it ended their interest in that season's competition.

The club's third venture in the Fairs Cup* in 1970, following a first-round victory over Grasshoppers Zurich, paired them with Sparta Prague. The first leg in the Czech capital was marked by the European debut of Hamish McAlpine*, who came on as a substitute for the injured Donald Mackay. The match ended with United on the wrong end of a 1–3 scoreline, but with the advantage of an away goal. However, two weeks later at Tannadice, despite constant pressure, an Alan Gordon strike was as much as Jerry Kerr's* team could manage, and the Czechs advanced on a 3–2 aggregate.

Thirteen years on, an altogether more experienced and accomplished

McAlpine returned to Prague. The team of which he was now part were well on the way to winning the League championship and, in retrospect, many Arabs now regard it as fortuitous that United's European progress was halted by Bohemians, allowing the players to concentrate on the pursuit of the championship. It did not seem that way at the time though, a 1–0 first-leg defeat poor return for a controlled United performance in Prague, but the return at Tannadice required the suspension of belief to accept their failure to score. Jim McLean's* team literally camped in the opposing half for the whole match, but just could not carve out the one goal which it seemed certain would have opened the floodgates.

The final occasion on which a club from Czechoslovakia would visit Tannadice was altogether less auspicious. Just five months after the emotion of the UEFA Cup final at Tannadice, United contrived to produce as dismal a performance on a European occasion as they have ever managed in 100-plus matches. Vitkovice's players, aware of United's record in the competition, could scarcely believe their good fortune and in truth should have departed with rather more than a 1–0 lead. United did improve in the second leg (it would have been impossible to do otherwise), but a 1–1 draw was not enough.

D

Christian DAILLY (born 1973)
He became the youngest player to appear for the club in the Premier Division on his debut at 16 in August 1990. He never quite found his true position at Tannadice, making his name as a striker, but then dropping back to a defensive role, and occasionally one in midfield.

The highlight of his career at Tannadice was unquestionably the Scottish Cup final of 1994, when his perseverance allowed Craig Brewster* to score the only goal. Having gained his first U-21 cap at the age of 16, he went on to establish a world record number of appearances at that level, with 34.

Despite his youth, manager Billy Kirkwood* made him club captain for season 1995/96 but he was transferred to Derby County for a fee of £500,000 during the close season of 1996. He quickly settled in the Premiership and in May 1997 won his first full international honour.

Dundee United playing record (1990–96)

	Appearances	Goals
Scottish League	143	18
Scottish Cup	15	
League Cup	10	2
League Challenge Cup	4	1
European competitions	6	
Scotland B	1	
Scotland U-21	34	5
Scotland youth	21	7

Scottish Cup winner 1994
BP Youth Cup winner 1990,1991

Herbert DAINTY (born 1879; died 1961)
One of four Englishmen in the Dundee FC team which won the Scottish Cup in 1910, centre half Dainty was a big favourite at Dens Park* for several years. He briefly departed Scotland to play for Bradford City, but

was lured back north of the border by Ayr United who offered him the job of player/manager in 1913.

It was in a similar role that he signed for Dundee Hibs in April 1915, and it was clear that his popularity in the city had endured, despite having 'crossed the road'. During the war, benefit and charity matches were held to fill the gap in the rather haphazard leagues which then existed, and Dainty became actively involved in organising teams which he called 'Dainty's XI' from any footballers who happened to be stationed in the Tayside or Fife area. Dundee Hibs were their opponents on several occasions.

Because of these activities, allied to the fact that the club had less need of a manager during the war, Dainty reverted to being simply a player. He retired from playing in 1918 and went into business in the city. It was through these connections that he was invited to become involved in running Dundee Hibs. He was co-opted onto the club committee in 1920 and was made chairman in 1922, though he did not hold the position for long. Towards the end of that year, with the club in serious financial difficulties, it was taken over by another group of businessmen who turned it into a limited company for the first time. Dainty's services were no longer required and this ended his involvement with the club.

Herbert Dainty, featured on a cigarette card issued in 1914, when he was with Bradford City. On the reverse he is described as having 'plenty of grit and dash'

DALLAS TORNADO FC

When United competed in the North American Soccer League* in 1967 and the International League* two years later, they assumed the identity (and colours) of the Dallas club. Their home matches were played at the Cotton Bowl, normally used for American football by the Dallas Cowboys. The purpose of these competitions was to generate interest in 'soccer' among a public addicted to baseball, basketball and American football. Although the matches did attract considerably higher crowds than the clubs were able to do in their own right, the experiment ultimately failed.

Most of the clubs, Dallas Tornado among them, went out of business in the early 1970s, though not before they had paid a visit to Tannadice to play a friendly in October 1969. This was, in effect, a return match as the clubs had met in Dallas the previous June, following the conclusion of the International League.

The link between the clubs was maintained through Lamar Hunt, the oil tycoon who owned Tornado, becoming a United shareholder in 1969. Though he still retains his investment, it is unlikely to add much to Hunt's fortune as it amounts to a single share!

DEFEATS

Most in succession

Counting only the major competitions, the most successive defeats sustained by Dundee United is seven between 14 December 1929 and 11 January 1930; all were League matches in Division One.

Longest run without a defeat

Between 8 May and 27 October 1982 United went 21 matches undefeated (10 Premier Division, 8 League Cup and 3 UEFA Cup). The next longest was 19 (14 Premier Division, 4 Scottish Cup and 1 European Cup Winners' Cup) between 2 November 1988 and 11 March 1989.

Most in a League season

The worst season in the club's history, 1931/32, saw 25 (66%) of the 38 League games lost. The Premier Division record is slightly better, standing at 18 (50%), established during the relegation season of 1994/95.

Heaviest

Few Arabs* can be unaware of the club's record 1–12 defeat at the hands of Motherwell in 1954. The following week's match programme reported it in terms which would do a modern-day spin doctor proud: '. . . the better team won, but never by anything like an 11-goal margin. We got every bad break going. Most of our players did well; everything came off for the homesters, nothing for us.' These sentiments were later immortalised in song by Morecambe and Wise! The best thing which can be said about the all-time record defeat at Tannadice was that it came during the uncertain period of wartime. Aberdeen* departed with a 9–1 North Eastern League* victory on 10 February 1945.

Scottish League (overall)

Home: 0–7 v Morton, Division Two, 2.3.57
      1–7 v St Bernard's, Division Two, 14.8.37
           v Alloa Athletic, Division Two, 16.4.58
      2–7 v Airdrie, Division One, 23.1.32
      1–6 v Motherwell, Division One, 20.2.32
Away: 1–12 v Motherwell, B Division, 23.1.54
      1–9 v Third Lanark, B Division, 26.9.53
      0–8 v Kilmarnock, Division One, 12.12.31
           v Ayr United, B Division, 19.3.49
      2–9 v Stenhousemuir, Division Two, 16.4.36
      2–8 v Berwick Rangers, Division Two, 21.2.59

Premier Division

Home: 0–4 v Rangers, 26.9.92
Away: 0–5 v Hibernian, 13.8.94

Scottish Cup
Home: 1–5 v Motherwell, 4.2.39
Away: 0–7 v Raith Rovers, 16.2.57

League Cup
Home: 0–5 v Motherwell, 12.8.53
Away: 1–8 v Clyde, 24.8.57

European competitions
Home: 0–4 v Vitesse Arnhem, UEFA Cup, 7.11.90
Away: 0–4 v Royal Antwerp, UEFA Cup, 17.10.89

DENMARK

Along with Holland, Denmark shares the distinction of being the destination most often visited by Dundee United.

It is as the home of one of United's all-time greats, Finn Dossing*, that Denmark has its main association with the club. Dossing was transferred from Viborg, and that club was, as a direct result, one of United's opponents on their first visit to the country in 1966. That was an end-of-season tour, but on two occasions more recently (1982 and 1996) the club has used Denmark to prepare for the new season, mainly meeting lower league opposition. However, in 1996 United beat the then Danish Cup holders, Aarhus, 2–1.

Denmark has also beckoned United on more serious business, although these occasions are not likely to feature in the club's role of honour. When they were drawn against KB Copenhagen in the UEFA Cup of 1977, Jim McLean's* emerging young team was not expected to encounter much difficulty in progressing, a view which scarcely altered despite the first leg at Tannadice producing no more than a 1–0 victory. Clearly, minds were not securely on the business in hand two weeks later, as United returned home shamefacedly, having been on the receiving end of a 3–0 beating.

Sixteen years were to elapse before the UEFA draw again paired United with Danish opponents. They turned out to be Brondby IF, whom United had beaten 3–1 in a friendly at Tannadice in March 1989. Ivan Golac* was still adjusting to his new charges and rather extravagantly – and none too wisely – predicted that United would emerge from the first leg in Copenhagen with a three-goal advantage. That may well have inspired the Danes, who were good value for their 2–0 lead. The second leg produced one of those nights for which Tannadice has become renowned, as United battled manfully to retrieve the deficit. They achieved it, taking the tie to extra-time, but the effort during the 90 minutes seemed to have taken more out of them because it was Brondby who scored first, and although United did manage a third, the Danes advanced on the away-goals rule.

Apart from Dossing, United had another Dane during the heady days of the Scandanavian invasion in the mid-'60s. Somewhat unfairly, Mogens Berg has never received the credit he was due for sterling performances over more than 80 games.

DENS PARK

The home of their city rivals has, in recent times, come to be regarded as something of a happy hunting ground for United. In addition to capturing the League Cup there in both 1979 and 1980, it was the venue of the derby match in which the Premier Division championship was clinched in 1983.

Various matches have seen Dens used as a neutral venue, including three cup semi-finals involving United and Aberdeen. The first occasion came in the Scottish Cup of 1967, which Aberdeen won through an own goal by Tommy Millar. Three matches were needed before United advanced to the final of the same competition in 1988, although the Dons extracted early revenge, winning there in the semi-final of the League Cup later the same year.

Dundee Hibs were fairly regular visitors to Dens Park; it was frequently used as the venue for Forfarshire Cup* finals and also for second replays in earlier rounds of what was at the time a very popular competition. This was a practice which continued intermittently until the 1960s. The ground was also used for a play-off involving United and Raith Rovers in the Supplementary Cup* in 1945.

In addition, United have played a 'home' match at Dens Park. On 5 March 1947, at the end of one of the most severe winters on record, Tannadice was still snowbound when United were due to face Rangers in the second leg of the League Cup quarter-final. Despite being a mere 200 yards distant, Dens was playable, so the tie was switched there.

DERBY MATCHES
See also Dundee FC

The clubs first met on 13 March 1915, in a friendly at Dens Park, while the most recent was a League Cup tie at Tannadice on 3 September 1996. Their next encounter will be the 200th city derby.

The complete record is:

	Overall	Scottish League	Scottish Cup	League Cup	Other Comps.	Testimonials & Friendlies
Played	199	98	17	13	58	13
Dundee Hibs/United wins	82	50	7	6	18	1
Dundee FC wins	78	29	3	4	32	10

Draws	39	19	7	3	8	2
Dundee Hib United goals 318	163	29	24	91	11
Dundee FC goals	353	123	21	23	142	44

Dundee United's biggest win   5–0 at Dens Park, Division One, 11 September 1965

Dundee FC's biggest win   8–1 at Dens Park, Forfarshire Cup, 19 August 1935

Biggest attendance at Tannadice Park   25,000 Division One, 3 January 1927
Scottish Cup, 4 February 1956

Biggest attendance at Dens Park   38,000 Scottish Cup, 27 January 1951

LOCAL DERBY AT DUNDEE

Campbell (Dundee United), on the ground, scoring his side's third goal at Tannadice, with Hamilton, of Dundee, looking on.

Action from the first city League derby after United won promotion in 1960

It's a fact: the most famous city derby of all was played at Dens Park on 6 December 1980. It was the League Cup final, the only time in the history of the competition that the first match has been taken away from Hampden Park. United won 3–0 in front of a crowd of 24,700.

DEWAR SHIELD

This competition involved the holders of the Aberdeenshire, Forfarshire*,

Perthshire and Stirlingshire Cups, all of which were, at the time, prestigious trophies. It was instituted in 1899 by a leading member of the Perth-based Dewar whisky family, with the winners proclaimed 'champions of the northern counties'. Apart from war years, it was held regularly between 1899 and 1946, but then took place on a less regular basis and seems to have petered out in the early 1970s.

Dundee Hibs never participated, and United only once won the trophy, despite participating in the competition on 12 occasions and reaching the final three times. A measure of the status accorded the tournament in its latter years can be gauged from the fact that United's success came in the 1965/66 final – which was played in November 1967!

The club's last match in the Dewar Shield was against Peterhead at Tannadice in February 1972.

Dave DODDS (born 1958)

A Scottish schools U-15 cap, he was signed from Sporting Club, Dundee, in May 1975; he made his debut at 17 against Arbroath in a League Cup tie the following year, scoring twice.

An early product of Jim McLean's* local scouting system, he was a vital part of the team which captured the club's first trophy and raised its standing to the point where the League championship came to Tannadice in 1983. He was the club's leading scorer in five of the seven seasons in which he was a first-team regular, one of these coming in the 1980 League Cup final. His 22 goals during the championship-winning season represent the only occasion on which a United player has exceeded 20 goals in a season in the Premier Division. Dave remains United's second top Premier Division scorer behind his team-mate Paul Sturrock, and they remain the only two to reach the hundred-mark.

He was transferred to the Swiss club Neuchatel Xamax in 1986, but did not stay long, returning to Scotland with Aberdeen. He ended his career on a high, joining Rangers in 1989 where he won his second Premier Division championship medal. He retired at the end of the following season to take up a position as coach with the Ibrox club, which he held until 1997.

Dundee United playing record (1976–86)

	Appearances	Goals
Scottish League	243	102
Scottish Cup	31	12
League Cup	54	25
European competitions	42	11
Scotland	2	1
Scotland U-21	1	
Scotland youth	9	3

Scottish champion 1982/83
League Cup winner 1979,1980
Scottish Cup finalist 1981,1985
League Cup finalist 1981,1984

Finn DOSSING (born 1941)

One of the greatest goalscorers in the club's history; only Arthur Milne* and Peter McKay* registered a higher goal-per-game average in League games, but in Dossing's case they were scored in Division One.

Signed by manager Jerry Kerr* from Viborg, the Dane made his debut along with Orjan Persson* in December 1964 at a time when United were under severe threat of relegation. With 21 goals in only 19 matches, Dossing was a huge influence in the club's moving into mid-table security.

Hugely popular at Tannadice, he scored 25 goals the following season as United qualified for European competition for the first time. Sadly, he did not adequately reap the reward of his efforts, as injury kept him out of both games against Barcelona

The legendary Finn Dossing

and the first against Juventus; typically, returning for the home leg against the Italians, he scored the game's only goal.

After almost three years, Finn took his leave of Tannadice as a hero. He returned to Denmark where he successfully ran his own gents' outfitters business in his home town of Viborg.

Dundee United playing record (1964–67)

	Appearances	Goals
Scottish League	86	60
Scottish Cup	8	5
League Cup	11	1
Summer Cup	9	9
European competition	1	1

Summer Cup finalist 1965

DRAWN MATCHES

Up to the end of season 1996/97 United had played a total of 2,524 League matches over 73 seasons. Of these, 574 (22.7%) were drawn.

The highest number of drawn matches during a League season was 20 (45.5%) in 1993/94.

The least number of drawn matches during a League season was one (4.5%) in season 1915/16. The fewest draws during a season in the Premier Division was seven (19.4%) in 1984/85.

The highest scoring drawn match involving Dundee United is 5–5. This occurred on four occasions: Airdrie (h), Division Two, 30.4.38; Arbroath (h), B Division, 23.10.48; East Stirling (a), Division Two, 17.9.55; Arbroath (h), Division Two, 18.9.57.

DRYBROUGH CUP

This was a pre-season tournament sponsored by the Scottish brewery. Instituted in 1971, it was open to the four highest-scoring clubs in Divisions One and Two. For that reason, United did not participate in the tournament's initial phase between 1971 and 1974.

When it was resurrected in 1979 the Premier Division had become established and United qualified for the only time. In the first round they disposed of Second Division Dunfermline Athletic* by 3–0 at Tannadice, then fell at the semi-final stage, going down 2–3 to Celtic* at Parkhead after extra-time. The competition lasted only one more season before being discontinued.

DUMBARTON FC

Dumbarton were early opponents of Dundee Hibs, the clubs sharing membership of Division Two from 1910 to 1913. Dundee United found themselves in the same division as the Boghead Park club for 27 out of 30 League seasons between 1923 and 1960 they also spent season 1945/46 together in Southern League* B Division. The two have since met in only three seasons in Division One and one each in the Premier Division and the First Division.

It's a fact: Dumbarton were the first–ever opponents of Dundee United. Three days after officially adopting their new name, they travelled to Boghead Park for a Division Two match on 27 October 1923, which Dumbarton won 3–0. Things could only get better; they did!

The playing record against Dumbarton in major competitions is:

Scottish League (total): P 70 W 29 D 13 L 28 F 155 A 131 (51%)

Premier Division: P 4 W 3 D 1 L 0 F 9 A 2 (88%)

Scottish Cup: the clubs have been drawn together just twice, in 1949 and 1955, the latter being in the 1955/56 competition.
Record: P 3 W 1 D 1 L 1 F 6 A 5

League Cup: the clubs were drawn together in 1946, 1949, 1952, 1957, 1976 and 1984.
Record: P 11 W 7 D 1 L 3 F 24 A 15

Notable transfers from: Tom McAdam (1975), John Bourke (1977)

DUNDEE FC

Over the years, the city's two clubs have had what might be described as a love–hate relationship. There is evidence that Dundee FC, as a top club in 1909 when Dundee Hibs were formed, regarded themselves a cut above their ragged-trousered neighbours from Tannadice. The toffee-nosed Dens Park* board tended to be from the jute-owning and commercial business class of the city, while those men responsible for forming the Hibs were small businessmen – such as secretary Pat Reilly*, who owned a cycle shop – and publicans. The Dundee FC directors were invited to attend Dundee Hibs' first match, which also formed the official opening of Tannadice, but only one turned up in what can be seen – in retrospect at least – as a token gesture.

Dundee's A team played in the Northern League* along with the Hibs and it was the second string which also met them in the Forfarshire Cup*. A sign that there was no love lost between the players is that *The Courier*'s report of a Forfarshire Cup semi-final at Dens Park in April 1912 was described as 'a Donnybrook'. The match ended 2–2 and the reporter observed that 'when the replay takes place it is to be hoped both teams will endeavour to subdue the physical tones in their picture'. That replay never did take place because Dundee FC protested at the inclusion of an ineligible Hibs player, and this incensed the Hibs committee to the extent that they withdrew their club from the competition (see Forfarshire Cup for a more detailed version of that incident, plus a similar one in the same competition in 1920).

So, by 1912, both players and officials already had a less than cosy relationship, and that was hardly improved when the clubs eventually met at first-team level. It was supposed to be a friendly match at Dens Park in March 1915. The Division One club, not surprisingly, won rather easily, but there was a clear edge between the players, as illustrated by the report which appeared in the *Saturday Evening Post*. It stated that '. . . the rivalry between the teams is shown by the number of stoppages for fouls'. This reached a climax when 'shortly before the close, Low and Cargill got to grips and the referee promptly ordered them to the pavilion'.

The absurd objections by Dundee FC to the Hibs directors' proposed name-change to Dundee City in 1923 was a further manifestation of the 'them and us' attitude of those in charge at Dens Park. The Tannadice club were clearly regarded as upstarts, so it must have come as a jolt to their air of superiority when Jimmy Brownlie's* team won promotion to Division One in 1926. The first city League derbies the following season were each won by the home club, but it would have been interesting to be a fly on the wall of the Dens Park boardroom when the occupants learned that United's average home attendance for the season was greater than Dundee FC's.

The clubs shared Division One status during United's three other seasons in the top League prior to 1932, and they met again in Division Two during 1938/39, following Dundee's unexpected relegation. Apart from the first two seasons following the war (see Southern League), further League meetings had to await United's promotion in 1960.

That event, following which United established themselves at the top level for the first time, marked a watershed in the relationship – and status – between the two clubs. In the period between 1915 and 1960, the clubs had met a total of 73 times, 50 of which had been won by Dundee FC and only ten by Dundee Hibs/United. Since 1960, there have been 126 meetings, 71 of which have been won by United and only 26 by Dundee FC, illustrating the extent to which, over the past three decades, United have taken over as the city's major club.

With one notable exception, there have been no public disagreements between the clubs at board level over that period, although that instance soured relations and very nearly ended up in the courts in 1992. Dundee FC chairman Angus Cook devised an audacious plan to buy into Dundee United, then merge the two clubs. This met with outrage and outright resistance in equal measure from chairman Jim McLean* and the United board and was equally vigorously opposed by supporters of both clubs. Cook was eventually sent away with his tail between his legs and he left the Dens Park board shortly after, the jeers of the city's football community ringing in his ears.

The clubs maintain a polite, if distant, relationship, though the media were in no doubt that Dundee FC's refusal to sell Neil McCann to United was 'politically motivated'. United were reported to have offered around £600,000 in March 1996; this was turned down, only for the player to be transferred to Hearts for little more than a third of that sum three months later.

Having lost their Premier Division place in 1994 (after being members for 13 out of the first 19 seasons) Dundee FC faced severe financial difficulties, which effectively prevented them making a return. The summer of 1997, however, saw the club's foreign owner sell to local businessmen and this may herald a change in their fortunes.

The obligatory bravado notwithstanding, most Arabs would probably prefer their arch-rivals to be in the Premier Division, if only because of the electric atmosphere which derby matches generate, allied to United's guarantee of the lion's share of League points!

Ironically, the clubs' most recent League meetings came at First Division level in 1996, during United's season 'downstairs'; true to form, nine out of the 12 points ended up at Tannadice.

The playing record against Dundee FC in major competitions is:
Scottish League (total): P 98 W 50 D 19 L 29 F 163 A 122 (61%)
Premier Division: P 52 W 29 D 12 L 11 F 90 A 45 (67%)
Scottish Cup: the clubs were drawn together in 1928, 1929, 1951, 1956, 1980, 1987 (semi-final), 1988, 1989, 1990 and 1991.
Record: P 17 W 7 D 7 L 3 F 29 A 21
It's a fact: The clubs being paired five years in succession between 1987 and 1991 is believed to be a record for the competition. United advanced on each occasion.
League Cup: the clubs were drawn together in 1956, 1962, 1964, 1965,

1966, 1987 and 1996. They also contested the 1980 final.

Record: P 13 W 6 D 3 L 4 F 24 A 23

Summer Cup: The clubs met in sectional ties in both 1964 and 1965.

Record: P 4 W 2 D 2 L 0 F 10 A 6

Instances of players who have been with one of the city clubs subsequently appearing for the other are not difficult to identify. However, direct transfers between the two clubs are not common; without claiming to be definitive the following list includes most of them:

Dens to Tannadice: Tim Dailly (1909), Thomas Flood (1909), Collie Martin*(1913), Fred Stoessell (1913) (all to Dundee Hibs), Jimmy Dickson (1947), Kinnaird Ouchterlonie (1948), Alex Stuart (1969), Duncan McLeod (1973), Bobby Robinson (1977), lain Phillip* (1978), Neil Duffy (1996).

Tannadice to Dens: George 'Piper' Mackay (1947), Jack Court (1948), Ian Scott (1970), Billy Williamson (1977), Tommy Coyne (1986), Jim Mclnally (as player/coach, 1997)

It's another fact: Dundee FC are one of only two clubs from a lower division to put United out of the League Cup; they were in the First Division when they won a second-round tie at Tannadice on penalties in September 1996.

DUNDEE CITY ATHLETIC COMPANY LTD

When Dundee Hibernian was bought by a group of city businessmen in November 1922, it was decided that a change of name, ending the overt Irish connection, was desirable. Various options were considered as an alternative, but eventually Dundee City FC was decided upon. Dundee Hibernian Football and Athletic Company Ltd was then dissolved and its assets were utilised to form a new company, for which debenture shares were issued in the name of Dundee City Athletic Company Ltd.

Prior to the change, Dundee Hibernian, having lost their League place at the end of season 1921/22, had applied to the Scottish League for re-election. It was made clear that, if the application were to be made under the name Dundee City, allied to the fact that the club had new owners, the League would regard the application as coming from an entirely new club and as such it would stand little chance of succeeding against the applications of the other well established clubs. The application therefore remained in the name of Dundee Hibs, there being no alternative to delaying the change of name.

By that time, the Board of Trade, the government department with responsibility for overseeing corporate matters, had already endorsed the new company name of Dundee City with the result that, for six months, all business and correspondence had to be conducted under the name Dundee City, while the club continued to play as Dundee Hibs! This bizarre state of affairs continued until the SFA Council meeting in October 1923, at which the club was finally given permission to change its name. Just to complicate matters further, however, they were refused permission (following an objection by Dundee FC) to adopt Dundee City, with Dundee United proving to be the compromise which broke the stalemate.

So Dundee City existed for some seven months, but only as a company; Dundee City FC never existed.

DUNDEE HIBERNIAN FC
The original name of the club which became Dundee United.

The year 1909 was not the first time a club of that name had emerged from within the city's Irish sporting fraternity. A club calling itself Dundee Hibernian had appeared in 1894, though this was largely a cloak of convenience. The Irish community's original 'representative' had been Dundee Harp, formed in 1879. That club met with considerable success in local competitions during the 1880s, but eventually succumbed to financial difficulties, culminating in its expulsion from the SFA in 1894 for the non-payment of match guarantees to visiting clubs.

The Dundee Harp committee then claimed to have disbanded the club, though in essence it re-emerged later that same year in the guise of Dundee Hibs. That this was a ploy to enable the former club to continue playing was revealed by the fact that, just a year later, the club changed its name – to Dundee Harp. It was never again a force, however, and eventually did go out of existence in 1906.

There was no ambiguity as to the purpose of those city businessmen who formed Dundee's new senior football club in March 1909: it was designed to provide a focus of sporting interest for the city's large Irish, Roman Catholic, community. They were simply following the example set by the leaders of the same community 30 years earlier, and indeed by the same communities in Edinburgh (1875) and Glasgow (1887) when Hibernian and Celtic were born. Therefore, giving their club the name Dundee Hibernian and adopting colours of green and white was both logical and consistent.

The men who established the new Dundee Hibs were described as 'Dundee Irishmen' and were mainly engaged in small businesses or the licensed trade. The club was run by a committee which comprised city councillor Bailie Thomas Hannick as president, Samuel Johnstone (vice president), Patrick Reilly* (secretary), Thomas Timmons (treasurer), and ordinary committee members Patrick Doyle, James Glover, Thomas Heraughty, John Kennedy, Thomas Malone and John Naulty. They were determined that their club would prove more durable than its predecessors and they certainly made quick progress. Having spent their inaugural season in the Northern League*, the Hibs were voted into the Scottish League in 1910, ahead of St Johnstone, who had been in existence for more than 25 years. That, however, was to be the level at which the club remained, never threatening to scale greater heights.

With the suspension of Division Two during World War One, the Hibs played in regional leagues, but the decision of the Scottish League not to reinstate a second division after the war came as a serious blow. Hibs could not hope to compete with the drawing power of Dundee FC, at the time one of Scotland's top clubs, and attendances at Tannadice were at an extremely low level, leading to serious financial difficulties. Although Division Two was eventually reintroduced in 1921, by finishing in second bottom place Dundee Hibs lost their League membership after just one season.

By this time, it was clear that the club commanded something less than the undivided attention of the city's Roman Catholic community, many of whom did not baulk at paying their money to watch top-class football at Dens Park*. Allied to the fact that the treaty providing for the partition of Ireland – for long a contentious matter in Scotland – had led to the civil war then raging in that country, it was clear that the Irish associations of Dundee Hibernian were becoming unwelcome baggage as far as the club's committee members were concerned.

Having lost their League place, it was not at all clear where – if at all – the Hibs would spend season 1922/23. Ironically, it was the Irish connection which came to their rescue. Celtic had decided to withdraw their reserve team from the Scottish Alliance* and suggested that the Hibs apply for the vacancy. The two clubs had always enjoyed a good relationship and, with Celtic's support, the Hibs were successful. However, the poorest season in the club's history saw them finish third bottom, with their future looking bleak.

In November 1922, the club had been bought by a group of city businessmen, most of whom carried neither the religious nor cultural attachments of their predecessors. A limited company was formed for the first time but, despite having the necessary finances to resurrect the club, the directors were unwilling to do so until League status had been regained. That they were able to achieve this is testament to their lobbying ability, because the playing standards then on view certainly could not have justified Dundee Hibs' return. Yet the club was re-elected to Division Two in May 1923 and the new board then appointed former Scotland goalkeeper Jimmy Brownlie* as player/manager. He was provided with funds to rebuild the team and this heralded a dramatic turnaround in the club's fortunes.

The final piece of the jigsaw was the most fundamental, though. To complete the new image, and draw a veil over the past, the board decided that all vestiges of the club's origins had to be removed. That meant a change of name and club colours, both of which required the permission of the Scottish League. The former was not straightforward and was delayed for several months, with the result that the new season commenced with Dundee Hibs playing in black and white. Dundee United eventually took the field for the first time on 27 October 1923, and a new era was born.

DUNDEE UNITED SPORTSMEN'S CLUB

Formed in August 1955, it was to all intents and purposes a United supporters club, although at that time the only one which existed.

More importantly, its stated aim was to raise money for Dundee United at a time when the club was in serious financial difficulties and lacking the resources to mount a meaningful promotion challenge. The Sportsmen's Club's major contribution was the formation of Taypools*, the success of which exceeded the expectations of even the most optimistic club committee member.

Various, more modest fundraising activities, many centred on social events, were an important part of the club's attempts to increase the active involvement of United supporters beyond turning up at Tannadice every fortnight. They began running a bus to away matches, and the club was really the forerunner of the travel clubs which developed during the promotion season of 1959/60 and beyond into Division One.

The Dundee United Sportsmen's Club was wound up during the 1960s, having made a vital contribution to their football club.

DUNDEE WANDERERS FC

Contrary to some suggestions, Dundee Wanderers had no connection with the club which became Dundee United. The only link Wanderers had with Dundee Hibernian was that, in 1909, the newly formed club took over the lease of Clepington Park*, which until then had been the Wanderers' ground.

In fact, the club with which Dundee Wanderers did have a direct link was Dundee FC. Wanderers were formed in 1885 by a breakaway group of players and officials from a club named Our Boys, then one of the top two clubs in Dundee; in 1893, Our Boys amalgamated with the city's other leading club, East End, to form Dundee FC.

Dundee Wanderers were original members of the Northern League* when it was formed in 1891, but they became the city's second Scottish League club (after Dundee FC) when they were elected to the new Division Two in 1894. However, after finishing second from last, they were voted out a year later. The club then rejoined the Northern League, achieving little of note, and were still in membership when Dundee Hibs were admitted in 1909. In fact, Wanderers were the first-ever opponents of Dundee Hibs in a competitive match, a Northern League fixture at newly named Tannadice Park on 21 August 1909.

At the time, the clubs were involved in a bitter dispute over the fact that the Hibs committee had, without warning, bought out the lease of Clepington Park, as the ground was known when the Wanderers had it as their home. It was therefore more than a little ironic that the Wanderers' first match of the new season should see them return to what they still believed should have been *their* home ground.

That there was little room even then for sentiment in the game is illustrated by the fact that the Wanderers were forced to live up to their name, being unable to find a suitable long-term alternative ground, a decisive factor in the club's ultimate demise in 1914.

DUNFERMLINE ATHLETIC FC

Dundee Hibs' first match against Dunfermline came in the Consolation Cup* in February 1911, though 18 months later they joined Hibs in Division Two. The clubs then followed the same path, continuing in the League until the First World War, joining the Eastern League* during it, the breakaway Central League* of 1920/21, and rejoining Division Two when it was reinstated the following year. They also met in the Qualifying Cup* in 1913.

Between 1923 and 1960 the two were opponents in 19 out of 30 League seasons, though only once (1926/27) in Division One they also spent season 1945/46 together in Southern League* B Division. Following United's return to the top flight they met Dunfermline in all but one of the 15 seasons which preceded the formation of the Premier Division, but have shared status on only five occasions since then.

The clubs met in the League Challenge Cup in 1995/96, United winning a third-round tie at East End Park 4–0.

The playing record against Dunfermline in major competitions is:
Scottish League (total): P 98 W 38 D 23 L 37 F 150 A 171 (52%)
Premier Division: P 20 W 12 D 6 L 2 F 28 A 11 (78%)
Scottish Cup: the clubs were drawn together in 1967, 1974 and 1996.
          Record: P 4 W 3 D 1 L 0 F 7 A 1
League Cup: the clubs were drawn together in 1954, 1961, 1968, 1972, 1983 and 1991.
          Record: P 11 W 6 D 1 L 4 F 18 A 14
Notable transfers to: Andy Rolland (1978), Billy Kirkwood* (1987), John Holt* (1987), Hamish French (1992)
Notable transfers from: Bill Paterson (1925), Jock Bain (1927), Duncan Hutchison* (1927), Pat Gardner* (1972)

EASTERN LEAGUE (1915–1917)

Formed after Scottish League Division Two clubs decided to abandon their competition to reduce travelling during wartime. Initially it comprised six Division Two clubs from the east of the country, plus the same number from the Central League*, although some had difficulty in completing their fixtures. This led to a reduction in the number of clubs, ten in 1916/17 and only seven the following season. Dundee Hibs competed each season, though without much success.

During its first season, the League ran a competition called the Eastern Cup (the Hibs lost to Leith Athletic* in the second round), but this was abandoned in 1916, again due to problems in finding suitable dates for the ties to be played.

EASTERN LEAGUE (1919/20)

This competition was formed to fill the gap left by the refusal of the Scottish League to reinstate Division Two after its suspension during the First World War. Its ten member clubs were all from either Fife or Tayside. It included the reserve teams of Dundee and Raith Rovers, but nonetheless provided Dundee Hibs with their first championship success. The League was wound up at the end of its only season, with the formation of the new Central League*.

There was also a League Cup for members of the Eastern League. The Hibs took three matches to dispose of St Johnstone, only for the competition to be abandoned due to an inability to agree dates for the remaining ties.

EASTERN REGIONAL LEAGUE

This competition began in October 1939, following the abandonment of the Scottish League on the outbreak of war. Basically, the clubs split into eastern and western sections to restrict travelling and the Eastern League was formed by eight teams each from Divisions One and Two.

Although Cowdenbeath pulled out midway through the season, the remainder of the programme was completed. However, a number of clubs then decided to go into hibernation for the duration of the war, making it impossible for the Eastern Regional League to continue.

EAST FIFE FC

The clubs first met in the wartime Eastern League* (1915–17) and were also part of the breakaway Central League* of 1920/21. Their first Scottish League meeting came in Division Two at Bayview Park in November 1921. They met regularly in the inter-war period, though never in Division One and also spent season 1945/46 together in Southern League* B Division, but with East Fife being in the top division for ten years from 1948, their meetings prior to United winning promotion in 1960 were rare. Since then, the clubs have had just three seasons together in Division One, the last League meeting being at Methil in March 1973.

It's a fact: Despite having been an ever-present during season 1936/37, goalkeeper Jimmy Milton was given a free transfer by United at the end of it. His disappointment must have been more than offset when he signed for East Fife and became a member of their Scottish Cup-winning team a year later.

The playing record against East Fife in major competitions is:
Scottish League: P 38 W 13 D 11 L 14 F 64 A 73 (49%)
Scottish Cup: the clubs were drawn together in 1928, 1938 and 1991.
              Record: P 5 W 2 D 2 L 1 F 6 A 9
League Cup: the clubs were drawn together in 1973 and 1980.
              Record: P 4 W 4 D 0 L 0 F 16 A 5
Notable transfers to: Jimmy Milton (1937)
Notable transfers from: Tommy Neilson (1959)

EAST STIRLINGSHIRE FC

East Stirling were in Division Two when Dundee Hibs were elected in 1910 and they remained there together until its suspension during the war. The clubs both played in the Eastern League* between 1915 and 1917 and also the breakaway Central League* of 1920/21.

When Dundee Hibs were re-elected to the Scottish League after a year's absence in 1923, they displaced East Stirling, the Hibs gaining 21 votes to the Falkirk club's 15. Thereafter they met regularly throughout the remainder of the 1920s and 1930s, but since World War Two, United and East Stirling have been in the same division only seven times. The last time the clubs met was at Firs Park in January 1964, during one of only two seasons in their history East Stirling have spent in the top division.

It's a fact: United's 12–1 victory over East Stirling at Tannadice in April 1936 stands as the club's record in a Scottish League match. The margin of victory was almost equalled against the same club in March 1938, but on that occasion United had to settle for 10–0. In all, four League matches involving the two clubs have produced ten or more goals, the other two being a 6–4 win for the visitors at Tannadice in October 1936 and a 5–5 draw at Firs Park in September 1955.

It's another fact: In 1959, United and East Stirling met on three consecutive days in their only Scottish Cup encounter thus far. The first-round tie had been postponed twice and the SFA decreed that it must be decided in time for the winners to meet Third Lanark* on 14 February, the appointed day for second round ties. The clubs drew 1–1 at Firs Park on Monday, 9 February and 0–0 (after extra-time) at Tannadice the following day – this being the pre-floodlight era, both matches took place in the afternoon. The Tynecastle Park lights meant that the third meeting at least had an evening kick-off, and United won it 4–0. Having played a League match the previous Saturday, when United's part-time players faced Third Lanark (then in Division One) at Tannadice, it was their fifth match in eight days – which perhaps went some way towards explaining their 0–4 defeat.

The playing record against East Stirlingshire in major competitions is:
Scottish League: P 46 W 20 D 11 L 15 F 121 A 85 (55%)
Scottish Cup: the clubs have been drawn together only once; see above.
League Cup: in this competition, too, there has been only one meeting,
          United winning 2–0 at Tannadice, also in 1959
Notable transfers from: Jimmy Smith (1934)

EDINBURGH CITY FC

Edinburgh City were formed in 1928 as an amateur club modelled on Queen's Park. A mere three years later they were elected to the Scottish League, following the resignation of Clydebank*. Over the seven seasons which followed they were fellow members of Division Two with Dundee United, and the first meeting between the clubs was a 1–1 draw at Marine Gardens, Portobello in November 1931.

That was one of three venues used by City during their League career. They ground-shared with Leith Athletic* at Marine Gardens between 1931 and 1936, then spent season 1936/37 at Powderhall Stadium (still in existence today as a greyhound track) in the Broughton district. In 1937 the club opened their own ground, City Park in the Pilton district (it is still in use, currently being shared by East of Scotland League clubs Craigroyston and Spartans).

The last meeting between the clubs took place at City Park in August 1939. United won 3–2 on what was the opening day of the new season, but it counted for nothing as the League was abandoned a month later following the outbreak of war.

Edinburgh City never again played as a Scottish League club, although they were members of C Division* between 1946 and 1949. That year the club adopted junior status, but disbanded in 1955.

It's a fact: In season 1934/35 the two League meetings between City and

United produced a total of 25 goals! The home win by the amazing margin of 9–6 for United is the highest-scoring match in the club's history, but the 8–2 victory at Marine Gardens merits no more than fourth place in the biggest away from home in the League.

The full Scottish League record against Edinburgh City was:
P 15 W 10 D 2 L 3 F 61 A 32

EMERGENCY WAR CUP

This trophy was instituted in 1940. Following the suspension of organised football in Scotland on the outbreak of the Second World War, regional leagues were introduced in order to cut down on travelling costs and time. However, it was felt by the SFA that a national cup competition should be retained, given the huge crowds which had flocked to Scottish Cup ties during the 1930s. Therefore the SFA instigated the Emergency War Cup for which all League clubs still in existence (some had gone into abeyance for the duration of the war) were eligible to participate. Non-League clubs were excluded. The other feature which distinguished the new competition from the Scottish Cup was that the first round was played on a home-and-away basis.

Dundee United had never progressed beyond the quarter-finals of the Scottish Cup and indeed had reached that stage on only one occasion (1929). Furthermore, with the club firmly established as also-rans in Division Two, nobody expected United to make any impact on the new competition. But the war had led to the cancellation of player registrations with the result that all were free agents. United's management had been assiduous in signing several players with Division One experience, and the results were soon obvious as the team began to produce a level of performance above that to which United supporters had become accustomed.

United met Partick Thistle in the first round, winning 4–2 at Firhill, then drawing 1–1 in the return before a crowd of 8,000, the wartime safety limit placed on Tannadice. The competition then reverted to a straight knock-out basis and United confounded pre-match forecasts by trouncing visitors Third Lanark* 7–1.

Demonstrating that it was no fluke, they then dismissed another of the big clubs from the west, Kilmarnock, 3–0 in the quarter-final, again at Tannadice and, for the third time in three weeks, in front of a capacity crowd. By way of comparison, it is interesting to note that in the season prior to the war United's average League attendance had been 4,600; the season before that it had been 1,700!

Their reward was a semi-final meeting with Airdrie at Easter Road, where 22,655 watched a 0–0 draw. Airdrie bent the rules to introduce a famous guest player for the replay, but even Stanley Matthews could not prevent United advancing to the final on a 3–1 scoreline. The final was played against Rangers at Hampden and attracted an attendance of around 90,000. Captain Jimmy Littlejohn* marshalled his team well and they gave an excellent account of themselves. United's Arthur Milne* had a goal disallowed before Rangers scored what proved to be the winner. All of the newspapers praised United's gutsy performance and most reckoned Rangers were fortunate to win.

The team which represented Dundee United at the club's first Hampden cup final was: Thomson, Miller, Dunsmore, Baxter, Littlejohn (capt.), Robertson, Glen, Gardiner, Milne, Adamson and Fraser.

ENGLAND

Dundee United have met the following English League clubs (all friendlies or testimonials unless indicated):

Home

Birmingham City* 1948; Crystal Palace 1952; Blackpool 1953; Burnley 1954; Newcastle United 1959; Derby County 1960; Sheffield United 1960; Manchester City 1962; Sheffield United 1967; Preston North End 1968; Newcastle United 1969 (Fairs Cup); Newcastle United 1970; Derby County 1971 (Texaco Cup); Leicester City 1972 (Texaco Cup); Sheffield United 1973 (Texaco Cup); Leicester City 1973 (Texaco Cup); Newcastle United 1973 (Texaco Cup); Sheffield Wednesday 1974; Preston North End 1975; Aston Villa 1979; Tottenham Hotspur 1979; Chelsea 1980; West Ham United 1980; Tottenham Hotspur 1980; West Ham United 1982; Southampton 1982; Everton* 1983; West Ham United 1983; Tottenham Hotspur 1983; Nottingham Forest 1984; Manchester United 1984 (UEFA Cup); Leicester City 1986; Tottenham Hotspur 1988; Stoke City 1994; Leicester City 1996; Wolverhampton Wanderers 1997.

Away

Bournemouth 1949; Swansea Town 1951 (twice); Millwall 1951; Barnsley 1951; Millwall 1961; Northampton Town 1964; Bury 1964; Carlisle United 1965; Crystal Palace 1967; Stoke City 1967 (North American Soccer League, Dallas); Sunderland 1967 (NASL, Vancouver); Wolverhampton Wanderers 1967 (NASL, Dallas); Huddersfield Town 1968; Preston North End 1968; Hartlepool United 1968; Wolverhampton Wanderers 1969 (USA, twice); Aston Villa 1969 (USA, twice); West Ham United 1969 (USA three times, one a friendly); Everton* 1969; Millwall 1969; Ipswich Town 1969; Newcastle United 1969 (Fairs Cup); Newcastle United 1970 (twice); Blackpool 1971; Derby County (Texaco Cup) 1971; Crystal Palace 1972; Bournemouth 1972; Leicester City 1972 (Texaco Cup); Southampton 1973; Sheffield United 1973 (Texaco Cup); Leicester City 1973 (Texaco Cup); Newcastle United 1973 (Texaco Cup); Everton 1976; Port Vale 1978; Tottenham Hotspur

1979 (Tokyo Cup, Japan); West Ham United 1983; Manchester United 1984 (UEFA Cup); Chelsea 1992 (Canada); Swindon Town 1995 (Finland); Blackburn Rovers 1997 (Sweden).

In addition, United paid visits to non-League opponents on two occasions – Cambridge City in 1961 and Guildford City in 1972.

ENTERTAINMENT

Through the years, football clubs have indulged in some bizarre activities to attract or hold the interest of supporters. At Tannadice, the early years of Jim McLean's* management were characterised by unusual events such as the issuing of free chocolate bars to school-age children and OAPs; free footballs kicked into the crowd (for the visit of Dumbarton* on 23 December 1972, though the crowd was still only 3,500); half-time pillow fights; and even pie-eating contests (really!).

For most Arabs, seeing their club win generally amounts to entertainment, though the hard taskmaster McLean did not always see it that way. Following United's 6–1 defeat of Motherwell* in the Scottish Cup quarter-final in March 1981, McLean reportedly fined his players for failing to entertain the paying customers. It subsequently emerged that, more accurately, the manager had withheld half of their win bonus because, after being 4–1 ahead at half-time, his players had 'eased off', scoring only twice in the second half!

EUROPEAN CUP

To date, United have participated only once in European football's most prestigious tournament. It occurred in season 1983/84, when participants were admitted only as a result of having captured their domestic championship. A 6–0 aggregate win over Hamrun Spartans from Malta* did not deserve special mention, though the same could not be said of the second-round opponents. Standard Liege were regarded as potential winners of the trophy, but their interest ended when United followed a goalless draw in Belgium* with a crushing 4–0 victory at Tannadice, inspired by a brilliant individual performance from winger Ralph Milne*.

The quarter-final draw sent the Scottish champions to Vienna, where the first leg resulted in a 1–2 defeat by Rapid. On an emotion-charged evening at Tannadice, United did enough to achieve the 1–0 margin which allowed them to qualify on the away-goals rule.

The club were now very much part of the big-time, being joined in the semi-final by Dinamo Bucharest, Liverpool and AS Roma. It was the Italians who were the visitors for the first leg at Tannadice for a match second only in prominence in the club's history to the UEFA Cup final three years later. The euphoria of a 2–0 first-leg lead evaporated at the Olympic Stadium when Roma, fired by the prospect of playing the final on the same ground, scored three times without reply. That everyone associated with Dundee United could be bitterly disappointed at failing to reach the European Cup final illustrated the level to which Jim McLean* and his players had raised the club's status.

EUROPEAN CUP WINNERS' CUP

This is not a competition in which United have ever distinguished themselves. The club have participated on three occasions, though only once in their own right.

In both 1974/75 and 1988/89 entry was gained as losing finalists because the Scottish Cup winners were also League champions. On the first occasion Jiul Petrosani of Romania* were beaten 3–2 on aggregate before an ignominious dismissal at the hands of the Turkish club Bursaspor, who scored the only goal of the tie. Fourteen years later, further embarrassment resulted, firstly through a laboured 1–0 aggregate win over Malta's Floriana, to be followed by elimination (including a home defeat) by Dinamo Bucharest.

In 1994, flushed with pride at the first bona fide qualification for the competition, more red faces resulted. Having struggled to a 3–2 home win over the unknown Slovakians of Tatran Presov, a first-minute goal in the second leg seemed to pave the way for victory. Not so. A mixture of goalkeeping blunders and defensive frailty saw three goals conceded for an aggregate 3–4 defeat.

EVER-PRESENTS

There have been ten Dundee Hibs players and 39 Dundee United players who appeared in every Scottish League match during a season.

The greatest number of ever-present seasons is eight by Doug Smith*, of which seven were consecutive. In fact, over nine seasons between 1962 and 1971, Smith established the remarkable record of missing just a single League match.

Not all that far behind come Paul Hegarty*, who was ever-present for seven seasons between 1976 and 1986, and Maurice Malpas*, who managed five between 1985 and 1992 (so far).

The greatest number of ever-presents in one season is four, in 1968/69.

EXTRA-TIME

In all, Dundee Hibs/United have been involved in matches which have gone to extra-time on 48 occasions. Remarkably, in almost half of them (23) the additional 30 minutes failed to produce a winner, necessitating either penalties or a replay. Of the remainder, United came out on top in 13.

Extra-time was first played by Dundee Hibs in May 1915 and it was decisive, Aberdeen A scoring the only goal in the final of the Dewar Shield* at Dens Park. The following 20 years produced only seven further instances. It is an illustration of the greater number of competitions, as well as a lower goal-scoring rate in modern football, that the 20 years between 1977 and 1996 produced 28 instances.

The biggest winning margin achieved in extra-time was United 4 Stenhousemuir 0 in a Scottish Cup fifth-round tie at Tannadice in February 1957.

Undoubtedly the most famous – and certainly the most important – instance of United triumphing in extra-time is one of the most recent. The dramatic equaliser scored by Brian Welsh just 40 seconds from the end of the second leg of the First Division promotion play-off against Partick Thistle at Tannadice on 16 May 1996 will take some beating for heart-stopping excitement. Though the club's return to the Premier Division was subsequently secured by Owen Coyle's 115th-minute winner, few Arabs would wish to repeat the experience!

F

FAIRS CUP

This competition was introduced in 1955 as the Inter-Cities Fairs Cup, originally involving clubs from cities which hosted trade fairs. Participation was by invitation only and the first tournament took three years to complete. The next one was spread over two years, but in 1960 both its name and its duration were shortened, although qualification by League position was not introduced until 1962.

It was in the 1966/67 Fairs Cup that Dundee United made their debut in European competition, famously defeating Barcelona (the holders) home and away before losing 1–3 on aggregate to Juventus.

Three years elapsed before United again qualified, only to exit at the hands of Newcastle United in the first round. The following season, the club fared rather better, defeating Grasshoppers of Zurich before losing to Sparta Prague.

By the time United next participated (1975/76) the competition had again been renamed, as the UEFA Cup.

FALKIRK FC

The first contact between the clubs came in the breakaway Central League* of 1920/21, though such was the standing of Falkirk at the time that it was their A team (and that of Hearts) which participated along with 16 of the smaller clubs, including Dundee Hibs.

A further five years elapsed until the clubs met at first-team level, following United's promotion to Division One. That was one of only five seasons the clubs spent together in the inter-war period (all but one in Division One) though they did meet again during World War Two in the Eastern Regional* and North Eastern* Leagues.

The clubs were virtual strangers after the war, Falkirk having only two seasons outside the top division, but following United's promotion in 1960 the clubs shared Division One status for all but two of the following years until the establishment of the Premier Division in 1975. At that level, Falkirk have been League opponents in only five seasons.

The playing record against Falkirk in major competitions is:
Scottish League (total): P 58 W 32 D 10 L 16 F 108 A 91 (66%)
Premier Division: P 20 W 15 D 2 L 3 F 37 A 19 (80%)
Scottish Cup: the clubs have been drawn together only twice, in 1966 and
again the following year.
Record: P 3 W 2 D 1 L 0 F 3 A 1
League Cup: the clubs were drawn together in 1951, 1959, 1964, 1982,
1991 and 1993.
Record: P 10 W 4 D 2 L 4 F 18 A 16
Notable transfers to: Tommy Gilroy (1927), Reggie Smith* (as manager,
1957), Scott Crabbe (1997)
Notable transfers from: Mickey Campbell (1925), Archie Aikman (1955),
Andy Irvine (1958)

FAMOUS FIVE
'The Famous Five' is a term usually associated either with books written by
Enid Blyton or with the Hibernian forward line of the late 1940s and early
1950s. However, if you were a Dundee United supporter in the post-war
era, the Hibernian version was regarded with much less esteem than the
Tannadice front five of Frank Quinn*, George Grant*, Peter McKay*, Andy
Dunsmore and George Cruikshank, and small wonder. They were together
for six seasons from 1948 during which time, collectively, they scored 303
goals in 679 League appearances! No other United forward line has even
approached the staying power of the Famous Five, whose achievement was
all the more remarkable when it is recalled that in all but two of these six
seasons United finished in mid-table, or worse, in B Division.

FANZINES
Fanzines first appeared in the late 1970s, emerging from the vibrant punk
music scene, which itself was a reaction to the bland, uninspired and
uninspiring disco-pop of that period.
    Around the mid-1980s, the fanzine culture began to develop among
football supporters, many of whom were equally dismayed by the
uninspiring match programmes produced by football clubs. Although
better than most, Dundee United's was nonetheless circumscribed by an
inability to be critical of external matters relating to other clubs and players
and – more importantly in the eyes of some Arabs – of internal club issues,
particularly the performance of players, the manager and the board.
    England led the way in the burgeoning fanzine scene, the first one of
note to appear north of the border being *The Absolute Game*, which covered
Scottish football in general, soon followed by *Not the View*, produced by
supporters of Celtic. Both first appeared in 1987 and were still going strong
ten years later. The first Dundee United fanzine was *The Final Hurdle* – a
title with which Arabs could readily identify – the inaugural issue appearing

in March 1988. It was less than enthusiastic about the way in which the club was run and received a predictably cool response from the management, unused as they were to criticism from within the club. But *The Final Hurdle* proved hugely popular, as evidenced by the fact that early issues, with a print run of 4,000, quickly sold out, while its letters pages overflowed with the opinions of Arabs who had no other outlet for their angst.

If the United board imagined that the craze would soon die out they were disappointed, as a plethora of others began to appear. Some were published by out-of-town supporters clubs, such as *When The Hoodoo Comes* (Falkirk), *One Team in Dundee* (Edinburgh & Lothians), and *Freakscene* (Glasgow), while *The United Review* and *Let's all laugh at Dundee* were independent of any grouping. *Utd United* was unique in that it was jointly published – for no obvious reason – by supporters of Dundee United and West Ham United. Most published only a few issues before disappearing, but all were characterised by a common theme of the need to communicate their passion and concern for United through a mix of criticism (usually constructive), humour, merciless attacks on Dundee FC and their fans, cartoons, wit and comment – all largely representative of Arabs.

New titles appeared during the 1990s, such as *The Arabian*, *Can I Bring My Dog?* and *Top Tier Fanzine*, but the one constant remained *The Final Hurdle*, which published its forty-second issue in March 1997. For most of its nine years it has been edited by Steve Malone and Martin Manzi, whose penetrating critique and biting wit were recognised in 1996 when it won *The Sunday Times* award for Scotland's fanzine of the year.

There can be few League clubs in Scotland or England whose fans have not produced at least one fanzine title and the invigorating effect which fanzine culture has had on the game over the decade since 1986 is reflected in the spread of their irreverent humour to the broadcast media. TV programmes such as *Only an Excuse*, *They Think It's All Over* and *Fantasy Football*, as well as BBC Radio Scotland's *Off the Ball*, would never have happened but for the fanzine revolution.

FATHER and SON
There have been only four instances of father and son playing for Dundee United.

Graham Honeyman was a winger who made three League appearances during season 1978/79 before emigrating to Australia. His son, Ben, returned from there to join United but played only twice for the first team in 1995/96, before joining Forfar Athletic.

Jimmy Irvine was an inside forward whose career spanned the club's rise from the obscurity of Division Two to a secure position in Division One between 1958 and 1964, he scored many times in the process. Twenty-three years later his son, Alan, signed for United from Liverpool for £100,000, but subsequently made only seven League appearances.

Frank Kopel played more than 400 times between 1972 and 1982, but son Scott managed just one appearance, in a UEFA Cup tie in 1990, while Malcolm and Sandy Robertson made only ten League appearances between them in 1981/82 and 1995/97 respectively.

Peter O'Rourke senior was manager of Dundee Hibs only from December 1922 until March 1923, but during that period his sons Michael and Peter junior both played for the club.

Paul Sturrock was one of Dundee United's all-time greats, playing well over 400 matches between 1974 and 1989. His son, Blair, may yet follow in his footsteps, having signed as an S-form player in 1996.

Duncan FERGUSON (born 1971)

Signed from juvenile side Carse Thistle in his home town of Stirling, he made his debut in 1990 and quickly established himself as a quick and fearless striker, remarkably nimble for his height (6ft 3in). Typical of his goalscoring style was the one which earned United a place in the 1991 Scottish Cup final; Ferguson started that match, but was substituted at half-time.

He had a stormy relationship with manager Jim McLean* culminating in his being fined and banned after a walk-out. Such a mild misdemeanour paled into insignificance compared to some of his later exploits but it hastened his departure from Tannadice. This brought United a British record fee of £4m from Rangers, good value considering his best years to date have been those he spent at Tannadice – despite the fact that he was a member of Everton's 1995 FA Cup-winning team.

Dundee United playing record (1990–93)

	Appearances	Goals
Scottish League	77	27
Scottish Cup	8	6
League Cup	3	2
Scotland	4	
Scotland U-21	7	1
Scottish Cup finalist 1991		
BP Youth Cup winner 1990		

FINLAND

United paid their first ever visit to Finland for a pre-season tour in 1995 and played three matches. One of these was against fellow tourists Swindon Town; United won 1–0. The two matches against Finnish League opposition resulted in a 3–0 win over Kings and a 2–2 draw with TPV.

United's only Finnish player was Mikka-Matti (Mixu) Paatelainen*. He arrived in October 1987 and soon established himself as a firm favourite with supporters. He played in the 1988 Scottish Cup final team, as well as winning many caps for Finland, before leaving for Aberdeen in 1992.

George FLEMING   (born 1948)

A midfielder who joined Hearts in 1966 and became the first player for whom Jim McLean* paid a transfer fee in January 1972. It involved only £10,000 but money was rarely better spent, George proving an invaluable bank of experience on which McLean's emerging young talent could draw. He stayed at Tannadice just long enough to be part of the team which won the club's first honour, the League Cup, in 1979. Transferred to St Johnstone as player/coach the following year, he later became their assistant manager, followed by a spell as manager of Arbroath. His playing career over he became, and remains, a publican in Broughty Ferry.

Dundee United playing record (1972–80)

	Appearances	Goals
Scottish League	257	31
Scottish Cup	19	3
League Cup	40	2
European competitions	11	

League Cup winner 1979

FLOODLIGHTS

Although floodlighting at a football match was first tried out in the late 1880s, it was not found to be a practical proposition until the 1950s. Prior to introducing floodlights, clubs advanced their kick-off times in winter, often to as early as 2.00 p.m. In terms of the major competitions, there were no scheduled midweek matches until the introduction of the Scottish League Cup in 1946, when some sectional ties were played with 6.30 p.m. kick-offs. In the early years of the Scottish Cup, replays took place the following Saturday, with League matches being postponed, but by the 1920s they were played on midweek afternoons, with the result that there was usually mass absenteeism from workplaces.

Dundee FC introduced their floodlights in 1959 but, being in Division Two at that time, United lacked the finances to do so. Following the club's promotion in 1960, the directors waited to see whether Division One status could be retained; when it was, resources were then made available for the building of a new stand and the installation of floodlights.

The Tannadice lights were switched on for the first time during the Division One match against Rangers on 10 November 1962. The first United player to score under the lights was Wattie Carlyle, in a 2–1 victory for United.

The first competitive match played by United under floodlights was a Scottish Cup second-round replay against Hibernian at Easter Road in 1958.

FOREIGN OPPOSITION
See also European Cup, European Cup Winners' Cup, Fairs Cup and UEFA Cup.
Despite having been in existence for 54 years, prior to touring southern Africa in the summer of 1963 Dundee United had never encountered foreign opposition. As all of the opponents on that tour were select sides, the first foreign club which United met was Fram Reykjavik on their tour of Iceland in June 1966. The first foreign club to visit Tannadice was Orgryte from Sweden in March 1965, as a result of the joint transfer of Orjan Persson* and Lennart Wing* from that club.

The only non-European visitors to Tannadice have been Dallas Tornado (1969) and the Australian Olympic XI (1994)

The club's first match in European competition was a 2–1 Fairs Cup win over Barcelona at the Nou Camp in October 1966. Their 100th was not quite in the same class, despite being a 9–0 Uefa Cup win over CE Principat of Andorra at Tannadice in July 1997.

The overall record of Dundee United in European competitions (22 entries) is :
P 102 W 45 D 26 L 31 F 160 A 102 (67.5%)

FORFAR ATHLETIC FC
County neighbours Forfar were one of Dundee Hibs' fiercest rivals in the club's early years. The two first met in the Northern League* of 1909/10, but were regular opponents in various local cup competitions, as well as the Qualifying Cup*, which produced epic encounters in 1912 and 1913. The first Scottish League meeting was in 1921/22 in Division Two and the clubs were regular League opponents at that level for most of the next 40 years. They last met in a League match at Tannadice in April 1960 during United's successful promotion campaign.

It's a fact: The Dundee Hibs–Forfar Athletic Qualifying Cup tie at Tannadice in November 1913 drew an attendance of 15,000 – more than twice the previous ground record.

The playing record against Forfar Athletic in major competitions is:
Scottish League: P 48 W 26 D 11 L 11 F 118 A 67 (66%)
Scottish Cup: the clubs were drawn together in 1955 (which was part of the 1955/56 competition), 1965 and 1987.
            Record: P 4 W 2 D 1 L 1 F 9 A 5
League Cup: the clubs were drawn together in 1955 and 1984.
            Record: P 3 W 3 D 0 L 0 F 13 A 4
Notable transfers to: Doug Berrie (1953), Scott Thomson (1991)
Notable transfers from: Tommy Adamson (1940), Donald Mackay (1962)

FORFARSHIRE CUP
The Forfarshire Football Association was founded in 1883 with 18 clubs in membership – 12 from Dundee, two from Arbroath and one each from

Broughty Ferry and Lochee (both then independent of Dundee), Coupar Angus and Montrose. The association immediately put up a trophy for competition between its member clubs.

At that time, cup competitions were the only form of organised football in Scotland. The county cups – there were also two for Glasgow – were regarded as even more prestigious than the Scottish Cup, with the result that they often attracted substantial crowds. As an example, when Dundee Harp met Our Boys (another city club and one of the forerunners of Dundee FC) in a Forfarshire Cup second-round tie in 1885, it drew a crowd of more than 10,000. Even when Dundee Hibs were formed in 1909 – almost 20 years after the Scottish League began – Forfarshire Cup ties drew crowds higher than the competing clubs had for most League matches, and were accorded in-depth coverage by local newspapers. For the 1911 final, several special trains conveyed supporters of Arbroath to Dens Park and they contributed to a crowd of more than 7,000, which saw their team lose by the only goal to Dundee Hibs. That was the first occasion on which the Hibs had won the trophy and manager Pat Reilly* regarded it as a major achievement.

At that time, being one of the top clubs in Scotland and quite literally in a different league from all other clubs in the county, Dundee FC entered their A team in the Forfarshire Cup, though that did not mean they failed to take it seriously. In 1912 they met Dundee Hibs in the semi-final at Dens Park and, following a 2–2 draw, Dundee protested to the Forfarshire FA that the Hibs had fielded an ineligible player. The FFA upheld the claim, banned the player for six months and ordered the Hibs to replay the match at Dens, thus depriving them of ground advantage. All this was too much for the Hibs committee and they refused to accept the ruling, not just withdrawing from the competition but also resigning from the Forfarshire FA. They returned after just a year in exile and contested the next two finals, both against Arbroath, losing in 1914 but gaining revenge the following year.

The next time the Hibs reached the final (1920) was to be their last. Again their opponents were Dundee A and again the match ended in acrimonious exchanges between the clubs. The Hibs won 1–0 before a crowd of 10,000 at Dens Park and were presented with the cup, but again Dundee protested, this time that their opponents had fielded a player of another club under an assumed name. It transpired that this was indeed the case and the Forfarshire FA ordered the final to be replayed. On this occasion the Hibs committee – no doubt somewhat embarrassed at being found guilty of sharp practice and perhaps relieved at not being thrown out of the competition – accepted the decision and the match was replayed a week later. The controversy may well have increased interest in the game because this time 12,000 turned up, but the loss of their 'guest' player proved no hindrance to Dundee Hibs who again triumphed by the only goal.

When Dundee United gained promotion to Division One in 1925 it became impossible for Dundee to continue entering their A team, and from then on the clubs met at first-team level in the competition. Dundee remain the club which has recorded most wins in the competition with 22, though United, including Dundee Hibs's three wins, have 19.

The competition proved remarkably durable until the mid-1980s, by which time it had become virtually impossible for United to find suitable dates for their ties. They asked the Forfarshire FA for permission to field their reserve team, but when this was refused the club withdrew from the competition as well as from the FFA. Shortly afterwards, Dundee FC followed suit and the Forfarshire Cup is now a four-way competition between Arbroath, Brechin City, Forfar Athletic and Montrose.

The last tie played by United was against Brechin City at Tannadice in August 1988.

George FOX (born 1913; died 1993)
Appointed to the board in 1955 along with Johnston Grant*, George Fox set about ridding Dundee United of the financial problems which had beset the club for as long as anyone could remember, and had effectively prevented it from mounting a serious promotion challenge in more than two decades.

As a chartered accountant, Fox was more than equal to the task, and in conjunction with the introduction of the club lottery, Taypools*, United's fortunes were turned around within the space of five years – just as the club won promotion to Division One after an absence of 28 years. It was only as a result of the groundwork of those five years under Fox's careful financial management that the club was able to go full-time, thereby enabling United to become established at the top level.

George Fox had two spells as Dundee United chairman. From 1965 until 1967 he oversaw the club's arrival on the European stage, then stepped aside, allowing Johnston Grant to take over. He never sought a return to the top job but, following the death of his great friend and colleague in 1984, his sense of duty to the club led to him resuming the chair at the age of 70. He eventually handed over the reins to Jim McLean* at the end of 1988, but remained a director, continuing to offer the benefit of his vast experience until his death in December 1993.

The board's decision to commemorate his Herculean efforts on behalf of Dundee United in the naming of the new stand at Tannadice was a fitting tribute to a man who was United through and through.

FRANCE
The French can claim to have been the inspiration for some of the definitive moments in the development of European and world football, instigating the founding of FIFA in 1904, as well as the introduction of the

World Cup in 1930 and the European Cup in 1955. Yet on the field they are the great under-achievers of European football, where at club level they have been less successful than Scotland, a country with only one tenth of its population.

France is one of the major European nations against which United have achieved a level of success above what might have been expected. United's comprehensive 5–2 defeat of AS Monaco in the principality in the 1981/82 UEFA Cup ranks as one of the club's outstanding European performances. It was a significant factor in establishing United's Euro credentials, bringing the club's name to the forefront for the first time since the defeat of Barcelona in 1966.

The same, curiously, can be said of the club's next meeting with French opposition five years later. RC Lens are not one of the bigger clubs in France, but they gave United serious problems in the first leg in Picardy to the extent that Jim McLean's* players were relieved to depart only 0–1 behind. Billy Thomson's heroics in goal were largely responsible, though United were well worth the 2–0 victory which propelled them over the first hurdle of that season's run to the UEFA Cup final.

The only other occasion United have visited France was in October 1988, when the club was invited to play a friendly against Bordeaux. They lived up to their European reputation by recording an impressive 2–0 victory over the previous season's French League runners-up.

G

Ally GALLACHER (born 1909; died 1964)

Gallacher has the unenviable record of occupying the manager's chair at Tannadice for the shortest period of all – a mere seven weeks.

He was manager of Tayside junior club Carnoustie Panmure when, in November 1954, he accepted United manager Reggie Smith's* offer of the job as his assistant. When Smith resigned to join Falkirk in January 1957, the United directors appointed Gallacher as his replacement although this was intended only as a temporary measure. He was clearly out of his depth and had the misfortune to preside over the most disastrous month in the club's history, United conceding seven goals in three consecutive matches, including a 0–7 home defeat by Morton. His resignation enabled Gallacher to commentate on his other role as an employee of Taypools*, which he had been instrumental in establishing. Not without some irony, he the combined it with a scouting role for Dundee FC, the young Kenny Cameron* being one of his recommendations. His son, Ken, is a leading journalist, becoming chief football writer with *The Herald* in 1996.

Kevin GALLACHER (born 1966)

A player with a fine pedigree: his grandfather was the legendary Celtic forward Patsy Gallacher, while his uncle, Tommy Gallacher, was a stalwart defender with Dundee FC in the post-war era, when the club twice won the League Cup.

Born in Clydebank, he was a schoolboy international (U-15) and joined United as an apprentice in 1983. He made his debut for United in Switzerland, in a UEFA Cup tie against Neuchatel Xamax in December 1985, and soon established himself with his fast and penetrating wing play.

Perhaps his most notable goal for the club came against Barcelona in another UEFA Cup tie, in March 1987, which gave United a 1–0 first-leg advantage. He won his first full cap for his country in 1988, but his star began to wane and he was no longer an automatic choice when Coventry City paid £950,000 to take him to England in January 1990.

His international career continued, as it did when he was transferred to

Blackburn Rovers, although he had the misfortune to suffer a number of serious injuries which led him to miss his club's Premiership title win in 1995.

Dundee United playing record (1985–90)

	Appearances	Goals
Scottish League	131	27
Scottish Cup	23	5
League Cup	13	5
European competitions	21	3
Scotland	4	
Scotland B	2	
Scotland U-21	7	2
Scotland youth	2	

UEFA Cup finalist 1987
Scottish Cup finalist 1987, 1988

Pat GARDNER (born 1943)

He was bought from Dunfermline in January 1972 as one of Jim McLean's* first signings, the new manager appreciating the need for some experience from which to develop his youth policy. Pat certainly fitted the bill, having previously been with Queen of the South, Airdrie and Raith Rovers. He had also played in Europe, having been one of Dunfermline's 1968 Scottish Cup-winning side.

Pat Gardner, featured on a bubblegum card issued in 1973

Season 1972/73 saw him finish as United's top scorer and the following one ended with Gardner again appearing at Hampden Park in the Cup final. He had been a driving force in United's progress to their first final as well as being an important inluence on the emerging young players such as Andy Gray* and Graeme Payne*.

In October of that year Gardner joined Motherwell and ended his playing career with Arbroath. He was later employed in a coaching capacity with Celtic and Motherwell.

Dundee United playing record (1972–74)

	Appearances	Goals
Scottish League	75	18
Scottish Cup	9	3
League Cup	18	2

European competition	2	1
Texaco Cup	8	
Scottish Cup finalist 1974		

GERMANY

Since German reunification in 1989, the only meeting with a Bundesliga club has been the pre-season friendly with Bayern Munich in Kuala Lumpur in July 1994. It ended in a 1–1 draw.

Only one German has played for United, and his stay was a brief one. Jochen Muller was a central defender signed from Bundesliga 2 club Waldhof Mannheim. He made his debut in a 3–4 opening-day League defeat by Celtic at Tannadice in 1991, but managed only a further four appearances before sustaining a serious injury which meant his career with United was over before it had properly begun.

GERMAN DEMOCRATIC REPUBLIC

United never met a club from the GDR (East Germany) either in European competition or in friendlies.

GERMAN FEDERAL REPUBLIC

By contrast, United met clubs from the GFR (West Germany) on three occasions in European competition and, to their great credit, emerged victorious each time.

The 5–0 demolition of Borussia Moenchengladbach in the 1981/82 UEFA Cup may have been dismissed by the German sports media as a freak, but the following season they were forced into a reassessment. In December 1982 United faced Werder Bremen in a third-round match and seemed to have left themselves with too much to do by conceding an away goal (they won 2–1). A crowd of 38,000 was in the Weserstadion on a freezing December night, confidently expecting their team to brush United aside. But Paul Hegarty*, playing a captain's part, took their breath away by heading in a Paul Sturrock* corner after two minutes, requiring the Germans to score three. In one of the most intensive onslaughts ever faced by a United defence, post and bar were each struck twice, efforts were cleared off the line by Hamish McAlpine* and his defenders, but only once did Bremen break through. A 1–1 draw – showing United had mastered the counter-attacking game needed to succeed in Europe – was a tremendous achievement and took United into the quarter-finals for the second successive season.

Thereafter, few people underestimated Dundee United in European competition. The Bundesliga was regarded as the best and its representatives the proving ground for those with pretensions to European trophies – and United had sent two of its finest packing.

The Germans, then, ought to have acknowledged history when United renewed their acquaintance with Borussia in the 1986/87 UEFA Cup semi-final. A 0–0 draw at Tannadice was the result of the Germans defending in depth and their reaction as they left the field suggested they believed their path to the final was assured. Not so. In what was arguably United's finest hour on European soil, they held Borussia at bay and scored twice on the counter to record a memorable – not to say thoroughly merited – 2–0 victory, and with it a place in the UEFA Cup final.

On two other occasions United visited West Germany and met Bundesliga clubs. The first was for a pre-season friendly in 1971. MSV Duisburg were the hosts, though they clearly did not hold out the 'welcome' mat, United being on the end of a 6–0 thrashing. A year later the Germans travelled to Tannadice for a rematch at the start of Jim McLean's* first full season in charge and on that occasion the spoils were shared in a 1–1 draw. In a clear reflection of the improvement which McLean achieved over the years which followed, a pre-season tour in 1984 included a fixture against 1FC Cologne, which United won 2–1.

Dennis GILLESPIE (born 1936)

Three months after Jerry Kerr* moved from Alloa to become United manager in 1959, he returned to his old club to secure the services of inside forward Gillespie. The fee was said to be £3,000; if so, it was one of the best pieces of business ever done by the club.

He stayed at Tannadice until 1971, making 400-plus appearances and scoring 120-plus goals before ending his career with Brechin City. In 1961 he won a Scottish League cap, becoming the first Dundee United player to play at that level.

Dennis was a huge favourite with Arabs, who turned out in force to provide him with the biggest-ever crowd (11,000) at a testimonial match for a United player.

Dundee United playing record (1959–71)

	Appearances	Goals
Scottish League	346	93
Scottish Cup	28	5
League Cup	55	13
Summer Cup	16	2
European competitions	8	
Scottish League	1	

Summer Cup finalist 1965

GOALKEEPERS

Dundee United have had a fair share of characters among their last line of defence, the first being the legendary Jimmy Brownlie*. He served the club as player, manager, secretary and director but was welcomed by Tannadice fans when he arrived in 1923 as the first real star the club had known as a result of his exploits with Scotland. Brownlie also played his last match for the club in February 1926 at the age of 40, two years after retiring!

Bill Paterson was signed from his home-town club, Dunfermline*, in 1925. A larger-than-life character, and not simply because he stood 6ft 3in tall and weighed 15 stone, he was an inspirational player who made a major contribution in the club's first seasons in Division One. His sense of humour no doubt had a therapeutic effect in the dressing-room, which he used as a means of honing his act as a stand-up comedian. This talent was actually secondary to one for which he was in great demand, as a fine singer, mainly of traditional Scots songs. As if that, along with his full-time occupation at Tannadice, were not enough he also ran a butcher's shop in the city's Hilltown, which needless to say was popular with United fans. Paterson's sudden transfer to Arsenal in 1928 was greeted with sadness by many beyond the football community.

Chic McIntosh was a Dundonian who joined United in 1931 and quickly became a huge favourite with the fans. Although only 5ft 7in he had great agility and at times extended this into a display of acrobatic skills. His pre-match work-out included cartwheels and handstands and once the match had begun his exuberance often saw him dive full-length to hold the ball, despite the fact that a simple pick-up was all that was needed. Equally, when the ball was at the opposite end he thought nothing of having a chat through his net with spectators, relying on them to let him know if play began to head in his direction! McIntosh made more than 100 appearances for United, his star going into steep decline when Jimmy Brownlie returned as manager in March 1934. The man who had earned the nickname 'the prince of goalkeepers' was not impressed with United's clown prince and McIntosh was soon on his way out of Tannadice, joining Preston North End later that year.

Hamish McAlpine* has the unique distinction of being the only Dundee Hibs/United goalkeeper to feature in the club's list of goalscorers. Between 1975 and 1977, as team captain, he had the responsibility of taking penalty kicks. He scored only three times, missing several more, which meant his colleagues were faced with a desperate rearguard action to keep the ball in the opposition half until Hamish had galloped back to his goal! In almost 700 appearances (the highest number by a United keeper) he established himself among United's all-time greats, sharing in all of the trophy wins between 1979 and 1983 as well as appearing in several unsuccessful finals.

Although Sieb Dykstra has, at the time of writing, been at Tannadice for little more than six months, he already shows signs of developing the kind of cult status with Arabs not seen since McAlpine's retirement. Like Hamish, he clearly understands the importance of establishing a rapport with supporters and his extrovert style equips him ideally for that role. Of course, without the necessary reliability to inspire confidence among his fellow defenders the inevitable 'blips' which accompany such flamboyance are not forgiven. In Dykstra's case he has already impressed with the kind of solid last line which any successful team needs, and the more established he becomes the more United will gain from it.

Although in the days before substitutes it was not unusual for an injured goalkeeper to play outfield rather than leave the pitch, Tom Muir – who played three League matches in goal during season 1946/47 – was also selected to play on the right wing against Leith Athletic* at Tannadice during that season. He was listed as 'Newman', his true identity only being revealed after the match, which United won 2–1.

One United goalkeeper who would rather not have entered the record books was Bob Morrison. Having missed a train, he failed to appear at Cowdenbeath for the Division Two match at Central Park in October 1935. Full back Dave Collington had to deputise but could not prevent the home side scoring seven, without reply. Morrison played in every other League match that season, but was given a free transfer at the end of it.

GOALS
Most/least in one season

The most goals scored by United during a Scottish League season was 108 in Division Two, 1935/36. With 34 matches played that season that meant an average of 3.2 goals per match, also a club record.

The lowest number of goals scored was 21, also in Division Two, in season 1911/12, their first as a League club. Only 22 League matches were played, giving an average of 0.95 per match. This is the only occasion on which the club has failed to average at least a goal per match during a Scottish League season.

United's most inept season defensively was 1931/32 when, not surprisingly, they were relegated from Division One. They conceded 118 at an average of 3.1 per match.

They had their tightest defence during season 1988/89 in the Premier Division, conceding only 26 at the miserly rate of 0.72 per match.

United's goalscoring record in the Premier Division was established in their championship season of 1982/83. It produced 90 goals, the same as runners-up Celtic. Thirty-six matches were played that season, for an average of 2.5 per match. Although Rangers scored 101 in 1991/92, they averaged only 2.3 as it was a 44-match season, so United share the record as the most prolific scorers in a season in the Premier Division.

The fewest goals registered by United in the Premier Division was 36 in season 1989/90, averaging exactly one per match.

The most conceded was 55 in the relegation season of 1994/95, an average of 1.6 per match.

The highest aggregate of goals for and against during a League season was in 1935/36, in Division Two. The club's followers certainly got their money's worth that season, watching United reach their record tally of 108, but at the same time they saw their goalkeeper retrieve the ball from his net on no fewer than 81 occasions. The total of 189 averaged out at 5.6 goals per match!

Most in one match

The highest number of goals to result from a match involving the club is fifteen. On 28 November 1934, United won a Second Division encounter against Edinburgh City* by nine goals to six – after being 2–4 down!

The next highest is the club's record win, 14–0 over Nithsdale Wanderers in a Scottish Cup first-round tie at Tannadice on 17 January 1931.

The club has been involved in two matches which finished 12–1, and it is a case of one for, one against. Not surprisingly, they represent United's record Scottish League victory and defeat. The thirteenth of April 1936 was the date on which Division Two visitors East Stirling were despatched by an 11-goal margin, while on 23 January 1954 United travelled to Fir Park, Motherwell, for a B Division match. They scored within 30 seconds, then produced what can at least be described as a balanced performance – they conceded six in each half!

Double figures

A total of 25 other matches involving United have produced ten or more goals:

10–2 v Stenhousemuir (h), Eastern Regional League, 3.4.39
 9–3 v Edinburgh City (h), Division Two, 18.11.33
 3–9 v Raith Rovers (h), North Eastern League, 8.11.41
10–1 v Alloa Athletic (h), B Division, 24.3.51
 9–2 v Arthurlie (h), Division Two, 14.1.27
      v Brechin City (h), Second Division, 22.12.34
 5–6 v Hearts (h), Scottish Cup, 17.2.68
 2–9 v Stenhousemuir (a), Division Two, 16.4.37
      v Hearts (h), Eastern Regional League, 18.11.39
10–0 v East Stirling (h), Division Two, 25.3.38
 9–1 v Airdrie (h), Division One, 5.10.63
 1–9 v Aberdeen (h), North Eastern League, 10.2.45
      v Third Lanark (a), B Division, 26.9.53
 8–2 v Edinburgh City (a), Division Two, 15.12.34
 2–8 v Berwick Rangers (a), Division Two, 21.2.59
 7–3 v King's Park (h), Division Two, 18.3.33
 3–7 v Dundee (a), League Cup, 12.9.56
 6–4 v Kilmarnock (h), Division One, 22.3.29
 5–5 v Airdrie (h), Division Two, 30.4.38
      v Arbroath (h), Division Two, 23.10.48

v East Stirling (a), B Division, 17.9.55
v Arbroath (a), Division Two, 18.9.57
4–6 v East Stirling (h), Division Two, 31.10.36
v Hibernian (h), North Eastern League, 31.10.42
v Dundee (a), Division One, 11.9.71

It's a fact: The climax to season 1935/36 produced United's most prolific goalscoring ever, with no fewer than 42 being registered in the last six matches. Scores of 6–3, 6–1, 6–1, 8–2, 4–3 and 12–1 established a record which no other club has achieved in the history of the Scottish League.

GOALSCORERS
See also Hat–tricks
Most in total
Between 1947 and 1954, Peter McKay* scored 201 goals for Dundee United (158 League, 12 Scottish Cup, 31 League Cup). He is also the club's leading Scottish League marksman, his 158 from 185 games working out at an average of 0.85 per game. In 1949, McKay scored in each of United's first eleven competitive matches of the season, a club record which still stands.

Although Arthur Milne* scored only 77 League goals for United, what is remarkable is that they were scored in a mere 73 appearances in three seasons between 1934 and 1937. He remains the only player in the club's history to record a career average of more than a goal per game. By means of comparison, the club's leading Premier Division marksman is Paul Sturrock*, with 109 in 385 League appearances, an average of 0.3 per game.

Most in one season
Johnny Coyle* holds the record with 43 (41 League, 1 Scottish Cup, 1 League Cup) netted in season 1955/56.

The most in a season since the Premier Division began is 28 (22 League, 5 League Cup, 1 UEFA Cup) scored by Dave Dodds* in 1982/83.

Most in one match
Albert Juliussen scored six of United's seven goals against St Bernard's* in a North Eastern League* Cup tie at Tannadice on 15 November 1941.

Collie Martin* scored five goals for Dundee Hibs in a Division Two match against Albion Rovers at Tannadice on 19 December 1914.

Only four Dundee United players have scored five times in one match. Tim Williamson against Nithsdale Wanderers in the Scottish Cup on 17 January 1931; Willie Ouchterlonie achieved the feat twice within a month in Division Two, against Edinburgh City* on 18 November and Leith Athletic* on 9 December 1933; Willie Black scored half of United's ten against East Stirling in a Division Two match on 25 March 1939; and Paul

Sturrock* against Greenock Morton in the Premier Division on 17 November 1984.

League's leading scorer

Occasions on which either Dundee Hibs or United have produced the League's leading scorer are few and far between. Collie Martin took the honours in Division Two in seasons 1913/14 and 1914/15; on the latter occasion he scored 29 of the Hibs' 48 League goals, from 25 appearances.

Duncan Hutchison* topped the Division Two charts in 1928/29, his 34 goals (35 games) helping United to the championship, but the club had to wait a further 27 years until Coyle's all-time record of 41 (36 games) saw him emulate Hutchie's feat.

The first United player to finish as top scorer in Division One was Kenny Cameron* in 1968/69, when he netted 27 from 34 appearances. Cameron's achievement remains unique to this day, although Andy Gray* shared the honour with 20 goals from 33 games in 1974/75. Ironically, his rival was Willie Pettigrew*, then with Motherwell, but who would join United four years later.

Ivan GOLAC (born 1950)

The appointment of the former Yugoslav international to the manager's job at Tannadice in July 1993 stunned Scottish football. Of all the Premier Division clubs, Dundee United would have been the last choice of most people to break the mould by introducing the country's first overseas manager. It was a bold decision by chairman Jim McLean* and his fellow directors, but their adventurous approach was rewarded with another mould being broken ten months later when Golac brought the Scottish Cup to Tannadice for the first – and, so far, only – time.

Golac had had a successful career in his native country as well as a spell with Southampton. Managerially he had earned his spurs with Partizan Belgrade, so he arrived with sound credentials. Unfortunately, Scottish football – and, as it turned out, the Tannadice board – were not ready to accept quite such a radical departure from the norm. Golac's unconventional training methods and his devil-may-care comments to the media made him more enemies than friends. The Cup triumph was almost certainly due to his ability to motivate the players for the big occasion, but he proved unable to repeat the act when it came to the bread-and-butter of the League.

In his first season, United finished only two points clear of relegation, a fact lost amid the euphoria of the Cup win. However, the following season's form was never convincing and it was clear that he did not command the respect of some of the players, particularly the senior ones. United's Premier Division status was under threat and when defeat at Hearts broke their hold on the Scottish Cup, the board acted quickly. Although it was reported that Golac had left the club 'by mutual consent', few doubted that, had he not agreed to do so, he would have been dismissed.

After less than two years, Ivan Golac was gone, but he will not be easily forgotten. Whatever their opinion of his reign as a whole – and they seem to embrace every description from saint to sinner – Golac did deliver the Holy Grail which many Arabs had all but given up hope of seeing: tangerine and black ribbons attached to the Scottish Cup.

Richard GOUGH (born 1962)

Although he went on to be recognised as one of the top central defenders in Britain, it was as a right back that Gough rose to prominence at Tannadice.

His father played for Charlton Athletic during the 1960s before emigrating to South Africa, where Richard was brought up. He initially experienced some difficulty settling in Scotland and during the winter of 1981/82 went home, vowing not to return. Not only did he do so, but he established himself in time to play a vital part helping United to win the Premier Division championship in 1983. That campaign saw what was arguably the club's best ever defence of Gough, Hegarty*, Narey* and Malpas*, and ironically it was that factor which ultimately prompted Gough to seek a transfer. He claimed his best position was as a central defender, but he had no chance of putting his theory to the test due to the impeccable form of Hegarty and Narey.

Doubtless other factors also came into play, but Gough, who since 1983 had been a regular in the Scotland team, got his wish with a £750,000 transfer to Tottenham in August 1986. Little more than a year later he was back in Scotland, Rangers having paid £1.1m to make him the rock on which was built their dominance of the Premier Division over the following decade. In May 1997 he moved to the USA, joining Kansas City Wizards.

Dundee United playing record (1981–86)

	Appearances	Goals
Scottish League	168	24
Scottish Cup	19	2
League Cup	36	9
European competitions	33	2
Scotland	26	
Scotland U-21	5	1

League champion 1982/83
Scottish Cup finalist 1985
League Cup finalist 1984

George GRANT (born 1923)

Born in Dundee, he was one of the United stalwarts of the post-war era, a dynamic player, then known as an attacking wing half who today would be described as a creative midfielder.

Creative he certainly was, from the moment he arrived from Arbroath in January 1946. In an era when United played attractive football while only rarely threatening to mount a serious promotion challenge, George was a consistently high achiever who had a telling ability to score vital goals, and it was surprising that he was not offered the opportunity of playing at a higher level before Falkirk signed him in 1954.

He regarded the famous Scottish Cup win over Celtic in 1949 as the most memorable match during his time at the club and he was a key factor that day. His long service and major contribution

George Grant, pictured in 1954

to United through what were often difficult times was recognised by the management when they gave him a testimonial – or, rather, half of one. In April 1954 the two city clubs met at Dens Park, the proceeds being shared between Grant and Dundee FC's Jimmy Toner.

Dundee United playing record (1946–54)

	Appearances	Goals
Scottish League	188	42
Scottish Cup	19	3
League Cup	36	5

Johnston GRANT (born 1915; died 1984)

He was a director in the family firm of haulage contractors when invited, along with George Fox, to join the board of Dundee United in 1955. Together they provided the impetus – and business/financial acumen – for the arduous task of turning Dundee United from Division Two also-rans into a club secure within Division One.

Boosted by the proceeds from the highly successful Taypools*, the club made speedier progress than Grant himself had anticipated, but he was always more willing to assume responsibility for taking the club forward and he became vice chairman in 1965. Never one to court publicity, he had to be convinced by his fellow directors (one of whom was his brother George) that he should assume the chairmanship two years later, a position he retained until his death in July 1984.

Under his chairmanship United not only achieved, but consolidated their position as one of the country's top four clubs, and Johnston Grant took great satisfaction in witnessing the arrival of the first trophies at Tannadice in 1979 and 1980. Even those achievements paled into insignificance three years later when the club captured the League championship, a feat beyond Grant's wildest dreams when he took up his seat on the board almost 30 years earlier. Those three decades had seen a metamorphosis of Dundee United and the effort and selfless dedication of Johnston Grant was a major factor in that change.

Andy GRAY (born 1955)

Andy Gray – complete with do-it-yourself hairdo – featured on a bubblegum card issued in 1974

One of Jim McLean's* early S-form boys, he signed as a professional in May 1973. Less than a year later, aged 18 years and five months, he was leading United's attack in the Scottish Cup final against Celtic.

There was a tremendous sense of loss among Arabs when he was transferred to Aston Villa in September 1975 for £110,000, the first six-figure fee received by United. Gray was such an immediate success that in 1977 he had the distinction, which remains unique, of being voted Player of the Year and Young Player of the Year in the same season by the PFA. He also won a League Cup winners' medal that year with Villa, a feat he repeated with Wolverhampton Wanderers in 1980. He had become one of the first million-pound players the previous year, Wolves paying £1.46m for his prodigious goalscoring capability.

His all-action style often bordered on the reckless and the many resultant injuries were largely responsible for restricting his haul of Scotland caps to a modest 20.

His greatest successes, however, came with Everton. They secured his services in 1983 for a fee of £200,000, a figure that reflected a return to something approaching sanity in the English transfer market rather than a diminution in the player's effectiveness. With Gray leading the line the Merseyside club won the League championship, the FA Cup and the European Cup Winners' Cup before he returned to Aston Villa to end his career.

But he still had one more medal to collect and he did so in an unlikely setting. Graeme Souness offered Andy the opportunity he had craved since boyhood of playing for Rangers and he was part of the team which won the League championship in 1988/89.

On retiring from the game he turned to a new career in the media, quickly becoming one of the most thoughtful, penetrating and amusing of television pundits. His tactical explanations and forecasts of future events on Sky TV's live matches are hugely entertaining and he doubtless earns more now than he ever did as a player!

Dundee United playing record (1973–75)

	Appearances	Goals
Scottish League	62	36
Scottish Cup	8	3
League Cup	14	9
European competition	5	
Scotland U-23	3	
Scotland youth	8	4
Scottish Cup finalist 1974		

Tommy GRAY (born 1926; died 1989)

A former Dundee FC player, he became United's third manager in the space of eight weeks when he was appointed in March 1957. At the time he was the part-time manager of Arbroath, then several places above United in Division Two, and in addition he had a secure and well-paid day job.

On being invited by United to take over as manager, he undertook to accept only if he was allowed to do it on a part-time basis; it is a measure of the lack both of foresight and ambition on the part of the Tannadice board that they agreed.

Tommy Gray, manager 1957–58

Any doubt as to the folly of such an appointment was removed when, in October 1958, and having made little impression during his year and a half in charge, Gray resigned due to what was described as 'pressure of business'.

GREECE

United have yet to meet a Greek club in European competition, although on two occasions they have travelled to that country for friendly matches. In May 1970 they lost 1–3 in Athens to Panathinaikos, who were to be the following season's European Cup finalists. In 1988, one of a number of invitations in the wake of United's run to the 1987 UEFA Cup final came from AEK Athens. United made the trip as part of pre-season preparations and recorded a 2–1 win over the club which had just finished runners-up in their championship.

GREENOCK MORTON FC

United did not meet Morton until achieving Division One status in 1925/26. The following season both were relegated, but they also bounced back together, with United as Division Two champions, in 1929. The next season, and then 1931/32, were the last which the clubs shared at the top level until 1963/64, although Division Two and B

Division meetings were fairly regular in the intervening period.

Since the introduction of the Premier Division in 1975, Morton have been members on only seven occasions. The last League meeting between the clubs was the First Division promotion decider at Cappielow Park in May 1996, in front of a crowd of 12,523. A 2–2 draw left them with the same number of points, allowing United to progress to the play-off because of a better goal difference.

It's a fact: United's record home Scottish League defeat was sustained when Morton won a Division Two match 7–0 in March 1957.

The playing record against Greenock Morton in major competitions is:
Scottish League (total): P 92 W 44 D 14 L 34 F 190 A 171 (55%)
Premier Division: P 28 W 18 D 4 L 6 F 66 A 21 (71%)
Scottish Cup: the clubs were drawn together in 1929, 1954, 1969, 1974 and 1986.
        Record: P 5 W 3 D 0 L 2 F 12 A 7
League Cup: the clubs were drawn together in 1953, 1958, 1969 and 1983.
        Record: P 8 W 1 D 2 L 5 F 12 A 24
Notable transfers to: Sammy Ross (1946), Tommy Traynor (1976)

It's another fact: In season 1984/85, United established their record aggregate score in Premier Division meetings with one club, scoring 18 times against Morton without reply. They won both matches at Cappielow Park by 3–0, while those at Tannadice ended 7–0 and 5–0.

George GREIG (born 1871; died 1940)

One of the larger-than-life characters which punctuate the club's history, Bailie Greig was a prominent Tory councillor on Dundee Corporation and a wholesale tobacconist when, in February 1934, he emerged as one of Dundee United's saviours.

Along with William McIntosh* (a former Dundee FC director), he put up the necessary finances to prevent Dundee United from going out of existence, when the directors had already raised the white flag by submitting the club's resignation from the Scottish League. The two reached agreement with the club's major creditors and re-scheduled the remaining debts; fortunately the League agreed to tear up the resignation letter.

This enabled the club to begin a slow recovery both on and off the park, but by the autumn of 1936 debts again began to rise. Clearly a wealthy man, Greig offered to underwrite these debts, but only in return for the other directors resigning, thereby allowing him to run the club as a one-man operation.

If that was unprecedented, Greig's next step was no less so. Despite having had no experience of professional football either as a player or as an administrator, he astonished everyone at Tannadice by dismissing legendary manager Jimmy Brownlie* in October 1936, taking over himself in a role he described as manager-director. He left all training and what tactics there were to trainer Johnny Hart, but Greig himself insisted on selecting the team each week. Amazingly, this arrangement continued for eighteen months, until the end of season 1937/38. At that point Greig made his exit, selling his shareholding and handing over to a new board of directors although he did remain a trustee of the club.

Neither Dundee United – nor indeed Scottish football – had seen anything quite like it, nor would again. Throughout it all the one constant was the performance of the team, which remained as it had throughout most of the 1930s – mediocre.

HAMILTON ACADEMICAL FC

Hamilton held a Division One place continuously from 1906 until 1947, thus restricting United's contact with them prior to World War Two to their four seasons in the top division between 1925 and 1932. Although the Accies were regular opponents in B Division and Division Two during the 1950s, their status as a club waned more or less as United's rose, with the result that since 1960 the clubs have spent just four seasons together. The last League meeting came in the First Division in April 1996, at Firhill Park, which Hamilton were using as a temporary home.

It's a fact: Hamilton are one of only two clubs from a lower division to defeat United in the League Cup, winning 2–1 at Douglas Park in August 1989.

The playing record against Hamilton Academical in major competitions is:

Scottish League (total): P 46 W 21 D 7 L 18 F 92 A 82 (53%)

Premier Division: P 8 W 6 D 1 L 1 F 20 A 3 (81%)

Scottish Cup: the clubs have been drawn together on only two occasions, 1976 and 1978.
Record: P 2 W 2 D 0 L 0 F 8 A 1

League Cup: the clubs were drawn together in 1948, 1964, 1979 (semi-final), 1981, 1989, 1993 and 1994.
Record: P 10 W 6 D 1 L 3 F 33 A 15

Notable transfers from: Duncan Ogilvie (1948), Paul Hegarty* (1974)

HAMPDEN HOODOO

From the mid-1980s, the Scottish football media seemed obsessed with the fact that, as Dundee United found it next to impossible to win at Hampden Park, they were somehow cursed by what was termed 'The Hampden Hoodoo'.

Did it really exist? Of course it did, eventually coming to be believed by some of the players, who admitted that it added to the pressures which already existed when facing a match at the national stadium. To some extent, therefore, it thus became a self-fulfilling phenomenon.

For those disinclined to believe in such things, the following statistics are offered as evidence. Between 1974 and 1991, including replays, Dundee United visited Hampden Park eight times for semi-finals (winning twice) and ten times for finals, winning not a single one. Spooky, or what?

On many of those occasions, United were expected to win so it was rather ironic that when the spectre of the hoodoo was finally exorcised in 1994 few observers gave them even a ghost of a chance. Ivan Golac's* team having disposed of Aberdeen after a semi-final replay (both matches at Hampden), Rangers lay in wait for what they and many others saw as the formality of adding the Scottish Cup to the League Cup and League championship trophies they had already collected that season. Prior to the final, Golac was asked by a journalist what he thought of the so-called Hampden Hoodoo. With a wave of his hand, he replied along the lines of 'that was then, this is now . . .', and the rest is history. So is the hoodoo.

David HANNAH (born 1973)

The youngest member of the Scottish Cup-winning team, he had made only seven first-team starts before the final and in all probability owed his place to the fact that Billy McKinlay* had been ruled out through suspension.

Having been in contractual dispute with the club for more than a year, he was transferred to Celtic for £650,000 in December 1996.

Dundee United playing record (1993–96)

	Appearances	Goals
Scottish League	66	7
Scottish Cup	8	2
League Cup	3	2
European competitions	2	1
Scotland U-21	16	2
Scotland youth		
Scottish Cup winner 1994		

HAT-TRICKS

See also Goalscorers

Firsts

The first player to score three goals in one match for the club was Willie Swan, in Dundee Hibs' 4–1 win at Tannadice over the Paisley club Abercorn* on 17 September 1910. Unfortunately, it didn't do him much good; despite scoring six goals in his eight League appearances that season, he was given a free transfer a year later.

The first player to score a hat-trick away from home was Dave

Scrimgeour, who got all of Dundee Hibs's goals in a Qualifying Cup* win over Forfar Athletic at Station Park on 21 September 1912.

Joe O'Kane scored the club's first Scottish Cup hat-trick in a 5–1 win over Aberdeen University at Tannadice on 24 January 1925. This was also the first ever hat-trick scored by a Dundee United player.

United's first hat-trick in the Premier Division was scored by Tom McAdam on 3 March 1976 in a 5–0 win over Ayr United at Tannadice.

Paul Sturrock* was the first to score three times in European competition, in the 5–2 Uefa Cup win against Bohemians in Dublin on 18 September 1985. In the same competition, Gary McSwegan hit three in each leg against CE Principat on 23 and 30 July 1997.

Most by one player
The greatest number of hat-tricks scored by a United player in one season is seven by Peter McKay* in 1948/49 – although two were in the Forfarshire Cup*. McKay also scored five hat-tricks in 1951/52, and all were in League and Scottish Cup matches.

Arthur Milne* scored six hat-tricks during season 1935/36; all were in League matches and two were in fours.

More than one in a match
There have been eight instances of two United players scoring three times (or more) in the same match.

On 17 January 1931, Tim Williamson scored five and George Bain three in United's 14–0 Scottish Cup win over Nithsdale Wanderers.

On 18 March 1933, Dave Laing and Willie Ouchterlonie each scored hat-tricks in a 7–3 win over the Stirling club King's Park*, in Division Two.

On 22 December 1934, Arthur Milne scored four and George Ross three in a 9–2 win against Brechin City in Division Two. The prolific Milne was at it again on 13 April 1936, both he and Duncan Hutchison* registering hat-tricks as East Stirling were the victims in United's biggest ever League win, 12–1.

On 12 January 1952, Peter McKay and Frank Quinn* each scored three as United beat Forfar Athletic 8–1 in B Division.

There was also an instance at Hampden Park though, sadly, not in a cup final! In much more mundane circumstances, Jim Irvine scored four and Dennis Gillespie* three as United beat Queen's Park 8–1 in Division Two on 12 September 1959.

At Tannadice on 30 December 1967, United beat Stirling Albion 9–0 in Division One, both Ian Scott and Ian Mitchell* registering hat-tricks.

Almost exactly 30 years had elapsed before a double hat-trick was again recorded by United players, Robbie Winters (four) and Gary McSwegan (three) contributing all but one of the goals against the amateurs of CE Principat in the UEFA Cup in Andorra on 23 July 1997.

Most unusual

On 22 February 1997, Ray McKinnon scored all of United's goals in a 3–2 Premier Division win at Kilmarnock. Each came direct from a free-kick, believed to be the first time this has happened in the history of the Scottish League.

HEART OF MIDLOTHIAN FC

The first contact between the clubs came in the breakaway Central League* of 1920/21, though it was Hearts A team (and that of Falkirk) which participated along with 16 of the smaller clubs, including Dundee Hibs.

A meeting at first-team level had to await Dundee United's promotion to Division One in 1925, but between then and World War Two the clubs met almost as often in the Scottish Cup as in the Scottish League. Indeed, following United's relegation from Division One in 1932, they did not meet Hearts in a League match until 1960. Since then there have been only five League seasons when they have not met, Hearts spending four in the First Division to United's one.

The playing record against Hearts in major competitions is:

Scottish League (total): P 106 W 37 D 32 L 37 F 146 A 130 (50%)

Premier Division: P 68 W 24 D 23 L 21 F 81 A 69 (52%)

Scottish Cup: the clubs were drawn together in 1926, 1935, 1938, 1967, 1968, 1974 (semi-final), 1984, 1986 (semi-final), 1995 and 1997.
Record: P 15 W 5 D 5 L 5 F 27 A 29

League Cup: the clubs were drawn together in 1962, 1969, 1970, 1977 and 1984 (semi-final).
Record: P 10 W 5 D 1 L 4 F 15 A 13

Notable transfers to: Willie Pettigrew* (1981), Eamonn Bannon* (1988)

Notable transfers from: Alan Gordon (1969), Tommy Traynor (1970), George Fleming* (1972), Scott Crabbe (1992)

It's a fact: When United and Hearts met in the Scottish Cup in 1926 two matches, including extra-time in the replay at Tynecastle, could not separate the teams. In anticipation of a larger crowd, United controversially conceded ground rights for the third game, then were faced with a crisis when goalkeeper Bill Paterson sustained an injury in the League match which preceded the tie. Manager Jimmy Brownlie*, who had officially retired as a player two years earlier, was still registered as a player and was the only other keeper on the books. At the age of 40 he had no alternative but to play, though his lack of match fitness was a major factor in United's 0–6 defeat.

It's another fact: In season 1988/89, all four League matches between the clubs ended goal-less, the only occasion on which this has occurred in the history of the Premier Division.

Paul HEGARTY (born 1954)

Signed from Hamilton Accies in November 1974 as a striker, few could have predicted the outstanding success Paul would have as a United player.

After three years manager Jim McLean* switched him to central defence, where he began to form the partnership with David Narey* which would endure for more than a decade of excellence. Hegarty soon earned the first of his Scotland caps and, as captain, led United to their League Cup and League championship triumphs as well as many cup finals and memorable European occasions.

His was an outstanding contribution to the club and this was recognised with a testimonial year and, in 1990, the waiving of a transfer fee when he moved to St Johnstone. His success continued when he won a First Division championship medal with them before moving to Forfar Athletic* as player/manager later that year. He remained for a year and a half, then was out of the game for a short spell before returning to Tannadice as a coach in 1992. He joined Hearts in the same capacity in 1995.

His total of 706 first-team appearances places him third in United's all-time list.

Dundee United playing record (1974–89)

	Appearances	Goals
Scottish League	493	51
Scottish Cup	58	7
League Cup	86	12
European competitions	68	12
Scotland	8	
Scottish League	1	
Scotland U-21	6	
Scottish League champion 1982/83		
League Cup winner 1979,1980		
UEFA Cup finalist 1987		
Scottish Cup finalist 1981,1985,1987,1988		
League Cup finalist 1981,1984		
Scottish PFA Player of the Year 1979		

HIBERNIAN FC

The Edinburgh club holds the distinction of being the first ever opponents of Dundee Hibs. The common name and Irish connection made the choice an obvious one and the clubs played out a 1–1 draw before around 7,000 spectators at Tannadice on 10 August 1909.

The first competitive meeting between the clubs came during United's Division One debut season in 1925. They also met at that level the following season as well as 1929/30, but Hibernian had been relegated by the time United reached the top division for the third time in 1931. That being but a brief visit, the clubs met again in Division Two in 1932/33 in what proved to be their last League encounter for 27 years.

Since 1960, the only seasons in which they have not met on League business were 1980/81, when Hibernian spent a season in the First Division, and 1995/96, when United suffered a similar fate.

It's a fact: The Scottish Cup second-round replay at Easter Road in February 1958 was the first occasion on which United had played a competitive match under floodlights.

The playing record against Hibernian in major competitions is:

Scottish League (total): P 116 W 45 D 33 L 38 F 151 A 142 (53%)

Premier Division: P 80 W 36 D 25 L 19 F 90 A 64 (61%)

Scottish Cup: the clubs were drawn together in 1924, 1932, 1958, 1976, 1982, 1985 and 1990.
Record: P 11 W 4 D 3 L 4 F 13 A 10

League Cup: the clubs were drawn together in 1963, 1971, 1972, 1986 and 1993 (semi-final).
Record: P 8 W 1 D 1 L 6 F 9 A 19

Notable transfers to: Alan Gordon (1972), Darren Jackson (1992), Michael O'Neill* (1993), Brian Welsh* (1996), Jamie McQuilken (1996)

Notable transfers from: Davie Hogg (1968)

HIGHLAND LEAGUE

Dundee Hibs/United have met the following Highland League clubs. These involved friendly matches (including testimonials) unless otherwise stated.

Home

Inverness Caledonian 1912 (Qualifying Cup); Inverness Caledonian 1913 (Qualifying Cup); Inverness Caledonian 1952 (Scottish Cup); Peterhead 1972 (Dewar Shield).

Away

Inverness Caledonian 1912 (Qualifying Cup); Inverness Caledonian 1913 (Qualifying Cup); Elgin City 1933; Fraserburgh 1933; Fraserburgh 1935 (Scottish Cup); Fraserburgh 1935; Forres Mechanics 1935; Inverness Thistle 1935; Elgin City 1935; Peterhead 1936; Elgin City 1947; Inverness Caledonian 1952 (Scottish Cup); Inverness Select 1961; Elgin City 1961; Keith 1966; Forres Mechanics 1971; Inverness Clachnacuddin 1974; Elgin City 1974; Fraserburgh 1975; Elgin City 1975; Peterhead 1989; Huntly 1995 (Scottish Cup).

It's a fact: When United were drawn against Huntly in the 1995 Scottish Cup, it was the first time in 43 years that the club had met non-League opposition in the competition.

HISTORY
Books

There has been a dearth of published material on Dundee United compared to Scotland's other major clubs. A club history was not published until 76 years after its formation in 1909. Prior to that there had only been *United through the Years*, a 28-page brochure/booklet published in 1948.

Rags to Riches: the Official History of Dundee United was written by Mike Watson and published by David Winter of Dundee in 1985. An updated version was published in 1992.

In addition, since the club began to win honours there have been several other publications about United and/or its players. Paul Hegarty's* autobiography *Heading for Glory* was published by John Donald in 1987 while journalists assisted Jim McLean* (*Jousting with Giants*, 1987) and Paul Sturrock (*Forward Thinking*, 1989) with theirs, both published by Mainstream. *A View From the Ground*, a diary of season 1992/93, was written by Gwen McIlroy, with match-by-match commentary by Dave Bowman. It was published by David Winter. The following year, the same publisher issued *Kissing Strangers*. Edited by Gwen McIlroy, it contained a wonderfully moving series of reminiscences by United players and supporters before, during and after the Scottish Cup triumph.

Milestones

1909   Founded as Dundee Hibernian
1910   Admitted to Scottish League
1913   First Scottish Cup tie
1923   Adoption of the name Dundee United and change of club colours from green and white to black and white
1925   Promotion to Division One after winning first championship flag.
1931   Record win, 14–0 at home to Nithsdale Wanderers
1935   Highest number of League goals scored (108)
1940   First national cup final (Emergency War Cup)
1940   Club closed down for a year
1945   Willie MacFadyen* appointed as manager
1954   Record defeat, 1–12 at Motherwell
1954   Willie MacFadyen resigns after a record nine years in charge
1954   Scottish League status retained on good average
1959   Jerry Kerr* appointed as manager
1960   Promotion to Division One after an absence of 28 years
1962   Dennis Gillespie* wins Scottish League cap, the club's first representative honour
1964   Scandinavian 'invasion' brings club's first full international caps
1965   Record League win over Dundee FC (5–0 at Dens*)
1966   First entry to European competition: Fairs Cup visit of Barcelona

creates Tannadice crowd record of 28,000

1971 Jerry Kerr moves out of manager's office (to become general manager) after a record 13 years; Jim McLean* appointed as manager

1974 First Scottish Cup final

1975 Inaugural members of new Premier Division

1976 Premier status retained on goal difference

1977 Dave Narey* becomes club's first full cap for Scotland

1979 First trophy win, the League Cup

1980 League Cup retained

1983 League champions in 75th year

1984 European Cup semi-final

1987 UEFA Cup final

1988 Jim McLean becomes chairman and managing director

1991 Reconstruction of Tannadice begins

1993 Jim McLean stands down as manager after a record 21 years and eight months (but remains as chairman)

1993 Ivan Golac* appointed; first foreign manager in Scottish football

1994 First Scottish Cup win

1995 Relegation for the first time in 63 years

1996 Return to Premier Division; Billy Kirkwood* sacked; Tommy McLean* appointed; second Scandinavian 'invasion'

HOLLAND

Holland has proved a popular destination for United and, on one special occasion, their supporters.

United's first contact with the Dutch came in 1967. One of their opponents in the North American Soccer League* was ADO Hague and United came out on top 2–1 in Dallas. In 1973 United first visited the country for a pre-season tour and met three Dutch First Division clubs. Honours ended even with a 1–1 draw at Dordrecht, a 1–0 win over Fortuna Sittard and a 1–2 defeat by Telstar Velsen.

The club's next appearance in Holland was altogether more notable. The 1982/83 UEFA Cup handed United a tough draw against PSV Eindhoven. Their task appeared even more arduous when the Dutch side left Tannadice with a 1–1 draw, but in the return one of United's finest away performances in Europe produced a superb 2–0 win. The large number of Arabs who had made the journey were ecstatic as goals from Paul Hegarty and Billy Kirkwood* made it a night to remember.

If that encounter represented one extreme of emotion, the next with a Dutch club, in the same competition, did the opposite. United emerged with some credit from a first-leg 0–1 defeat against Vitesse Arnhem, having seen nothing to make them believe the deficit could not be overturned at Tannadice. However, 7 November 1990 turned into the heaviest and most comprehensive home defeat suffered by the club in almost fifty European ties. In scoring four without reply, the Dutch served up a devastating display which left United's players chasing shadows, exposing a gulf in skill and technique between the teams which was as alarming as it was apparent.

Such was the effect that the Arnhem defeat had on Jim McLean* that he decided to learn from football in Holland and appointed a coach from that country on a temporary basis. Abe Grittner worked with the players on what was described as 'flexibility of movement and action, allied to maximising skills'. McLean had long been an admirer of the Dutch approach to football, especially its coaching and training methods, and for that reason took his squad to that country for pre-season training in 1990 and 1991. In the main, non- or lower League clubs provided the opposition.

He also signed three Dutch players. In 1989 full back Freddy van der Hoorn joined from Den Bosch for £200,000 and became a huge favourite with Arabs, with whom he was a great communicator. His five years at Tannadice included an appearance in the 1991 Scottish Cup final, but he had fallen from favour with Ivan Golac by the time he was transferred to the Belgian League club Aalst in 1994. Goalkeeper Guido van de Kamp* was also popular with the fans at Tannadice following his arrival from BVV Den Bosch in 1991. He was a member of United's 1994 Cup-winning team, but never played another competitive match for the club.

Gijs Steinmann was a much less successful signing. He joined from FC Utrecht for £100,000 in the aftermath of the Arnhem defeat in November 1991, but played only 16 League games during his stay. He then sought to return to Holland, but when his request was refused he walked out on the club and was never seen again.

In December 1996 manager Tommy McLean* paid Queen's Park Rangers £100,000 to renew acquaintance with goalkeeper Sieb Dykstra, who had played for him at Motherwell.

John HOLT (born 1956)
Born in Dundee, he joined United as an apprentice from school in 1972 and made his first-team debut in January 1974, just two months after his seventeenth birthday. A hard-working and tough-tackling midfielder, he went on to make in excess of 400 appearances over 14 years at Tannadice, sharing in all of the club's successes, as well as many cup final disappointments.

Shortly after the UEFA Cup final of 1987 he was transferred to Dunfermline Athletic, and a year later to Dundee FC. John tried his hand at management, first as player/manager with Forfar Athletic then as manager of Deveronvale and Montrose before the wheel turned full circle with his return to Tannadice as one of the SFA Community Development Officers.

Dundee United playing record (1974–87)

	Appearances	Goals
Scottish League	271	17
Scottish Cup	38	3
League Cup	47	5
European competitions	44	
Scotland youth	2	

League champion 1982/83
League Cup winner 1979,1980
UEFA Cup finalist 1987
Scottish Cup finalist 1981, 1985, 1987
League Cup finalist 1981, 1984

HUNGARY

United have visited Hungary on only one occasion. They met Diosgyori VTK from the provincial city of Miskolc in the UEFA Cup of 1979/80. Having eliminated Anderlecht in the first round, hopes were high that the Hungarians would follow, but they were probably underestimated, always a dangerous mistake. In fact, Diosgyori not only eliminated United on a 4–1 aggregate, but became only the second club (Newcastle United were the first, in 1969) to win at Tannadice and also to win both legs of a European tie.

Duncan HUTCHISON (born 1903; died 1973)

Although Dundee United has produced its fair share of characters over the years, it is no exaggeration to say that no player captured the imagination of the fans at Tannadice to the same extent as the man they nicknamed 'Hurricane Hutch'.

That aptly summed up his all-action style of powerful running and explosive shooting which brought him goals at a startling rate. His 64 in only 73 League games between 1927 and 1929 led to United receiving a bid which they could not refuse from Newcastle United, and sadly Hutchison left Tannadice after only two years; it was a decision which provoked a furious reaction among supporters, including match boycotts.

When, after spells at Derby County and Hull City, Hutchison returned to Tannadice in June 1935, the tremendous enthusiasm of his initial stay was instantly re-created. He showed that, despite being 32, he remained a prodigious goalscorer, adding 55 over the following four League seasons.

When his playing career came to an end Duncan, having no interest in entering management, became proprietor of a bar in the city centre and re-named it, with characteristic flourish, the United Bar; it remained for many years a magnet for United fans or anyone else who wanted to reminisce about 'the good old days' with one of the club's all-time greats.

Duncan Hutchison's link with United was restored in 1953 when he became a director. He remained on the board, having a brief spell as chairman in the mid-'60s, until his death in 1973.

Dundee United playing record (1927–29 & 1935–39)

	Appearances	Goals
Scottish League	196	119
Scottish Cup	16	5
Division Two champion 1928/29		

William HUTCHISON

A publican who was one of the group of city businessmen which bought out the Dundee Hibs committee in November 1922. He became club treasurer, a vital position given the club's precarious financial state.

Hutchison was a driving force in 'modernising' the club. He was in no doubt that the Irish connection represented excess baggage which was preventing its development and stated publicly that he was aware of people in Dundee who were willing to invest in the club, but would not do so until its image was changed and it had regained its Scottish League membership. Both aims were eventually achieved, though not, in respect of the latter, without intensive lobbying of other clubs, primarily by Hutchison, at a time when Dundee Hibs could scarcely justify its claim for a League place. Had League membership not been regained, the necessary finance to restructure the club would not have been forthcoming and it is quite likely the club would have gone out of existence – and Dundee United would never have existed.

William Hutchison is, in fact, one of the two men responsible for introducing the name Dundee United to Scottish football. When Dundee FC objected to the use of the name Dundee City, it was Hutchison and chairman James Dickson who travelled to Glasgow for a meeting with the SFA Council on 17 October 1923 to suggest the name United as a compromise.

He continued to play a leading role on the board, and was chairman between 1925 and 1929. He then resumed his previous position as treasurer, but resigned as a director in 1932 in protest at the board's decision to dismiss manager Jimmy Brownlie*.

That was not the end of his involvement, however. He returned to the board, as chairman, in June 1938 as the result of another takeover and remained there until the wartime close-down of season 1940/41.

I

ICELAND

An end-of-season tour in 1966 represented United's first contact with Iceland. It was the club's inaugural venture into Europe (though they had visited southern Africa in 1963) and the match against Fram Reykjavik was the first European club side ever faced by Dundee United. That and the following two matches were won before the party continued the tour in Denmark.

In 1975 United returned to the island on UEFA Cup duty, beating IBK Keflavik 2–0 in the first leg, followed by a 4–0 win at Tannadice.

A further 15 years were to elapse before any further contact, the UEFA Cup first-round draw of 1990 sending United to meet Hafnafjordar. The first leg ended with Jim McLean's* men 3–1 to the good, but was notable for the 'crowd' of only 263, the lowest ever to watch a European tie involving Dundee United. The return did not provide one of Tannadice's more memorable European nights, a lapse in concentration allowing the Icelanders to take most of the credit from a 2–2 draw.

INTER-LEAGUE MATCHES

These began in 1892 as a challenge between the Scottish and Football Leagues. The following year the Irish League was added and matches involving the three – the League of Ireland participated from 1947 – were played each season, with the exception of wartime, for almost 80 years. Caps were awarded.

Only clashes between the Scots and the English proved capable of attracting a sizeable crowd and the series was dropped in 1970 as new demands began to be made on the international calendar.

Dennis Gillespie* became the first Dundee United player to receive representative honours when he was selected to play for the Scottish

Stewart Fraser, scorer of a hat-trick for the Scottish League

League against the League of Ireland in 1961. The following season left half Stewart Fraser was selected and, despite his position, scored a hat-trick against the same opponents in an 11–2 landslide.

The only other United players capped at Scottish League level were Jackie Copland, Paul Hegarty*, Jim Henry, Dave Narey* and Andy Rolland.

INTERNATIONALISTS
Given the large number of United players at all levels who have represented their country over the past 20 years, it is easily forgotten that, until Dave Narey* came on as a substitute for Scotland against Sweden at Hampden Park in April 1977, no United player had ever won a full cap for Scotland.

The club's first internationalists were in fact Orjan Persson* and Lennart Wing*, who represented Sweden on several occasions (often together) while at Tannadice during the mid-1960s.

In total, 18 players have gained full international recognition while at Tannadice – twelve for Scotland, two for Sweden and one each for Finland, Northern Ireland, Trinidad & Tobago and Yugoslavia.

INTERNATIONAL LEAGUE (USA)
This invitation tournament was played during May 1969, with clubs from various countries adopting the identities of US cities in an (ultimately failed) attempt to stimulate interest in 'soccer' in that country.

As in 1967 with the NASL*, United played as Dallas Tornado, though on this occasion their group involved only four other clubs: Aston Villa (Atlanta), Kilmarnock (St Louis), West Ham United (Baltimore) and Wolverhampton Wanderers (Kansas City). United did not fare particularly well, winning two, drawing two and losing four of the matches.

INTERNATIONAL XIs
Club matches against international teams are officially discouraged by the SFA, but providing they take place abroad a blind eye is usually turned. United have met the following on their travels: Mexico XI, 1970; South Korea, 1971; Burma, 1979; Japan B, 1979.

The Second World War was responsible for introducing international sides to Tannadice, although they clearly comprised players chosen on the grounds of availability rather than ability. There were challenge matches against a Polish Army XI in December 1941 and a Norwegian Forces XI in April 1944.

The only international side United have met at Tannadice was the Australian Olympic team, for a pre-season match in 1994.

IRELAND
See also Northern Ireland and Republic of Ireland
Ireland has a special place in the history of the club, given that it grew from

roots within Dundee's substantial Irish immigrant community, and its offspring, in the early years of this century.

A letter which secretary/manager Pat Reilly* sent in May 1909 to all Scottish League clubs seeking support for the new club's application to join the League, included the following passage:

> The promoters of the club were actuated chiefly by the fact that in Dundee there is a very large population of Irish extraction estimated at fully 30,000 and experience shows that a football club which appeals to the sense of national patriotism receives their wholehearted and enthusiastic support. We recall with pleasure the career of Dundee Harp FC, and our belief is that the new Irish organisation will fill the place which has been vacant since the days of the Harp.

Dundee Harp had gone out of business in 1906 and adopting the name of Dundee Hibernian was a similarly explicit message, though the fact that the club was never sectarian in nature, either in terms of its committee or players, showed that it had no intention of excluding those from outside that community.

Despite the mention of 'patriotism' in Reilly's letter, the club was not intended as a vehicle for Irish nationalism. The Dundee Irish did retain a keen sense of their identity, though culture, and in particular sport, was seen by the founders of Dundee Hibs as an adequate means of expressing it.

However, it was largely as a result of the struggle for Irish independence and the divisions (and often violence) which that generated in the west of Scotland that the Dundee Irish tended to distance themselves from the issue. When the Irish civil war erupted in 1922 it came at a time when support for Dundee Hibernian was at an all-time low. Had strong feelings of Irish nationalism existed within the city, then the Hibs could have provided a focal point – perhaps even a rallying point – for those of Irish origin keen to express their support for their homeland's right to self-determination. That no such voice was heard may be evidence that, for the Dundee Irish, being Dundonian was beginning to carry as much importance as their Irish ancestry, not least since many in the community were by then of the third generation to have been born in the city. It is pleasing to record that the city has never produced the sectarianism rife for so long in the west of, as well as parts of central, Scotland.

Certainly, when the men who had taken over Dundee Hibs in November 1922 announced their intention of radically altering its name and image there is no evidence of any protests, nor indeed of any attempts by supporters or the wider Irish community to resist the new regime or its plan. The facts were that, as with any football club, those who support it by attending matches – or, more importantly those who might be enticed to do so – are primarily concerned with the quality of football on offer. With

Dundee Hibs then at the lowest point in the club's history, few people in the city, no matter what their origins may have been, much cared about what was happening at Tannadice. The club was in terminal decline and, without the takeover, would have died. Honourable as they undoubtedly were, by 1922 the club's Irish roots were both an anachronism and a liability; the time had come to move on.

Despite their origins, Dundee Hibernian never met Irish opposition, home or away, although it should be stressed that such exchanges were extremely rare in those days. Until drawn against Bohemians of Dublin in the UEFA Cup of 1985, Dundee United had never visited the island of Ireland. They have not since returned to the Republic, though UEFA Cup duty has taken them to Northern Ireland on two further occasions.

United first met Irish opposition when Portadown from Northern Ireland visited Tannadice for a friendly in October 1958.

United's first encounter with a League of Ireland club came in the USA. They beat Shamrock Rovers 5–1 in a North American Soccer League* match in Boston in June 1967.

Sam IRVING (born 1893; died 1969)

Irving was a cultured wing half who played at the top level in all four corners of the UK. He was a Scottish Cup finalist with Dundee FC in 1925 and went one better with Cardiff City, being a member of their FA Cup-winning team in 1927. He later played for Chelsea and won a total of 18 caps for Northern Ireland, ten of them while at Dens Park*.

His heart must have remained in Dundee, however, because he returned to live in the city when his playing career was over. He set himself up in business, obviously with some success, because he was one of a group of businessmen which bought out George Greig at Tannadice in 1938. This led to him becoming a director and, for one season, joint director/manager of Dundee United with Jimmy Brownlie*. The two stood down when Bobby McKay* was appointed manager in July 1939, but remained as directors until the club went into hibernation in 1940.

ITALY

United's defeat of holders Barcelona in the Inter-Cities Fairs Cup of 1966/67 had as its reward a confrontation with Italian giants Juventus in the next round. This was the first time Italian opposition had been faced and it was disappointing when the first leg in Turin's Stadio Communale ended in a 3–0 defeat. Although the deficit could not be retrieved in the return at Tannadice in March 1967, a 1–0 win (the goal scored by Finn Dossing*) conferred considerable respectability on a club which had emerged from part-time football in Division Two a mere seven years earlier.

The club's European exploits had the effect of bringing it to the notice of football people around the world, and one tangible benefit was the invitation to compete that summer in the North American Soccer League*. That included a meeting in Chicago with the Italian League side Cagliari, which resulted in a 1–0 win.

Two years later, the invitation was repeated and United returned to the USA. Following the tournament, United played some friendly matches, one of which saw them renew acquaintance with Juventus. In Jersey City, United achieved the satisfaction of recording a second 1–0 win over the Italian club.

Another end-of-season jaunt to far-off places provided an opportunity of testing Jim McLean's* emerging young team against one of Serie A's best sides. Along with United, Fiorentina were invited to participate in the Japan Cup* tournament in 1979 and the clubs met in the semi-final. With extra-time having failed to alter the 1–1 scoreline, penalties were called for and it was United's players whose nerve held as they advanced to the final.

A semi-final was also the setting for the most recent meeting with a Serie A club. Champions AS Roma were intent on reaching the 1984 European Cup final, not least because it was to be played at their own Olympic Stadium. A 2–0 triumph by United rocked them and their desperation to overturn it was all too obvious in the gamesmanship – and, indeed, venom – which met Jim McLean and his players, plus United supporters, in Rome for the return. Although on the day the Italians were good value for the 3–0 result they craved, the club was later fined for attempting to bribe the match referee.

J

JAPAN CUP
It was an honour for Dundee United to be invited to participate in the Japan Cup tournament held in May and June 1979. The club acquitted itself well, accounting for both the Burmese national side and Japan B in Hiroshima, as well as drawing with Argentinians San Lorenzo in Kyoto. This allowed them to progress to the semi-finals where they ended the interest of Fiorentina (in Osaka) after extra-time and penalties. In the final they lost 0–2 to Tottenham Hotspur in Tokyo's Olympic Stadium.

JOHNSTONE FC
This Renfrewshire club played at Newfield Park and were members of the Scottish League for eight seasons between 1912 and 1926; for six of them Dundee Hibs/United were fellow members of Division Two. There was little to choose between the clubs in their League exchanges, home advantage usually proving decisive.

Johnstone's last season as a League club was spent in Division Three, and when that division ended in 1926 the club disappeared with it.

The full Scottish League record against Johnstone was:
P 12 W 5 D 2 L 5 F 26 A 15

JUNIOR FOOTBALL
See also United Juniors FC
Dundee Hibs/United played the following matches against junior clubs or select teams: St Joseph's 1919; Dundee North End 1919; Dundee Junior XI 1920; Forfarshire Junior Select 1921; Dundee Junior League Select 1933; Dundee Junior League Select 1936; Perthshire Junior League Select 1940; Midland Junior League Select 1943; St Andrews United 1984; St Andrews United 1985; Dunbar United 1992.

Jacky KAY (born 1908; died 1963)

Lanarkshire-born, he was signed from the junior ranks by manager Jimmy Brownlie* in the close season of 1927. Kay was one of several signings as Brownlie sought to rebuild his team following relegation, and within two years the club regained Division One status, with Kay a powerful influence.

He struck a rich seam of goals along with Duncan Hutchison* during their two seasons together, and Kay felt the effects of Hutchie's transfer more than most. Only Hutchison scored more goals for the club than Kay in the inter-war years, but no other player made more appearances for United during that period.

Over his nine years at Tannadice, Jacky Kay was a big favourite with the fans, who were shocked and disappointed when he was given a free transfer in 1936, at the age of 28. That he still had plenty to offer was shown by the fact that he was signed by English club Chester, with whom he stayed until the outbreak of the Second World War.

He returned to Dundee and was a trainer with Dundee FC for several years until the mid-1950s.

Dundee United playing record (1927–36)

	Appearances	Goals
Scottish League	193	82
Scottish Cup	25	7

Division Two champion 1928/29
Division Two runner-up 1930/31

Jock KAY (born 1899; died 1979)

An attacking full back, he signed for Third Lanark* in 1920, where one of his colleagues was goalkeeper Jimmy Brownlie*. When Brownlie was appointed manager at Tannadice three years later, Kay was one of the first signings for his new club.

Jock immediately established himself as an essential element in the

United team which within two years won promotion to Division One for the first time in the club's history. His popularity with the fans and his consistently excellent service were recognised in 1928 when Hearts played a benefit match for him – one of only three Tannadice players to receive a testimonial in the club's first 50 years. Later that year he returned to his native Stirlingshire, joining Stenhousemuir. He retired from playing in 1931 and became postmaster at Denny.

Jock had no further formal connection with football, but his son played for Greenock Morton* in the 1950s.

Dundee United playing record (1923–28)

	Appearances	Goals
Scottish League	177	4
Scottish Cup	14	1
Division Two champion 1924/25		

Jerry KERR (born 1912)

Jerry Kerr, manager 1959–71

It would be difficult to overestimate the contribution Jerry Kerr made to Dundee United. He it was who guided the club from Division Two obscurity to an established position in the top division and, though it took Jim McLean* to carry the club's development to the stage where honours were won, without the astute management of Kerr, the solid platform which McLean inherited simply would not have been in place.

Kerr was a full back of modest ability, but his playing career (which included a brief spell with Rangers) took him to Alloa Athletic, St Bernards* and Motherwell before becoming one of new United manager Bobby McKay's* first signings during the close season of 1939. He was made club captain, but with the storm clouds of war ominously gathering, only four League matches of season 1939/40 were played before the competition was abandoned.

Kerr was one of only three players who remained with United after the outbreak of war, but the relaxed registration conditions of the time enabled a much stronger squad to be assembled. They progressed to the semi-final of the Emergency War Cup* (which, to all intents and purposes, was the Scottish Cup), where their captain was unlucky to sustain a shoulder injury which kept him out of the final at Hampden.

It was when he moved into management that Jerry Kerr's true strengths began to emerge. His first post was as player/manager with the East of Scotland League club Peebles Rovers, followed by a spell at Berwick Rangers before being appointed manager of Alloa, a club which knew him well.

As the directors of another of Kerr's former employers surveyed their club's situation in the summer of 1959, what met their gaze was not a pretty sight. Their manager (the fifth in less than five years) had just resigned after leading the part-time club to third bottom place in Division Two and there was little on offer to suggest that it might regain the Division One status it had not known for 27 years. More in hope than expectation, Dundee United advertised for a new manager; the man given the apparently thankless task of reviving the club was Jerry Kerr.

The records show that less than a year later Kerr had taken Dundee United into Division One and in so doing had more than doubled attendances at Tannadice. They doubled again the following season as United – following Kerr's insistence that his players must be full-time – retained their place and, through shrewd entries into the transfer market, Kerr achieved the gradual improvement which led to qualification for European competition in 1966. It was an astonishing achievement and one which stands as a landmark in the club's history.

By 1971 Kerr, then aged 59, had taken Dundee United as far as he reasonably could. In November of that year he assumed the post of general manager, the job which he had transformed into one of the most sought-after in Scottish football going to Jim McLean. It seems Kerr was never comfortable with his new duties and perhaps, in retrospect, it might have been more appropriate had he been offered a seat on the board instead, or as well. Certainly, it would have been more than justified, but it did not happen and he left the club, with the minimum of publicity, at the end of season 1972/73.

It was an exit which did not do justice to his contribution to Dundee United over a period of twelve and a half years, and it seems odd to say the least that his achievements were not recognised by the board granting him a testimonial match at which Arabs could have paid due tribute.

He did return briefly to management, taking charge of Forfar Athletic for two years from 1974, but thereafter his involvement in football was restricted to scouting.

Dundee United playing record (1939–40)

	Appearances	Goals
Scottish League	4	
Emergency War Cup	5	2
Eastern Regional League	25	5

KILMARNOCK FC

Prior to 1947, League meetings between the clubs had been restricted to United's four seasons in Division One between 1925 and 1932. They came together for seven seasons in B Division until Kilmarnock won promotion in 1954, then did not meet again until United achieved the same feat six years later. Until the advent of the Premier Division they were perennial adversaries, but since 1975 Kilmarnock have spent only nine seasons there.

In 1969 the clubs also met in Dallas and St Louis while competing in the International League*.

The playing record against Kilmarnock in major competitions is:
Scottish League (total): P 78 W 31 D 18 L 29 F 147 A 132 (51%)
Premier Division: P 28 W 14 D 9 L 5 F 56 A 19 (66%)
Scottish Cup:　the clubs were drawn together in 1932, 1986 and 1997 (semi-final).
　　　　　　　Record: P 6 W 1 D 3 L 2 F3 A 6
League Cup:　the clubs were drawn together in 1953, 1971, 1972 and 1975.
　　　　　　　Record: P 8 W 4 D 0 L 4 F 11 A 15

Notable transfers to: John Bourke (1978)
Notable transfers from: Kenny Cameron* (1968)

It's a fact: After winning promotion in 1960, United did not record a Division One win at Rugby Park until their thirteenth visit there in 1973; the previous nine had all ended in defeat.

KING'S PARK FC

The Stirling club were regular Scottish League opponents of Dundee Hibs/United during the inter-war period. However, the clubs first met in a Dewar Shield* tie at Forthbank Park in April 1911 and renewed their acquaintance in the Central League* of 1920/21. Both were admitted to the new Division Two the following season and their first Scottish League meeting occurred in October 1921 at Tannadice.

Dundee United had the better of the exchanges over 12 subsequent seasons before the outbreak of the Second World War brought Division Two to an end. The last Scottish League meeting between the clubs was at Forthbank Park in April 1939.

They did meet the following season in the Eastern Regional League*, but King's Park was forced to withdraw from that competition after its ground suffered bomb damage in 1940. The club never re-formed after the war.

It's a fact: King's Park were the last ever opponents of Dundee Hibs. The Hibs won 3–2 in a Division Two fixture at Forthbank Park on 20 October 1923, and two days later officially changed their name to Dundee United.

The full Scottish League record against King's Park was:
P 26 W 14 D 6 L 6 F 61 A 41

Billy KIRKWOOD (born 1958)

He had gained two U-18 schoolboy caps (together with Derek Stark*) when he joined from school in 1976. Within a year he had broken through to the first team to begin a distinguished Tannadice career. Billy went on to make more than 400 League appearances, winning two League Cup winners' medals and being a vital part of the squad which won the League championship three years later. He was also a member of the the UEFA Cup final side and was a cup finalist on five other occasions.

Having departed for Hibernian in the close season of 1986, he returned to Tannadice after only six months, joining Dunfermline the following year. In February 1988 he was transferred to Dundee FC, with whom he became a coach at the end of his playing career. He built up an impressive coaching reputation, which was further enhanced after he joined Rangers in 1991.

United was his first managerial appointment, in March 1995, at a time when the club was in freefall towards the First Division. Although he did restore Premier Division status a year later, he was never quite convincing in his role and, following a poor start to the season, was dismissed in September 1996. Later that year he was appointed to a coaching position in Hong Kong and in August 1997 he joined Hull City as assistant manager.

Dundee United playing record (1977–86 and 1987)

	Appearances	Goals
Scottish League	261	44
Scottish Cup	34	5
League Cup	58	14
European competitions	44	5

Scottish League champion 1982/83
League Cup winner 1979, 1980
UEFA Cup finalist 1987
Scottish Cup finalist 1981, 1985
League Cup finalist 1981, 1984

Frank KOPEL (born 1949)

Falkirk-born Frank joined Manchester United from school, but made only ten first-team appearances for the Old Trafford club before being transferred to Blackburn Rovers. He arrived at Tannadice in January 1972 and was a member of both League Cup-winning teams as well as the Scottish Cup final teams of 1974 and 1981. He made more than 400 League appearances before joining Arbroath, where he had a spell as player/coach.

After retiring in 1984, Frank was a coach with United for some time and his son, Scott, joined the club as an apprentice, but made only one first-team appearance before being freed, then joining Forfar Athletic.

Dundee United playing record (1972–82)

	Appearances	Goals
Scottish League	284	7

Scottish Cup	28	
League Cup	61	1
European competitions	22	2

League Cup winner 1979, 1980
Scottish Cup finalist 1974, 1981

Miodrag KRIVOKAPIC (born 1959)

Signed from Red Star Belgrade for £200,000 in the summer of 1988, the international defender took some time to settle but then developed into an indispensable part of United's defence over the three seasons which followed.

In 1991 he was transferred to Motherwell, against whom he had played for United in that year's Scottish Cup final, and his fitness and athleticism allowed him to prolong his career at the top level beyond the point where retirement normally beckons. After joining Raith Rovers in 1996 as player/coach he was appointed to a similar post with Hamilton Accies the following year.

Dundee United playing record (1988–91)

	Appearances	Goals
Scottish League	82	1
Scottish Cup	17	
League Cup	6	
European competitions	3	
Yugoslavia	1	
Yugoslavia B	1	

Scottish Cup finalist 1991

L

LEAGUE CHALLENGE CUP

This tournament was instituted in 1990 as the B&Q Centenary Cup, to mark the first 100 years of the Scottish League. When B&Q's sponsorship had run its course in 1995, its name was changed to the League Challenge Cup. It proved impossible to attract a new sponsor, but the popularity of the competition with clubs and supporters led the League itself to underwrite the tournament costs and guarantee prize money, thus enabling it to continue.

Entry has always been restricted to League clubs outside the Premier Division. As a consequence, United have participated on only one occasion, 1995/96. They beat Stranraer 2–0, Clydebank 1–0 and Dunfermline Athletic 4–0, all away from home, to reach the final. It was played at McDiarmid Park, Perth on Sunday, 7 November, and United's opponents were Second Division Stenhousemuir. The scoresheet remained blank after 120 minutes, following which there was a penalty shoot-out, won 5–4 by Stenhousemuir.

LEAGUE CUP

The suggestion of a cup competition different in nature from the Scottish Cup was first made in the late 1930s and during the Second World War it was instituted as the Southern League Cup. Its distinguishing feature was that clubs were drawn in sections of four, playing each other on a home-and-away basis, with the winners progressing to quarter- and semi-finals played on the customary knock-out basis.

That format proved popular, with the result that it was retained after the war, being renamed the Scottish League Cup in 1946/47. Played at the beginning of the season, with the final in October, it was kept apart from the Scottish Cup. Over the years the format has changed on several occasions, and in 1984 the concept of sudden death was introduced, with no replays. This breathed new life into what had been an ailing competition.

The League Cup was the first of the three major competitions to attract sponsorship. It became known as the Bell's League Cup in 1979, the Skol Cup in 1984, and the Coca-Cola Cup in 1994.

For many years, United failed to make any impression on the tournament. Although in the post-war period as a B Division club they were placed in a section with other clubs from that division, they qualified for the knock-out stages only twice (1951 and 1956) in the 14 seasons before their promotion to Division One in 1960.

Nor did the club's fortunes in the League Cup improve thereafter: in the 15 seasons which followed, until the sectional format was abandoned in 1977, United won their section only twice (1964 and 1972). In that first instance the club did reach the semi-final stage, losing 1–2 to Rangers (after extra-time) at Hampden Park. So, in 29 attempts, United progressed from the sectional stage of the competition on only four occasions, a truly dreadful record.

The club's performance did, however, change dramatically soon after. Not only did they reach their first final in 1979, they took the trophy by beating Aberdeen 3–0 in the replay at Dens Park*, having drawn 0–0 at Hampden Park. The following year the trophy was retained, again at Dens Park and again by a winning margin of 3–0. This time Dundee were the victims in the most famous city derby of all.

In 1981 United made it three finals in a row, which was, and remains, the only occasion that this has been achieved in the competition by a club other than Celtic or Rangers. It was Rangers who were their opponents at Hampden Park, but although Jim McLean's* fine young team took the lead, the Glasgow club – for whom Hampden is always 'home' territory – scored twice in the latter stages.

United reached the semi-final the following two years and in 1984 made another final appearance. It was the first time the competition had been played on a Sunday and the first time it had been shown live on television. As in 1981, Rangers were their opponents at Hampden Park and, as in 1981, the Ibrox club took the trophy by the narrowest of margins, on this occasion 1–0.

Thereafter, the club's brief flirtation with the League Cup went into decline. They did reach the semi-final stage in 1985 and 1986 (to complete eight in a row), but since then further semi-finals in 1988, 1990 and 1993 have proved the summit of the club's achievements.

These are the players who won League Cup winners' medals with Dundee United:

1979: McAlpine, Stark, Kopel, Phillip, Hegarty, Narey, Bannon, Sturrock, Pettigrew, Holt, Payne. Substitutes – Fleming, Murray.

1980: McAlpine, Holt, Kopel, Phillip, Hegarty, Narey, Bannon, Payne, Pettigrew, Sturrock, Dodds. Substitutes – Kirkwood, Stark.

Biggest wins

Home   8–0 v Hamilton Academical, 9.9.64
        6–0 v Airdrie, 27.8.49

v Queen of the South, 11.8.92
6–1 v Ayr United, 11.8.56
v Dunfermline Athletic, 24.8.83

Away 6–2 v Hamilton Academical, 24.11.79 (semi-final)
5–1 v Albion Rovers, 23.8.77
4–0 v Queen's Park, 29.8 59
v Clyde, 28.8.68
v Arbroath, 5.10.77
v Hamilton Academical (away), 2.9.81
v Dumbarton, 29.8.84
v Cowdenbeath, 20.8.95

Biggest Defeats
Home 0–5 v Motherwell, 12.8.53
2–6 v Stirling Albion, 13.8.52
0–4 v Cowdenbeath, 21.8.57

Away 1–8 v Clyde, 24.8.57
1–7 v Motherwell, 17.8.55
1–6 v Stirling Albion, 27.8.52
v Cowdenbeath, 27.8.58

Only twice have United been dismissed from the League Cup by a club from a lower division. On 23 August 1989 they lost 1–2 to Hamilton Academical at Douglas Park and on 3 September 1996 they drew 2–2 (after extra-time) with Dundee at Tannadice, the Dens Park club winning 4–2 on penalties. On both occasions their opponents were in the First Division.

The overall record of Dundee United in the League Cup, 1946–96 (51 seasons), is:

P 304 W 152 D 43 L 109 F 590 A 482 (57%)

LEITH ATHLETIC FC
Leith Athletic were founder members of the Scottish League in 1890 and spent a total of 45 seasons as a League club, being expelled in 1953 for refusing to complete fixtures. They were in Division Two when Dundee Hibs joined it in 1910 and Leith Athletic were the club's first ever Scottish League opponents, winning 3–2 at Tannadice on 20 August.

With the exception of season 1931/32 when both clubs were in Division One, all League meetings were in the lower division. The Division Two match at Tannadice on 2 September 1939 was the day before Britain declared war on Germany, following which the League programme was abandoned.

Incredibly, the Edinburgh club used no fewer than 12 different grounds throughout their history. Their clashes with Dundee Hibs/United took place at Logie Green (1910–15), Marine Gardens (1927–36), Meadowbank (1936–39) and New Meadowbank (1947/48).

The clubs also met during wartime: in the Eastern League*, and in its sister competition the Eastern Cup, during 1915/16, and in the North Eastern League* of 1941/42. The Scottish League Cup also brought them together at the sectional stage in season 1947/48, Leith's last as a League club. They ended their League encounters with United as they had begun, with a win.

Leith were playing in C Division* when the two clubs met for the last time, United winning a Scottish Cup second-round tie 4–1 at New Meadowbank in February 1952.

The full Scottish League record against Leith Athletic was:
P 33 W 14 D 7 L 12 F 75 A 65

Willie LINN (born 1890; died 1959)
Few of the players who helped Dundee Hibs become established as a League club stayed sufficiently long at Tannadice to write themselves into the annals of the club's history. In those days there was a high turnover of the playing staff, but one of the exceptions was Willie Linn.

Born in Dundee of Irish parents, Linn was small and fast, a natural winger. He preferred to play on the left side and he was an effective player

Willie Linn, in the strip worn by Dundee Hibs from 1913–20

who scored a few goals, but supplied many more to his team-mates. He was a member of the Qualifying Cup* final team of 1913 and might well have been lost to the Hibs, as were most of his colleagues, on the outbreak of the First World War. He joined the forces, but was fortunate not to be posted overseas, as a result of which he was able to return to Tannadice once the conflict had ended.

He continued to give sterling service to the Hibs and became the first player to make more than 100 Scottish League appearances for the club. This was recognised when he became the first player to be given a testimonial by the club in 1922.

Dundee Hibernian playing record (1911–15 and 1919–22)

	Appearances	Goals
Scottish League	105	27
Scottish Cup	3	
Qualifying Cup	15	4
Qualifying Cup finalist 1913		

Jimmy LITTLEJOHN (born 1910; died 1989)

Shares the distinction with Jimmy Brownlie* of having been player, manager and director with Dundee United.

A Glaswegian, Littlejohn was a centre half of some distinction, principally serving St Johnstone during the mid-1930s, when they were an established Division One club. After a spell with Cowdenbeath, he arrived at Tannadice in 1939 following the outbreak of war and was a stalwart in the team which reached the final of the Emergency War Cup* in 1940. Indeed, due to an injury to captain Jerry Kerr*, it was Littlejohn who led United against Rangers at Hampden and, by all accounts, he was man of the match and very unfortunate not to lift the trophy.

That was the only season he played for the club, but he had made a good impression and was invited back as manager in 1944. His was a brief tenure of the manager's office (August to November), following which he accepted the offer of a directorship at Tannadice, bringing a welcome infusion of (relative) youth into the boardroom. He was unusual in that he was not himself in business, but was employed for most of his life after he retired from playing as a commercial traveller. Indeed, the exigencies of his job necessitated his standing down from the board for two years in the mid-1950s, but he returned to play what proved to be a vital role in improving the traditionally parlous financial state of the club.

He was the director charged with the responsibility of assessing the viability of Nottingham Forest's football pools scheme and, on his return from viewing the English club's set-up at first hand, he recommended the establishment of a similar venture by Dundee United. As the first club in Scotland to do so, they were ahead of the field and Taypools*, as it was known, proved to be a huge success.

Jimmy Littlejohn continued to play an important supportive role as a director as United moved onwards and upwards following promotion, though he was always behind the scenes, his name probably known by few United supporters. That was the way Jimmy himself preferred it, and he continued to serve on the board until his death in 1989.

Dundee United playing record (1939–40)

	Appearances	Goals
Eastern Regional League	26	
Emergency War Cup	7	
Emergency War Cup finalist 1940		

LIVINGSTON FC

Dundee United have not met Livingston since the club changed its name from Meadowbank Thistle in 1995 and moved to the newly built Almondvale Stadium. This continues a remarkable trend since, during the 21 years of their existence, Meadowbank played at the Commonwealth Stadium in Edinburgh, yet United never set foot in it. Indeed, United's 3–1 win in a Scottish Cup third-round tie at Tannadice in 1992 was the only occasion on which the clubs met.

LOCHGELLY UNITED FC

The Fife club had their home at the Recreation Ground and were members of the Scottish League for a total of six seasons between 1914 and 1926.

In 1914/15, 1921/22 and 1923/24 they were in Division Two along with Dundee Hibs, though the clubs also met in the Eastern League* from 1915–17 and 1919/20.

Lochgelly spent their last two seasons as a League club in Division Three between 1924 and 1926, but disbanded in 1928.

The full Scottish League record against Lochgelly United was:
P 6 W 3 D 2 L 1 F 11 A 6

M

Hamish McALPINE (born 1948)

Signed from Butterburn Youth Club (with whom he had won three amateur youth caps) in 1966, Hamish made his first-team debut in March 1969, the first step towards becoming a Tannadice icon. Over the next five seasons he vied, first with Donald Mackay then with Sandy Davie, for the keeper's jersey, finally claiming it as his own in 1974.

A great communicator, his rapport with the fans was a feature of his guardianship over the following 12 years, which just happened to coincide with the most successful period in the club's history! The only goalkeeper to score for United, he often induced palpitations among team-mates, manager and Arabs* alike when his attempts from the penalty spot went agley – as they not infrequently did.

His sustained reliability was belatedly recognised at international level when he was awarded U-21 caps as an over-age player, and indeed a full cap and a Scottish Cup winners' medal were the only honours to elude this club man *par excellence*.

He joined Raith Rovers in 1986, but his heart remained at Tannadice and when he finally drew down the curtain on his playing career he took up promotional work with United. His contribution as one of United's greatest characters over almost two decades at Tannadice was immortalised in Michael Marra's song 'Hamish the Goalie' in 1983.

Dundee United playing record (1969–86)

	Appearances	Goals
Scottish League	487	3
Scottish Cup	45	
League Cup	103	
European competitions	52	
Scotland U-21	5	
League champion 1982/83		
League Cup winner 1979, 1980		
Scottish Cup finalist 1981, 1985		

League Cup finalist 1981, 1984

Andy McCALL (born 1908; died 1979)

He was appointed Dundee United manager in October 1958, following the resignation of Tommy Gray*. An Ayrshireman, McCall had been a player of some distinction with Ayr United, St Johnstone, Huddersfield Town, Nottingham Forest and Dundee FC and was later a coach at Dens Park* for several years. Despite his experience, he never really came to grips with the job at Tannadice. Under his managership United plummeted to third bottom of Division Two and his resignation at the end of the season, after only six months, was not unexpected.

Willie MacFADYEN (born 1904; died 1971)

He took over as manager at Tannadice in October 1945 and remained in the post for what was then a club record of almost nine years.

An accomplished player, he spent most of his career with his home-town club, Motherwell, for whom he scored 52 times on the way to winning the League championship for the only time in that club's history in 1931/32. He also played in Motherwell's losing Scottish Cup final teams of 1931 and 1933 as well as gaining two Scotland caps. He later played for Huddersfield Town (collecting another runners-up medal in the 1938 FA Cup final) and Clapton Orient.

Willie MacFadyen, manager 1945–54

MacFadyen put his experience to good use, but throughout his period in charge was hamstrung by a lack of finances to buy players, despite United consistently being one of the best-supported clubs in the lower division. On only two out of his nine seasons as manager did United mount a serious promotion challenge, and he finally threw in the towel after the club had finished second last in B Division in 1954, avoiding the ignominy of C Division* only on goal difference.

MacFadyen did not seek another job in football, instead using his qualifications as a chiropodist and physiotherapist to establish his own practice.

Charlie McGILLIVRAY (born 1912; died 1986)

He was an inside forward with United when, in November 1944, his manager, Jimmy Littlejohn*, resigned. It seems that Charlie was as surprised as anyone when invited to take over, but he accepted and occupied the manager's office for the eleven months which followed. He remains the club's youngest manager.

Pre-war, McGillivray had played for Dundee FC and was their leading scorer in 1938/39, but he had no particular credentials for the job at Tannadice and, to be fair, would not in all probability have held the position but for the special conditions of wartime.

Under his leadership United had the misfortune to suffer several heavy reverses, including 1–9 to Aberdeen at Tannadice in February 1945, which remains the club's record home defeat. It seems the directors were not impressed with McGillivray's efforts and, when they let it be known towards the end of the season that they were seeking a full-time manager from outside the club, he got the message and resigned.

Jim McINALLY (born 1964)

Came to Tannadice from Coventry City in the summer of 1986 in a joint transfer with Dave Bowman*. He had begun his career with Celtic in 1982 as a full back; while there he won youth caps and spent a period on loan with Dundee FC. Jim was transferred to Nottingham Forest in 1984 and joined Coventry 18 months later.

At Tannadice he quickly became an effective attacking midfielder and played an important part in United's run to the UEFA Cup final in his first season. This brought him international recognition and he won the first of ten Scotland caps the next year. A solid, if unspectacular, performer over the following seven seasons, he won a Scottish Cup winners' medal in 1994, in his fourth final with the club.

In 1995 he joined Raith Rovers where he was player/coach, but he returned to Tannadice the following year as one of manager Tommy McLean's* first signings. In June 1997 he moved across the road becoming player/coach with Dundee FC.

It's a fact: Jim played for Nottingham Forest against United in Jim McLean's* testimonial match in August 1984.

Dundee United playing record (1986–95 and 1996–97)

	Appearances	Goals
Scottish League	302	18
Scottish Cup	51	1
League Cup	17	1
European competitions	25	2
Scotland	10	
Scotland U-21	1	

Scottish Cup winner 1994
Scottish Cup finalist 1987, 1988, 1991
UEFA Cup finalist 1987

William McINTOSH (born 1881; died 1955)

A genuine Jekyll and Hyde character as far as his involvement with Dundee

United was concerned. The proprietor for many years of the Opera Bar in the city's Gellatly Street, McIntosh was a director of Dundee FC from 1912 until 1933. In that guise, he was cast in the role of villain through his attempts to prevent Dundee Hibs being re-elected to the Scottish League in 1923. He is said to have argued that the city could not support two League clubs, but clearly did so with the intention of protecting Dundee FC's interests. Fortunately, his spoiling tactic failed, but once the Hibs had been readmitted, McIntosh then led the objections to the proposed change of the club's name to Dundee City, offering the spurious (to say the least) reasoning that it could cause 'confusion' in relation to the two clubs' correspondence! Despite the fact that any such problems had apparently been overcome in Bristol, Bradford and Manchester, the SFA upheld the objection and only when a compromise suggestion of 'United' was proposed did McIntosh and his fellow directors relent.

Although McIntosh had left the board at Dens Park in 1933, he retained his shares in the club. It therefore came as quite a surprise when it emerged that he was one of those who had put together the financial package which rescued Dundee United from bankruptcy in 1934. Today, SFA rules prohibit anyone holding shares in more than one member club, but McIntosh became a United shareholder and indeed retained his shares in the city's two clubs until his death 21 years later.

Not only did he join the new board at Tannadice, he became chairman in July 1934, a position which he retained until the club's next financial crisis in October 1936. He returned to the board in 1945 and remained a member for the rest of his life.

The indefatigable McIntosh's remarkable double life was further exemplified by the fact that he was a member of the SFA Council and the Scottish League Management Committee on separate occasions with each club.

Bobby McKAY (born 1900; died 1977)

Through no fault of his own, the club played fewer matches under his tenancy than that of any other manager at Tannadice. Appointed in July 1939, he had no previous managerial experience, but most of his playing career had been spent at the highest level. A former Scotland inside forward, he was a member of Morton's 1921 Scottish Cup-winning team and also played with Rangers, Newcastle United (where he won a League championship medal) and several other English clubs.

He may unwittingly have played a significant part in the future of Dundee United long after his own departure, because one of his first signings as manager was full back Jerry Kerr*. McKay clearly spotted what he regarded as leadership qualities, appointing him team captain. However, Kerr and his colleagues were to play only four League matches under McKay before the outbreak of war caused the suspension of the competition in September 1939. Confusion reigned over the path which football in Scotland should follow, but when it was decided to abandon the League programme McKay's contract was terminated and he left the club, just three months after arriving.

Peter McKAY (born 1925)

From Newburgh in Fife, McKay was playing for the local junior club, West End, when he was signed by United manager Willie MacFadyen* in 1947. Over the next seven years the little centre forward wrote himself into the history books by becoming the club's all-time record scorer. After netting only (!) 14 times in 19 matches in his first season at Tannadice, his annual tallies thereafter in League matches illustrate his consistency. From 1948/49 until 1953/54 they were: 25, 21, 32, 28, 15 and 23.

In more than one sense, he was the leading member of the Famous Five*, who had the kind of scoring record which ought to have lifted the club to a higher level. That was certainly a level at which McKay's talents ought to have been tested, but two factors seem to have conspired to deny him. Firstly, his height (he was only 5ft

McKAY

Peter McKay, featured on a cigarette card issued in 1950

5in), and secondly, United's lack of prominence throughout his career at Tannadice, during which time the club only twice managed to mount a serious challenge for promotion. The problem was that, no matter how fast McKay and his colleagues fired goals into opponents' nets, a bungling United defence would contrive to concede at least as many, and frequently more!

In the close season of 1954, Peter signed for Burnley for a fee of £3,000 and he quickly confounded those who doubted his ability to transfer his goal-scoring ability from Scotland's B Division to England's Division One. He scored a hat-trick on his debut and eventually totalled 35 in 60 appearances for the Lancashire club over the following two seasons. He did return to Scotland with St Mirren, in 1957, but after some time in English non-league football, he settled in Northamptonshire.

Will Arabs ever see his like again? It is an enticing prospect, though a combination of much better organised defences and different tactical formations make it unlikely. Peter McKay's style came close to being unique and the great pity was that he never had the opportunity of illuminating A Division with his explosive shooting power – and even more of a pity that he did not do so in a United strip.

Dundee United playing record (1947–54)

	Appearances	Goals
Scottish League	185	158
Scottish Cup	16	12
League Cup	39	29

Billy McKINLAY (born 1969)

One of the products of the club's highly efficient scouting and coaching network in the west of Scotland, McKinlay was signed from Hamilton Thistle in 1986. He won a place in the 1988 Scottish Cup final side at the age of 19, despite previously having made just 12 League appearances, and he performed with an assurance beyond his years.

An energetic and perceptive midfielder, he took some time to claim a regular first-team place, but when he did was a most effective link man. If he had a shortcoming, it was that he did not often enough force himself into scoring positions. He suffered a major disappointment in May 1994 when a caution for an innocuous tackle in a League match carried him over the points threshold and led to him being suspended when United achieved their historic first Scottish Cup triumph.

He took rather longer than might have been expected to become a full international, but went on to win 14 caps while at Tannadice, the last two as a First Division player. He is one of only three players from that division to play at full international level for Scotland since League reconstruction in 1975.

Following United's relegation he asked for a transfer and got his wish when Blackburn Rovers paid £1.75m for him in October 1995.

Dundee United playing record (1988–95)

	Appearances	Goals
Scottish League	220	22
Scottish Cup	26	4
League Cup	21	3
League Challenge Cup	2	1
European competitions	15	1
Scotland	14	
Scotland B	3	
Scotland U-21	6	1
Scotland youth	14	

Scottish Cup finalist 1988, 1991

Andy McLAREN (born 1973)

Another youngster who was nurtured through the club's coaching network, he was a Scottish schools cap at U-16 and signed for United in 1989. He made his debut two years later at 18, though he did not become a first-team regular until the arrival of manager Ivan Golac* in 1983. That confidence was amply rewarded when McLaren produced a scintillating display in the 1994 Scottish Cup final, his powerful running and accurate crossing leaving the Rangers defence in disarray.

For many Arabs, it remains a mystery as to why he seems unable to produce that kind of form more regularly, because it cannot be denied that, when on his game, Andy is a match for any wide player in Scotland. Still young enough to fulfil his potential, and that should include full international recognition.

Dundee United playing record (1991–97)

	Appearances	Goals
Scottish League	130	8
Scottish Cup	13	3
League Cup	11	1
League Challenge Cup	3	
European competitions	3	
Scotland U-21	4	
Scotland youth	8	

Scottish Cup winner 1994
BP Youth Cup winner 1990, 1991
League Challenge Cup finalist 1995

Jim McLEAN (born 1937)

No one has managed a League club in Scotland for longer in the post-war period and few if any can have had as dramatic an effect on his club's standing during his tenancy.

As an inside forward, Jim's playing career between 1956 and 1970 took him to Hamilton Accies, Clyde, Dundee and Kilmarnock, making a total of 473 appearances, scoring 170 times. He returned to Dens Park in a coaching capacity in July 1970, the post which he held when appointed United manager in December 1971, at the age of 34.

Jim McLean

McLean immediately laid the foundations of the youth policy which was to produce so many fine young players over the two decades which followed. In the short term, he used his knowledge of the Scottish scene to buy experienced players who would allow him to re-shape both the squad and the style of play in line with his approach to coaching.

He led the club to its first Scottish Cup final in 1974 and, despite defeat, it proved an important psychological step in the club's development. As the first of the young players began to emerge, McLean's team mounted a challenge for the League championship in 1978/79, something of which the club had never previously proved capable. It was now becoming clear that Dundee United were serious contenders for domestic honours, and that was confirmed a few months later.

In December 1979, McLean guided his team to triumph in the League Cup and retained it a year later. All the while, he was gradually building the club's reputation in Europe, the counter-attacking style which he had developed proving ideally suited to that stage. Despite the progress he had made, however, few believed that United were potential Premier Division champions, Aberdeen at that time providing a third hurdle to be cleared in addition to the Old Firm. But in 1983, profiting from a late run which left those clubs in their wake, that is precisely what McLean's largely home-grown side did, playing exhilarating attacking football in the process.

The following year United's progress was maintained. It took a penalty kick to deny them a place in the European Cup final, and in 1986/87 arguably the best team United have ever assembled went one better in the UEFA Cup. Jim McLean was by now recognised as one of the finest coaches in Europe and his success had led Rangers (in November 1983) and Newcastle United (in June 1984) to offer him the manager's job. That he was able to turn both down was a reflection of his total commitment to the club which, under his guidance, had been transformed. Largely as a result of spurning these approaches, he was given the rare tribute for a manager of a testimonial match.

The one disappointment of McLean's tenure was that the club had a poor record in cup finals, but the critics who cited that as a failing on his part ignored the fact that Dundee United had reached a solitary major cup final prior to his arrival, and even that occurred under the artificial conditions of wartime. Few of the thousands of Arabs who had made several sombre return journeys from Hampden Park did not subscribe to the Tennysonian theory that it was far better to have loved and lost than never to have loved at all. They knew that, were it not for Jim McLean, their club would never have reached the heights it did under his shrewd leadership.

The Dundee United board were equally appreciative and had marked their debt to McLean by making him a director in 1984; four years later he became chairman and managing director. He retained those joint responsibilities until stepping down as manager in July 1993, after a marathon reign of 21 years and seven months. He remains chairman and in that role is clearly the decisive voice on all matters relating to the running of the club.

It has to be said, however, that - in common with many people who reach the top of their profession - James Yuille McLean is a complex and idiosyncratic individual. His intense, perfectionist nature has led to difficulties in dealing with certain players, their representatives and the media, with whom it is not unfair to say he has had an often stormy relationship over the years. The widespread reporting of contractual disputes and fraught employee relations, coupled with the banning of some journalists from Tannadice Park, have contributed to a poor public relations image.

It is difficult to imagine Dundee United without Jim McLean, though not to imagine how the club might have fared had he never arrived. His contribution has been a massive one and, though it is not yet complete, his legacy is already visible: a status for the club throughout Europe and beyond which no one believed possible, and a stadium fit for the twenty-first century.

It's a fact: Jim McLean's debut for Dundee FC came in the city derby at Dens Park on 11 September 1965. That match just happened to be the one in which United recorded their most decisive victory over their rivals, winning 5–0.

Tommy McLEAN (born 1947)

Brother of Jim, he was appointed United manager in September 1996 and none of his predecessors came to Tannadice with a better pedigree.

Tommy began his career with Kilmarnock, winning a League championship medal at the age of 17, and was transferred to Rangers in 1971. At Ibrox he won a clutch of honours in all three domestic competitions and was a member of the team which won the European Cup Winners' Cup in 1972. Capped at youth, amateur, Scottish League and full international levels, he was quickly in demand when his playing career ended. He became assistant manager at Ibrox, then managed Morton, Motherwell (winning the Scottish Cup in 1991) and Hearts. He had a spell out of the game after leaving Tynecastle and was manager of Raith Rovers for just a few days before accepting the offer to follow Billy Kirkwood* at Tannadice.

His arrival sparked a remarkable turnaround in United's fortunes. From bottom position, having collected a single point from the first six Premier Division matches, he led them to qualification for the UEFA Cup by finishing in third place. Astute signings, predominantly from abroad, allied to McLean's exceptional tactical awareness, rejuvenated the team, the club and by extension the many Arabs who, prior to his arrival, had been contemplating a quick return to the First Division.

MALAYSIA

United visited Malaysia in July 1994, having been invited to play in the match which marked the official opening of the new national stadium in Kuala Lumpur. A crowd of more than 100,000 was inside the Shah Alam Stadium to see United share a 1–1 draw with Selangor, the country's leading club; this is the largest attendance at a match involving Dundee United.

United returned to the same venue four days later to meet Bayern Munich, but this match attracted rather less interest, another 1–1 draw being watched by under 10,000!

Maurice MALPAS (born 1962)
A Scottish schools U-15 cap, he signed from Leven Royals in 1979. Despite making his first-team debut in November 1981, he did not become a full-time player until the completion of his BSc degree in Electrical Engineering two years later. Maurice soon developed into one of the best attacking full backs in Scotland, a fact recognised when he won the first of his caps in 1984. He went on to exceed 50, thus becoming the only United player so far to enter the SFA's Hall of Fame.

Consistently outstanding, his good fortune in avoiding serious injury has helped him build the club's all-time record for appearances. That figure is still increasing because, at the age of 35, he remained a first-team regular and playing well enough to have the media speculating in the spring of 1997 on his recall to international duty.

Though that is unlikely, he has already signalled his intention of entering management when his playing career comes to a close – which his then manager Jim McLean* may have anticipated occurring rather earlier, as he appointed Maurice player/coach as far back as 1991!

Dundee United playing record (1981–97)

	Appearances	Goals
Scottish League	543	19
Scottish Cup	75	4
League Cup	54	2
League Challenge Cup	4	
European competitions	56	
Scotland	55	
Scotland U-21	8	
Scotland youth	3	

Scottish League champion 1982/83
Scottish Cup winner 1994
UEFA Cup finalist 1987
Scottish Cup finalist 1985, 1987, 1988, 1991
League Cup finalist 1984
League Challenge Cup finalist 1995
Scottish Football Writers' Association Player of the Year 1991

MALTA
United have paid two visits to the Mediterranean island, both on European business. In 1983 they went as League champions to meet Hamrun Spartans in a first-round European Cup tie. They won comfortably 3–0 and

repeated the scoreline at Tannadice. Unusually, the club shared the charter flight with Rangers, who met Valetta in the UEFA Cup on the same day and indeed at the same venue, the Ta'qali Stadium being the only grass-covered pitch on the island.

Five years later, on UEFA Cup duty, United encountered much greater difficulty in progressing. They could manage only a 0–0 scoreline at the Ta'qali and struggled no less at home, a late goal from Raphael Meade proving the only one of the tie, but failing to save United's blushes.

MANAGERS

From 1909 until 1967, the position of manager at Tannadice Park also included the duties of club secretary. The only exceptions to this were Herbert Dainty*, Jimmy Brownlie* in his spell with Sam Irving*, and those who briefly held the post during the Second World War.

Date	Manager	Reason for vacating post
Jun 1909 – Apr 1915	Pat Reilly	Stepped down but remained secretary
Apr 1915 – Mar 1917	Herbert Dainty (player/manager)	Stepped down but remained a player
Mar 1917 – Dec 1922	Pat Reilly	Resigned
Dec 1922 – Mar 1923	Peter O'Rourke	Resigned
Mar 1923 – Apr 1931	Jimmy Brownlie	Resigned
Jun 1931 – Mar 1934	Willie Reid	Dismissed
Mar 1934 – Oct 1936	Jimmy Brownlie	Dismissed
Oct 1936 – Apr 1938	George Greig (managing director)	Retired
Jul 1938 – Jun 1939	Jimmy Brownlie & Sam Irving (joint manager/directors)	Resigned
Jul 1939 – Oct 1939	Bobby McKay	Contract terminated on outbreak of war
Nov 1939 – Jul 1940	Jimmy Allan	Resigned
Season 1940/41	Club closed down	
Jun 1941 – Aug 1944	Arthur Cram	Stepped down but remained secretary
Aug 1944 – Nov 1944	Jimmy Littlejohn	Resigned
Nov 1944 – Oct 1945	Charlie McGillivray	Resigned
Oct 1945 – Aug 1954	Willie MacFadyen	Resigned
Sep 1954 – Jan 1957	Reggie Smith	Resigned
Jan 1957 – Mar 1957	Ally Gallacher	Resigned
Mar 1957 – Oct 1958	Tommy Gray	Resigned
Oct 1958 – Apr 1959	Andy McCall	Resigned
Jun 1959 – Dec 1971	Jerry Kerr	Resigned to become general manager
Dec 1971 – Jul 1993	Jim McLean	Retired but remained chairman
Jul 1993 – Mar 1995	Ivan Golac	Left 'by mutual agreement'
Mar 1995 – Sep 1996	Billy Kirkwood	Dismissed
Sep 1996 –	Tommy McLean	

Collie MARTIN (born 1890; died 1917)
One of relatively few players in the club's history to join direct from Dundee FC, he signed for Dundee Hibs in the close season of 1913. He proved to be a highly effective centre forward, leading the Division Two scoring charts on each of his two seasons at Tannadice.

His goals helped fire the Hibs to the Qualifying Cup* final in 1913. They lost, after two replays, to Albion Rovers but Martin took his revenge the following season, scoring five times against the Coatbridge team in a Division Two encounter at Tannadice. He ended that season with an amazing 29 goals from 25 League matches, and averaged a goal per game over his two seasons with the club.

Sheffield United wanted to sign him in 1914, but Martin gave them no encouragement, although the Hibs would doubtless have welcomed the income. The following year Division Two was abandoned due to the war and Collie Martin never played another match for the club. Like so many of his generation he went to war, but did not return.

Dundee Hibernian playing record (1913–15)

	Appearances	Goals
Scottish League	47	47
Scottish Cup	1	
Qualifying Cup	11	5
Qualifying Cup finalist 1913		

MEXICO
United's sole visit to Mexico took place immediately prior to the 1970 World Cup, which that country hosted. The trip was no doubt memorable as far as the players were concerned off the pitch, but on it they did themselves little credit. What was effectively the full Mexican international side won the first match in the massive Aztec Stadium 6–0, and four days later a select team representing Toluca came out on top by 2–0.

The next meeting with Mexicans was no more successful. It occurred in 1987 in Los Angeles, where United were competing in the Gold Cup invitation tournament. The players of Guadalajara may have had the advantage of being more accustomed to the heat, but they got the better of United, winning 2–0.

Arthur MILNE (born 1915)
Signed from Brechin Vics in 1934, the 19-year-old had a sensational start to his senior career, scoring four times on his debut, something which no other Dundee Hibs/United player has achieved.

That proved to be just the first of many records as he quickly established a reputation as a natural goalscorer, finishing his first season with 23 from only 18 League matches. Nicknamed 'L'il Arthur', along with Bobby Gardiner he also became known as one of the Mighty Midgets (both being under 5ft 6in) and they hunted very effectively as a pair.

There has never been a more productive scorer in the club's history. Although he spent less than three years at Tannadice during peacetime, he scored 85 times in 81 matches to become the only player to average more than a goal per game over his career at Tannadice. That total included six instances of scoring four times, plus five hat-tricks, and he would have scored many more had his stay not been cut short following a pay dispute with managing director George Greig*.

That led to United losing a considerable amount of money. Milne went on trial with Liverpool in March 1937 but this resulted in a registration mix-up which left the player a free agent; he was then signed by Hibernian for nothing. United could have expected a fee of around £2,000, but had to make do with compensation from Liverpool of around one third of that.

There was great disappointment among Tannadice fans at losing their hero, though Milne did rejoin United after the outbreak of the Second World War in 1939 and was a member of the team which lost to Rangers* in the Emergency War Cup* final the following year.

The little centre forward was thirty when the war ended, yet he retained enough of his ability and sharpness to serve St Mirren with distinction until 1950. His career over, he settled in Edinburgh, where he was for many years a traffic warden.

Dundee United career (1934–37 and 1939/40)

	Appearances	Goals
Scottish League	73	77
Scottish Cup	9	9
Eastern Regional League	17	14
Emergency War Cup	5	7

Emergency War Cup finalist 1940

Ralph MILNE (born 1961)
Signed in August 1977 from Dundee Celtic Boys Club, his debut in July 1979 presaged some of the most exciting and effective wing play of the modern era at Tannadice. On his day he was virtually unstoppable, and he reserved some of his best performances for the European arena.

No Arab will ever forget his breathtaking goal in the match which secured the League championship in 1983, and Ralph was a significant influence on the trophy coming to Tannadice, ending the season as second top scorer.

It seemed that the championship would be the first of many honours he would win, both individually and with United; in retrospect, it is astonishing that his international recognition did not progress beyond Under-21 caps. Many believed he would enjoy a long career with the full Scotland team and indeed he ought to have, just as he ought to have had many more years thrilling Tannadice fans with his speed and power.

However, he proved something of a wayward genius, his off-field activities all too often reducing his ability to perform with consistency, or even to appear consistently. This is illustrated by the fact that he played in 34 League matches, scoring 16 times, during the championship season yet appeared only 76 times, scoring a paltry 11 goals, throughout the four seasons which followed.

His was a talent which, sadly, never fully flowered and he left Tannadice in 1987, at the age of 25, to join Charlton Athletic, later playing for Bristol City and, briefly, Manchester United under Alex Ferguson.

Dundee United playing record (1979-86)

	Appearances	Goals
Scottish League	179	45
Scottish Cup	22	
League Cup	43	14
European competitions	41	15
Scotland U-21	3	
Scotland youth	6	1

Scottish League champion 1982/83
Scottish Cup finalist 1981, 1985
League Cup finalist 1984

Ian MITCHELL (born 1946; died 1996)

Signed from juvenile football in his native Falkirk after winning schoolboy caps, Mitchell became – and remains – the youngest player ever to make a first-team appearance for Dundee United. He was aged 16 years and four months on his debut in a Division One match against Hibernian in September 1962.

An outside or inside left, he was a regular from that point onwards and scored frequently, becoming one of only five players ever to register more than 100 League goals for the club. He had a brief spell in England, joining Newcastle United for what was then United's record fee of £50,000 in 1970, but returned a year later and remained at Tannadice until 1973.

Sadly, he died at the age of 50 after a long illness.

Dundee United playing record (1962–70 and 1971–73)

	Appearances	Goals
Scottish League	238	101
Scottish Cup	23	9
League Cup	34	16
Summer Cup	11	6
European competitions	6	1
Scotland U-23	2	1
Scotland youth	8	3

Summer Cup finalist 1965

MONTROSE FC

Dundee Hibs' first ever win at Tannadice was recorded against Montrose in a Northern League* fixture on 28 August 1909.

Having been regular rivals from that era until Dundee United won promotion in 1960, the clubs have met competitively just once since then, a League Cup tie at Tannadice in 1991, which United won 3–2.

The only occasion on which the clubs were drawn together in the Scottish Cup was 1927, three years before they first met in a Scottish League match. Having been postponed several times, the tie at Tannadice was eventually played on a Wednesday afternoon. Montrose, as they were entitled to do at the time, sold the ground rights for the replay in anticipation of a bigger crowd, but they may have regretted their decision as United, then in Division One, won 3–1, though only after extra-time had been played.

It's a fact: When United visited Links Park for a Division Two match in March 1960, both clubs were involved in the promotion chase. A new attendance record was created, but many more saw United win 3–1. *The Sporting Post* reported: 'the official crowd was 6,000, but this did not include several hundred who broke in through the main gate at the start'.

The playing record against Montrose in major competitions is:
Scottish League: P 26 W 12 D 4 L 10 F 63 A 54 (54%)
Scottish Cup: see above
League Cup: the clubs were drawn together in 1959 and 1991.
Record: P 2 W 1 D 1 L 0 F 4 A 3

Notable transfers to: Bill Masson (1936), Kenny Cameron* (1974), Archie Knox (1976).

MOTHERWELL FC

The club were one of Scotland's strongest in the inter-war years, as evidenced by the fact that they were the only one to break the Old Firm's stranglehold on the League championship throughout that period.

As a consequence, meetings were restricted to United's four seasons in Division One between 1925 and 1932, when Motherwell developed a nasty habit of handing out heavy defeats. Between those years, results at Fir Park were 4–0, 6–0, 6–1 and 5–0 and, for good measure, in 1931/32 they won 6–1 at Tannadice as well! Given that experience, United supporters could have been forgiven a sense of relief at their club's absence from the top division sparing them further embarrassment over the following 21 years, though they may have greeted Motherwell's unexpected relegation to B Division in 1953 with some trepidation. If so, their fears were fully confirmed as United suffered their all-time heaviest defeat, conceding 12 goals at Fir Park the following January.

However, things did improve after United returned to Division One in 1960, since when they have had distinctly the better of exchanges at league level, where meetings have been regular; on only six out of 37 seasons have the clubs not been in the same division.

It's a fact: Quite apart from the record 12–1 demolition of 1954, the Fir Park club were responsible for what remain United's record home defeats in both the Scottish Cup (1–5 in 1939) and the League Cup (0–5 in 1953).

The playing record against Motherwell in major competitions is:

Scottish League (total): P 106 W 48 D 31 L 27 F 171 A 137 (60%)

Premier Division: P 68 W 33 D 21 L 14 F 117 A 66 (64%)

Scottish Cup: the clubs were drawn together in 1939, 1962 (in the 1962/63 competition), 1981, 1986, 1994 and 1997. They also met in the 1991 final.
Record: P 8 W 4 D 1 L 3 F 18 A 17

League Cup: the clubs were drawn together in 1953, 1955, 1961, 1964, 1965, 1971, 1973, 1974, 1980, 1981, 1983, 1990 and 1995.
Record: P 24 W 10 D 3 L 11 F 38 A 50

Summer Cup: the clubs met in the final of the 1965 competition, which Motherwell won 3–2 on aggregate.

Notable transfers to: Billy Thomson (1991), Miodrag Krivokapic* (1991), Owen Coyle (1997)

Notable transfers from: Willie Pettigrew* (1979), Jamie Dolan (1997)

It's another fact: United have played more League Cup ties against Motherwell than against any other club.

Steve MURRAY (born 1944)

Steve Murray was a Scotland international who had won honours with Celtic when he was forced to retire through injury in 1975. It seems bizarre, then, that he should qualify for inclusion on these pages by dint of being a member of United's League Cup-winning squad of 1979 (he received a medal even though he did not participate in the replay, having come on as a substitute in the first match at Hampden Park).

He had joined the club as a scout earlier that year, but discovered, having had acupuncture treatment, that he was fit enough to resume a playing career at the age of 35. He played only three League matches for United, but has the distinction of having appeared in League Cup finals with both Dundee clubs, his winners' medal being added to the runner-up badge he received in 1968 as a team-mate of Jim McLean*.

When he finally did give up playing he set what is thought to be a world record for the shortest managerial stint at a League club, lasting just three days with Forfar Athletic in 1980! He did manage Montrose for rather longer, before taking up a career in banking, but returned to Tannadice as assistant manager in July 1989, only to leave four months later following a serious disagreement with McLean, as a result of which Murray won a substantial sum in a court action.

Dundee United playing record (1979/80)

	Appearances	Goals
Scottish League	3	
League Cup	2	

League Cup winner 1979

N

NADIR

The lowest point in the history of the club in a playing sense was surely season 1922/23. At the end of the previous season Dundee Hibs had finished second bottom of Division Two; because the number of clubs was to be reduced, the last two clubs lost their League membership, so the Hibs were out in the cold.

For some time it appeared they might have no other league to join and, had that been the case, the club would undoubtedly have closed down. A solution came when the Hibs were allowed to fill the vacancy caused by the withdrawal of the Celtic reserve team from the Scottish Alliance*. All other members of that competition were Division One reserve sides, but even then the Hibs could do no better than finish third from bottom. In doing so, they suffered some heavy defeats, the worst being 0–7 at the hands of Airdrie.

As if that were not embarrassing enough, the club's interest in the Scottish Cup was ended by Nithsdale Wanderers – and at Tannadice, for good measure. With manager Peter O'Rourke* resigning before the end of the season, just four months after taking up his post, and attendances often failing to reach 500, the club was in total disarray. Had the new board – which had bought control of the club the previous November – decided to lock the doors at Tannadice and throw away the key, few would have blamed them.

In fact, the key which turned the club round was the appointment as manager of Jimmy Brownlie* in June 1923. Earlier that month Scottish League status had been regained and from that point the club began to move upwards; it was the only direction they could have taken!

From a financial viewpoint, the club has known several crises, the most recent one in the mid-1950s. However, the most serious occurred in 1934. Shareholders of The Dundee United Football Company Ltd had been advised in writing in February of that year that, without an immediate influx of new capital, the company was in danger of going out of business. No cash injection was forthcoming, following which the board attempted to reschedule the club's debts of around £18,000, a massive sum for the time. This also was to no avail, the creditors unwilling to accept a reduction in the payments they were due.

At a board meeting on 19 February it was decided that United would be unable to complete the remaining eight Division Two fixtures and a letter was sent to the Scottish League announcing their resignation. *The Courier* and *Advertiser* reported the following day:

> It was stated that there was barely sufficient money in hand to pay the players' wages last week and no money to meet the [match] guarantee for Saturday or to meet wages for the incoming week. The decision to wind up the club was carried unanimously.

With the club facing oblivion and supporters mystified by events, white knights appeared on the scene in the form of city businessmen George Greig* and William McIntosh*. They undertook to guarantee the necessary finance to allow United to complete their remaining matches, while entering new negotiations with creditors. Application was made to the Scottish League to withdraw the letter of resignation and this was granted on 28 February. Jimmy Brownlie was brought back as manager and Dundee United continued, though the club had come perilously close to extinction.

Dave NAREY (born 1956)

At the age of 15, Dave was one of manager Jim McLean's* first signings in January 1972 and he began as an apprentice the following year. He made his first-team debut in 1973 at the age of 17 and was soon a regular from 1974/75; he quickly matured into a defender of great distinction, a fact recognised by the representative honours he gained at all levels. He holds the unique distinction of becoming the first ever Dundee United player to win a full cap for Scotland, which he achieved in 1977.

In 22 years Dave established the record number of appearances for the club with 866, as well as records for each of the individual competitions. Given modern trends and the effects of the Bosman judgment, it is likely that some, if not all, of these will never be exceeded.

An era came to an end in 1994 when he left Tannadice on a free transfer to join Raith Rovers, adding to his impressive array of honours by helping them win the Coca Cola Cup and the First Division championship. He then retired and severed his connection with the game, spurning offers of coaching posts.

Dundee United playing record (1973–94)

	Appearances	Goals
Scottish League	612	22
Scottish Cup	70	1

League Cup	108	6
European competitions	76	6
Scotland	35	1
Scottish League	1	
Scotland U-23	3	
Scotland U-21	5	
Scotland Youth	9	1

Scottish League champion 1982/83
Scottish League Cup winner 1979,1980
UEFA Cup finalist 1986/87
Scottish Cup finalist 1981,1985,1987,1988,1991
Scottish League Cup finalist 1981,1984

NEUTRAL VENUES

Not surprisingly, the neutral venue most often used in Scotland is Hampden Park, though few Arabs would accept it as such when the opponents are either Celtic or Rangers. In all, United have appeared at Hampden on 24 occasions: seven Scottish Cup finals and one replay; six Scottish Cup semi-finals and three replays; three League Cup finals; two League Cup semi-finals; the Emergency War Cup* final; and, rather more obscurely, a League Cup play-off against Ayr United in 1946!

Without a doubt, United's favourite 'other' ground must be Dens Park, which has also been called into use as a neutral venue on a total of 24 occasions since Dundee Hibs first used it in 1911. Other venues used have been Tynecastle Park (on nine occasions), Easter Road Stadium (five), East End Park and Gayfield Park (three each), Ibrox Stadium (twice), and McDiarmid Park and Station Park (once each).

Tannadice Park has also been used as a neutral venue for representative matches. Scotland have yet to play a full international at the ground, although Under-21, youth and schoolboy sides have done so on numerous occasions. League Cup semi-finals have been played at Tannadice on two occasions; in 1967 Dundee beat St Johnstone, but 20 years later they lost to Aberdeen.

On three occasions the ground has been used as a neutral venue for Scottish Cup second replays. Brechin City beat Peebles Rovers in 1955; Cowdenbeath beat Arbroath in 1966; and Motherwell beat Brechin City in 1986. Although Inverness Caledonian Thistle met Rangers in a third-round match at Tannadice in 1996, that was a 'home' match for the Highland club, whose own ground was ruled unsuitable to stage the tie.

Jerren NIXON (born 1973)

Signed by Ivan Golac* from ECM Motown of Trinidad in December 1993, he was a left-sided striker with a wicked turn of speed, which frequently left defenders with no option but to pull him down. Excellent ball skills, too, often took him past three or four defenders, although he did have a tendency to want to beat one too many. One of four 20 year-olds in the Scottish Cup-winning side, along with Dailly*, Hannah* and McLaren*, he came on as a substitute in the latter stages. He was less impressive during 1994/95, the season which culminated in United dropping to the First Division. New manager Billy Kirkwood* decided that Nixon was a luxury at that level and he was transferred to FC Zurich during the close season of 1995 for £200,000.

Dundee United playing record (1993–95)

	Appearances	Goals
Scottish League	43	7
Scottish Cup	11	1
League Cup	3	
European competitions	2	2
Trinidad & Tobago	5	1
Scottish Cup winner 1994		

NON-LEAGUE OPPOSITION
See also Junior Football
Throughout the years, Dundee Hibs/United have met the following non-League clubs. Unless stated otherwise, all matches were friendlies or testimonials:

Home
Arbroath 1910; Montrose 1911 (Consolation Cup); Montrose 1911 (Forfarshire Cup); Dunfermline Athletic 1911 (Consolation Cup); King's Park 1911 (Dewar Shield); Forfar Athletic 1911 (Qualifying Cup); Forfar Athletic 1912 (Consolation Cup); Dundee Wanderers 1912 (Consolation Cup); Dundee Wanderers 1912 (Forfarshire Cup); Dunfermline Athletic 1912 (Loftus Cup); Montrose 1912 (Qualifying Cup); Brechin City 1913 (Qualifying Cup); Forfar Athletic 1913 (Qualifying Cup); Forfar Athletic 1914 (Qualifying Cup); Brechin City 1914 (Forfarshire Cup); Aberdeen University 1925 (Scottish Cup); Arbroath Athletic 1927 (Scottish Cup); Vale of Leven 1927 (Scottish Cup); Montrose 1927 (twice: Scottish Cup, both at Tannadice); Nithsdale Wanderers 1931 (Scottish Cup); Forfar Athletic 1947 (Forfarshire Cup); Montrose 1948 (Forfarshire Cup); Brechin City 1948 (Forfarshire Cup); Montrose 1949 (Forfarshire Cup); Brechin City 1950 (Forfarshire Cup); Brechin City 1951 (Forfarshire Cup); Montrose 1953 (Forfarshire Cup); Brechin City 1953 (Forfarshire Cup final); Brechin City 1953 (Forfarshire Cup); Montrose 1954 (twice: Forfarshire Cup replays); Montrose 1955 (Forfarshire Cup).

Away

St Johnstone 1910; Arbroath 1910 (Qualifying Cup); Montrose 1911 (Consolation Cup); Dunfermline Athletic 1911 (Consolation Cup); Arbroath 1911 (Forfarshire Cup final, Dens Park); Forfar Athletic 1912 (Consolation Cup); Dunfermline Athletic 1912 (Consolation Cup); Forfar Athletic 1912 (Qualifying Cup); Broxburn United 1912 (Qualifying Cup); Arbroath Amateurs 1912; Arbroath 1914 (twice: Forfarshire Cup final and replay, Dens Park); Arbroath 1915 (Forfarshire Cup final, Dens Park); St Andrews United 1928; Stranraer 1930; Armadale 1933 (Scottish Cup); Wick Academy 1936; Brora Rangers 1936; Brechin City 1947 (Forfarshire Cup); Montrose 1948 (Forfarshire Cup); Brechin City 1948 (Forfarshire Cup); Montrose 1949 (Forfarshire Cup); Berwick Rangers 1951 ; Leith Athletic 1952 (Scottish Cup); Montrose 1953 (Forfarshire Cup); Brechin City 1954 (Forfarshire Cup); Montrose 1954 (Forfarshire Cup); Montrose 1955 (Forfarshire Cup); Golspie Sutherland 1975.

The fixtures here relate only to those periods when Dundee Hibernian/United were playing in the Scottish League, viz. 1910–1915, 1921/22, 1923–39, 1946 – date, excluding Highland League* and select teams, but including clubs in C Division* (1946–55).

NORTH AMERICAN SOCCER LEAGUE (NASL)

United's exploits in their first season of European competition – victory over Barcelona and honourable defeat by Juventus – brought them an invitation to participate in the NASL.

The competition was spread over six weeks between the end of May and early July and involved clubs from Europe and South America, each

United players training in the Cotton Bowl, Dallas, during their participation in the NASL. Leading off are (left to right) Jackie Graham, Dennis Gillespie, Walter Smith and Billy Hainey

of which represented the NASL club from the city in which they were based. United played as Dallas Tornado* and met Aberdeen* (Washington), ADO Hague (San Fransisco), Bangu of Brazil (Houston), Cagliari (Chicago), Cerro of Uruguay (New York), Glentoran (Detroit), Hibernian (Toronto), Shamrock Rovers (Boston), Stoke City (Cleveland), Sunderland (Vancouver), and Wolverhampton Wanderers (Los Angeles).

Bangu were the only club United played twice, but they did not exactly cover themselves in glory, winning three, drawing three and losing six of the matches. Perhaps the most notable aspect of their visit was that they played in Dallas Tornado's tangerine shirts and shorts; two years later these were adopted as United's official club colours.

NORTH EASTERN LEAGUE
Following the collapse of the Eastern Regional League* in 1940, Dundee United's management decided that the club, having no alternative league in which to play, should close down for the following season.

A year later, United were one of seven east of Scotland clubs which together formed the North Eastern League. The others were Aberdeen, Dunfermline Athletic, East Fife, Leith Athletic*, Raith Rovers and St Bernard's* and Rangers also joined despite continuing to run a team in the Southern League*.

The North Eastern League continued for the next four seasons and was characterised by two innovations. Firstly, the competition was split into two halves, all clubs playing each other home and away prior to the end of the year, then beginning afresh in January. This was to some extent recognition that the turnover of players due to the exigencies of wartime was so great that separate championships were appropriate. Not that it made much difference to United, who never managed to finish higher than fourth in any of the eight competitions.

The second unusual feature was that bonus points were awarded, though only in the second series of each season. In 1942 and 1943 a bonus point was awarded for an 'aggregate' win over home and away matches, while in 1944 and 1945 three points were awarded for an away win and two points for an away draw.

During the League's first three seasons, its members also competed for a knock-out trophy called the North Eastern League Cup.

NORTHERN IRELAND
See also Ireland and Republic of Ireland
United have met only three clubs from Northern Ireland, though one of them, Glentoran, on no fewer than four occasions.

The first encounter took place in United's Second Division days. Portadown were the visitors to Tannadice for a friendly on the Dundee October fast holiday in 1958, United winning 5–1. Nine years later saw the first meeting with Glentoran, in the unlikely setting of Detroit. It was a North American Soccer League* match in June 1967 which saw the Irish side triumph 1–0.

Two decades passed before United finally ventured to the Six Counties. It was a first-round tie in the UEFA Cup of 1987/88, and the draw took the previous season's finalists to Coleraine. United made heavy weather of it, an Iain Ferguson goal the only one of the first leg, but a 3–1 margin at Tannadice saw them through comfortably.

In 1989, the draw gave the club its second visit to the province, this time to Belfast to meet Glentoran. United had waited 22 years to erase the memory of that defeat in Detroit, and they made the most of it, winning 3–1 at The Oval and 2–0 at Tannadice. The friendship formed between the clubs over these two ties led to United returning to The Oval a year later to play a testimonial for two Glentoran players. The match ended 2–0 to United.

Strictly speaking, United did meet another club from Northern Ireland in 1992. They visited Derry City to play a pre-season friendly (drawing 0–0), although Derry are members of the League of Ireland (covering the Republic) and not the Irish League, as the Northern Ireland equivalent is known.

Given the number of players from Northern Ireland who have played in Scotland over the years, it is perhaps surprising that only one has joined United. Michael O'Neill* – who had played against United for Coleraine in those UEFA Cup ties in 1987 – became the club's record signing when he joined from Newcastle United for £350,000 in August 1989.

NORTHERN LEAGUE
Started in 1891, the first championship was shared by East End and Our Boys, who merged two years later to form Dundee FC.

Dundee Hibs were admitted to the Northern League just weeks after their formation in March 1909. The club spent their first season there and remained in the competition even after joining the Scottish League the following season. This was possible partly because there were only 22 Division Two matches, but was equally due to the fact that the Northern League itself had only seven members and was generally used as a means of filling in blank Saturdays; its fixtures were rarely completed, and Dundee Hibs never played more than 11 in one season.

The Hibs participated in 1910/11 and 1911/12, withdrew the following season, but returned for 1913/14 and 1914/15. The Northern League suspended its competition for the First World War and never resumed.

NORWAY
United's first connection with the country of mountains and fjords came during World War Two. Many members of the Norwegian armed forces

were stationed in Scotland and among them were the international footballers Boye Karlsen and John Sveinsson. They guested for United on a number of occasions and were popular with Tannadice patrons. Both also played against United; they may have wished they had remained in the club's black and white hoops because as members of a Norwegian Forces XI which played United in a challenge match at Tannadice in April 1944 they were on the receiving end of a 6–0 defeat.

Two decades later, Dundee United's Scandinavian colony included Finn Seemann. A seasoned international signed from Lyn Oslo in 1965, Seemann was a strong, attacking winger who had three seasons at Tannadice before joining DWS Amsterdam for £25,000 in July 1968. He later played for FC Utrecht, then returned to Norway and his original club. He was tragically killed in a car crash in September 1985 at the age of only 40.

International midfielder Erik Pedersen was one of Tommy McLean's* first signings for the club. He joined from Viking Stavanger in October 1996 and made an immediate impact.

Seemann's old club was one of three faced by United on an end-of-season tour to Norway in 1968; they were also one of two clubs (Brann Bergen was the other) who beat United. The single victory came against Viking Stavanger, who would be United's opponents on the club's next visit to the country in 1982 for a UEFA Cup first-round tie, which United won 3–1 on aggregate, though as all the goals came in the first leg in Stavanger, the Tannadice return was not one of their better European performances.

That remains the only occasion on which United have met Norwegian opposition in a competitive setting, although a return was made to the country for a pre-season tour in 1987. Three matches were played, including one in Tromso, home to Europe's most northerly League club, several miles north of the Arctic circle.

NUMBERS

Along with most other Scottish League clubs, Dundee United first numbered their shirts for season 1946/47. They were first worn in a League Cup sectional tie against Arbroath at Gayfield Park on 5 October 1946.

OLDEST

Gordon Wallace* is the oldest player to play in a first-team match for Dundee United. He was aged 50 and was club coach when a long injury list saw him drafted into the team against a Tobago XI during the club's Caribbean tour in June 1994. He played the full match and United won 4–2.

The oldest player to make a competitive appearance also did so *in extremis*. At the age of 40 years and eight months, Jimmy Brownlie* was manager during the club's second season in Division One when regular goalkeeper Bill Paterson was ruled out through injury for the Scottish Cup replay with Hearts at Tynecastle in February 1926. In those days, United had no reserve team and goalkeeping injuries were covered by fielding a trialist. Only signed players being eligible in Cup ties, Brownlie – who had given up playing two years earlier but remained as a signed player – was forced to emerge from retirement. Ring-rusty he undoubtedly was, and was reported to be at fault for the loss of three goals, although as Hearts scored six without reply his contribution was hardly decisive!

The oldest player to make a scheduled competitive appearance was also a goalkeeper. Former England international goalkeeper Peter Bonetti's last match for United came in the Premier Division in September 1979, when he was aged 38 years and two days.

Michael O' NEILL (born 1969)

The Irishman became United's record signing when he joined from Newcastle United for £350,000 in August 1989. He had first come to manager Jim McLean's* attention playing against United for his hometown club, Coleraine, in the UEFA Cup in 1987.

Unfortunately, O'Neill failed to make much impact during his four years at Tannadice, managing a total of only 63 League appearances. To some extent he was hampered by injury but, having been signed as a striker with international experience, his return of a mere eleven goals was well short of what he was capable of.

He was transferred to Hibernian for a fee of £400,000 in 1993, and three years later moved back to England with Coventry City.

Dundee United playing record (1989–93)

	Appearances	Goals
Scottish League	63	11
Scottish Cup	3	
League Cup	6	2
European competitions	5	1
Northern Ireland	12	

Peter O'ROURKE, Snr (born 1874; died 1956)

Despite being one of the club's shortest-serving managers – he was in charge of Dundee Hibs between December 1922 and March 1923 – O'Rourke came to Tannadice with one of the most distinguished records.

Born in Ayrshire, he won a Scottish junior international cap and played for Celtic, Burnley, Lincoln City, Third Lanark* and Bradford City before taking on the role of manager at his last club. He remained with Bradford for 14 years, all but three of which were spent in the First Division, and he led the club to what remains their only FA Cup win in 1911.

O'Rourke had dropped into non-League football when the call came from the new board which had just taken over at Tannadice, but at the time Dundee Hibs were themselves a non-League club, playing in the Scottish Alliance*. He agreed to lend his vast experience to help turn the club round, but soon recognised that, without the necessary finance to bring in good quality players, the task was beyond him. It is not clear whether the board denied him the kind of money they made available to his successor, Jimmy Brownlie*, but there were suggestions that, given the board's determination to change the club's name and drop all associations with its Irish roots, having a manager named O'Rourke was seen as unhelpful to that process. That may have been the case, but it begs the question as to why he was appointed in the first place.

O'Rourke departed, along with his sons Michael and Peter junior, whom he had signed as players, but was soon in demand back in England. He subsequently managed Bradford Park Avenue, Bradford City again, and finally the Welsh club Llanelli, before retiring in 1933.

OVERSEAS TOURS

Dundee United have been regular tourists since the mid-1960s, frequently by invitation, either to play in end-of-season tournament or as part of pre-season preparations. The following list includes a wide variety of destinations, with South America the most obvious absentee.

Nyasaland, Rhodesia and South Africa 1963; Iceland and Denmark 1966; USA 1967; Norway 1968; USA 1969; South Korea 1971; Nigeria 1972;

Holland 1973; Spain 1975; Japan 1979; Sweden and Denmark 1982; Spain 1983; German Federal Republic and Switzerland 1984; USA 1987; Norway 1987; Holland 1990; Holland 1991; Canada 1992; Trinidad & Tobago 1994; Malaysia 1994; Finland 1995; Denmark 1996.

OWN GOALS

The highest number of own goals in a season from which United has benefitted is seven (six League, one League Cup) in 1961/62. The club has never conceded more than three in a season.

Own goals, of course, come in all shapes and sizes and are either comical or disastrous, depending on which end they occur at. One of the most spectatcular ever seen at Tannadice was scored by Stewart Fraser in Division One match with Airdrie in October 1963. Having received the ball around twenty-five yards from his own goal, he spun round and sent it soaring into the top corner, leaving goalkeeper Sandy Davie helpless. As United won the match 9–1, Fraser drew a huge cheer from United fans!

In what is probably the only such occurrence in a Scottish Cup semi-final, United scored two own goals against Aberdeen at Tynecastle Park in April 1990. Freddy van der Hoorn and Mixu Paatelainen's efforts contributed to a thoroughly forgettable day as United went down 0–4. United were equally philanthropic in February 1994, Dave Bowman and then Freddy van der Hoorn again giving Motherwell a 2–1 victory in a League match at Tannadice.

Rangers' Terry Butcher scored a spectacular late winner for United in a Premier Division meeting at Tannadice in September 1990. It may be no more than coincidence, but he never again played a first-team match for the club.

Richard Gough scored several headed goals for United, but few gave Arabs as much pleasure as the one which he scored in the Premier Division match at Tannadice in December 1996. An Andy McLaren cross was punched by Rangers' Andy Goram onto Gough's head, from where it rebounded into the net for the game's only goal.

One of the costliest own goals was that scored by United full-back Tommy Millar in the Scottish Cup semi-final against Aberdeen at Dens Park in April 1967. After only three minutes, Millar was unfortunate to deflect the ball into his own net and there was no further scoring.

P

Mixu PAATELAINEN (born 1967)

Signed from the Finnish League club Valkeakosken Haka for £100,000 in 1987, he was the first of the wave of foreign imports brought in by Jim McLean. He was also the most successful, making an immediate impact. Later that season he won a place in the 1988 Scottish Cup final team, as well as winning the first of many caps for Finland.

Although never the club's top scorer, he did have a habit of getting important goals and he revelled in the big occasion. Throughout his five years at Tannadice he became a firm favourite with Arabs* who enjoyed his all-action style and never-say-die spirit.

He was transferred to Aberdeen for £400,000 in 1992, and two years later moved south to Bolton Wanderers, with whom he played in the Premiership. In 1997 he joined Wolverhampton Wanderers.

Dundee United playing record (1987–92)

	Appearances	Goals
Scottish League	133	33
Scottish Cup	21	8
League Cup	10	5
European competitions	9	1
Finland	32	6

Scottish Cup finalist 1988

PARTICK THISTLE FC

The first meeting between the clubs was a Scottish Cup tie at Firhill Park in 1925, which Thistle won decisively, 5–1. The following season United did rather better in the first of four which the clubs spent together in Division One between 1925 and 1932, but, with the exception of the Scottish Cup, the clubs did not come into contact again until United returned to Division One in 1960.

From that point, United met Thistle every season in Division One until 1970, when the Glasgow club lost the top division place they had held

154

continuously since 1902. They returned after only one season, but in the 22 years' existence of the Premier Division, Thistle have been members in only ten.

The clubs' most recent encounters came in the tension-filled play-offs at the end of season 1995/96, when United required a last-minute equaliser, then an extra-time winner, to secure promotion.

It's a fact: When United met Partick Thistle at Firhill in a Premier Division match in February 1993 it produced one of the most bizarre incidents in the history of Scottish football. With United leading 1–0, striker Paddy Connolly shot for goal; the ball beat the Thistle goalkeeper and hit the stanchion inside the goal before rebounding into the six-yard box. As Connolly, his team-mates and United fans began to celebrate a Partick Thistle defender picked up the ball and threw it to his goalkeeper, who then kicked it downfield for the match to be re-started. The only person in the ground who did not see the ball enter the goal was referee Les Mottram, who waved play on! Despite vehement protests from United players, the match continued, with Mottram refusing demands to consult his linesman. Even if he had missed the 'goal', he ought to have awarded a penalty after the defender picked up the ball; he claimed to have missed that, too! Luckily, Mottram's outrageous gaffe did not affect the outcome of the match, which United eventually won 4–0, but the incident frequently returned to haunt him – at the time, he was regarded as Scotland's top referee, and officiated at the 1994 World Cup – for the remainder of his career. It deserved to!

The playing record against Partick Thistle in major competitions is:

Scottish League (total): P 74 W 35 D 20 L 19 F 124 A 95 (60%)

Premier Division: P 36 W 21 D 11 L 4 F 68 A 35 (74%)

Scottish Cup: the clubs were drawn together in 1925, 1927, 1930, 1948, 1950, 1960 and 1981.
Record: P 8 W 1 D 1 L 6 F 8 A 28

League Cup: the clubs were drawn together in 1975, 1977, 1981, 1987, 1988, 1989 and 1990.
Record: P 10 W 7 D 1 L 2 F 17 A 8

Summer Cup: the clubs met in the quarter-final of the 1965 competition, United advancing on a 3–0 aggregate score

Notable transfers from: Billy Hainey (1966), Ian Gibson (1980)

Graeme PAYNE (born 1956)

One of the first graduates from the Jim McLean* academy of excellence and, like many of those, Dundee-born. He broke into the first team in 1973 at the age of 17 and made an immediate impact, his lack of bulk more than compensated for by his jinking wing skills.

A member of United's first Scottish Cup final team in 1974 at the age of 18 years and two months, he is the youngest United player to appear in a final. Graeme was also in both League Cup-winning squads and was voted SPFA Young Player of the Year in 1978. Capped three times at U-21 level, he ought to have won more representative honours in a career which many Arabs felt was left disappointingly unfulfilled. He was unable to command a regular first-team place from 1981 and eventually left the club for a loan spell with Greenock Morton, later transferring in March 1984 to Arbroath, for whom his elder brother Kenny had earlier played.

He became an insurance salesman when his playing career was over.

Dundee United playing record (1973–83)

	Appearances	Goals
Scottish League	199	11
Scottish Cup	17	3
League Cup	49	5
European competitions	21	1
Scotland U-21	3	
Scotland youth	6	3

League Cup winner 1979, 1980
Scottish Cup finalist 1974

PENALTIES

Joe Hannan scored the club's first-ever penalty. It came at Tannadice in Dundee Hibs' first competitive match, a Northern League* encounter with Dundee Wanderers* on 21 August 1909.

Dundee United's first was scored by Eddie Gilfeather in a Division Two fixture against St Johnstone at Muirton Park on 22 December 1923.

The greatest number of penalties scored by Dundee Hibs/United in a League season is eleven in Division Two, 1927/28. In the Premier Division the greatest number is seven, in 1981/82.

Are referees becoming more reluctant to award penalties? Prior to 1993/94, United had never gone through a League season without scoring at least one, yet they scored none at all over the next three seasons. In fact, between 13 February 1993 and 14 December 1996, United did not score a penalty in a League match.

Penalty shoot-outs are a relatively recent means of settling a cup-tie which remains level after extra-time. They make for great TV entertainment, providing your team is not involved! The live action is rarely enjoyed by the fans of the participating teams, but there is no fairer way of deciding a winner. United's first experience of a penalty shoot-out came in the Texaco Cup* against Leicester City at Tannadice in September 1972; the English club won. Since then there have been nine further instances, four of which have been won and five lost.

Orjan PERSSON (born 1942)

Has the distinction (shared with fellow countryman Lennart Wing*) of being the first Dundee United player to win a full international cap. He also has the singular distinction of being the first overseas player to join the club, when brought from Orgryte by manager Jerry

Finn Dossing, Mogens Berg, Orjan Persson and Lennart Wing pictured during the close season of 1965 when they worked as agents for the CIA!

Kerr* in November 1964. There being no professional football in Sweden at that time, Kerr did not have to pay a fee for him.

Six feet tall, Persson was a fast and penetrative left winger who scored more than his fair share from that position. He was immensely popular with Arabs*, who were mightily disappointed when he was transferred to Rangers (in exchange for winger Davie Wilson and wing half Wilson Wood) in 1967.

Dundee United playing record (1964–67)

	Appearances	Goals
Scottish League	77	15
Scottish Cup	8	1
Scottish League Cup	12	
European Competitions	4	
Sweden	9	

Gordan PETRIC (born 1969)

Became the club's record signing when bought by Ivan Golac* from Partizan Belgrade for £650,000 in November 1993.

Golac had been his manager at Partizan, where Petric was a member of the team which won the Yugoslav League championship once and the Yugoslav Cup twice. He also played several times for his country at U-21 level (scoring against Scotland in 1989) and had one full international cap. Petric was unable to add to that total while at Tannadice, as Yugoslavia were suspended from membership of UEFA at the time because of the civil war in Bosnia.

The central defender was an immediate success at Tannadice, his height and bulk enabling him to command the penalty area but he also demonstrated remarkable skill on the ground.

He was an influential figure in the club's run to the 1994 Scottish Cup final, where he turned in a near flawless performance which justifiably saw him win the man of the match award.

He was, however, noticeably less effective the following season and as United headed for relegation his form dipped alarmingly, particularly following the departure of Golac in March 1995. His transfer to Rangers (for a fee of £1.5 million) in August of that year was seen to be in the best interests of both player and club. He won several honours at Ibrox, but it is fair to say that he never reproduced there the form shown in his first season at Tannadice.

Dundee United playing record (1993–1995)

	Appearances	Goals
Scottish League	60	3
Scottish Cup	12	
League Cup	3	
European competitions	2	1
Scottish Cup winner 1994		

Willie PETTIGREW (born 1953)

Signed from Motherwell in August 1979 for £100,000, his goals helped secure the League Cup, the club's first-ever trophy, just three months later, earning him cult status among Arabs. He won a string of representative honours, being capped for his country at schoolboy, youth, U-23, League

Willie Pettigrew scoring against St Mirren at Tannadice in 1980, acclaimed by Dave Dodds.
Opposing players Billy Thomson and Jackie Copland also played for United

and full international level. Strangely, he failed to add to that total while at Tannadice, though he did gain a second League Cup winners' medal in 1980 and was a member of the 1981 Scottish Cup final team.

He scored his most famous goals in cup-ties, netting twice in the 1979 League Cup final replay and getting all four against Dundee FC in a Scottish Cup third round tie at Tannadice in 1980.

His stay at Tannadice was, however, brief. He departed for Hearts in a joint deal with Derek Addison (reported to be worth £150,000) in September 1981, and later played for Greenock Morton and Hamilton Academical.

Dundee United playing record (1979–81)

	Appearances	Goals
Scottish League	58	21
Scottish Cup	5	4
League Cup	21	8
European competition	7	3

League Cup winner 1979,1980
Scottish Cup finalist 1981

Iain PHILLIP (born 1951)

After winning U-18 schoolboy caps, Iain joined Dundee FC but was transferred to Crystal Palace for £72,500 in 1972. He returned to Dens Park barely 12 months later and was a member of Dundee's League Cup-winning team that year.

Transferred to United for £25,000 in November 1978, he was a first-team regular up until the start of the championship season and was a member of all four cup final teams between 1979 and 1981. Although he did not play in the 1979 replay he received a medal as he had played in the first game, thus having the unique distinction of having won winners' medals in the competition with both city clubs.

He moved to Raith Rovers in 1983, where he finished his playing career.

Dundee United playing record (1978–82)

	Appearance	Goals
Scottish League	85	1
Scottish Cup	11	
League Cup	33	
European competitions	15	

League Cup winner 1979, 1980
Scottish Cup finalist 1981
League Cup finalist 1981

PLAY-OFFS

The first occasion on which United took part in a play-off was in 1946 – and they did so twice within eight weeks, in different cup competitions.

Having lost 0–3 at home to Raith Rovers in the Supplementary Cup*, they surprised everyone (including, no doubt, themselves) by winning the return leg 4–1 at Kirkcaldy. This necessitated a third match, which took place at Dens Park; it ended 3–3 and Rovers won on the toss of a coin*. United manager Willie MacFadyen* remonstrated with the referee, arguing that extra-time should have been played, but there was apparently no provision for this. His case was not helped by the fact that he did not do so before the toss took place! United went as far as lodging a protest with the SFA, but to no avail.

In April, having finished level with Ayr United at the top of their section in the Southern League Cup, the clubs were obliged to play-off for a place in the quarter-finals. The game was played at Hampden Park, Ayr winning by the only goal.

In 1959, United met Falkirk in what was officially known as the supplementary round of the League Cup. In fact, it was a play-off between the winners of two of the sections, in order to reduce the number of qualifiers to eight for the quarter-finals. United earned a 1–1 draw at Brockville Park in the first leg, but were well beaten at Tannadice (0–3) two days later.

The play-offs introduced in 1995 were not the first the Scottish League had used to determine promotion and relegation. Between 1890 and 1915, what were termed 'test matches' were used on occasion (not every year) to separate candidates for promotion and relegation in the days before automatic movement between the divisions was introduced.

May 1996 saw United pitched into two nail-biting matches with Partick Thistle to decide which club would play in the Premier Division the following season. The first leg at Firhill Park ended 1–1 and Tannadice was filled to capacity four days later. After Thistle had taken the lead from a penalty during the second half, United appeared to be condemned to a second season in the First Division as the match entered its 90th minute. But drama beyond the imagination of the most creative scriptwriter was about to unfold. A mere 40 seconds remained when Brian Welsh* headed an equaliser to take the match into extra-time. Owen Coyle's winner was a classic example of a team snatching victory from the jaws of defeat – but neither manager Billy Kirkwood* nor the ten thousand Arabs there that evening would wish to witness a repeat of such brinkmanship!

For Coyle, that play-off experience was nothing new. A year earlier he had played for Bolton Wanderers in the play-off final at Wembley and on that occasion, too, he scored and his club were promoted.

POLAND

Although none of the many Polish servicemen stationed in Scotland during World War Two appear to have guested with United, the club did act as host for a challenge match against the Polish Army in December 1941. It attracted a large crowd, which saw an entertaining contest won 3–0 by United.

The only other contact the club has had with Poland took the form of a UEFA Cup tie against Slask Wroclaw in season 1980/81. United returned from the Polish coalfields with a creditable goalless draw, then ran riot in the return at Tannadice. The 7–2 scoreline was, until 1997 the biggest margin of victory achieved in Europe.

PORT GLASGOW ATHLETIC FC

The Renfrewshire club was one of the original members of Division Two of the Scottish League in 1893 and spent eight years in Division One between 1902 and 1910. Coincidentally, their eighteenth and last season as a League club was Dundee Hibs' first. The Division Two meetings in season 1910/11 were both won by the Hibs, 4–1 at Tannadice and 2–1 at Clune Park. Port Glasgow hit financial difficulties and resigned from the League at the end of that season; they appear to have gone out of business shortly thereafter.

PORTUGAL

Perhaps surprisingly, United have been drawn against Portuguese opposition only once in Europe. That occurred in the second round of the UEFA Cup of 1975/76 when FC Porto were their opponents. This was a tie United ought to have won, but they shot themselves in the foot by giving away two goals in the first leg at Tannadice, despite dominating the match. They acquitted themselves rather better in the return, but a 1–1 draw allowed Porto to advance on a 3–2 aggregate.

The only transfer between United and a Portuguese club involved the Brazilian Sergio Gomes from Amora in January 1995.

PREMIER DIVISION

Established in 1975, United were one of only four clubs to have enjoyed unbroken membership over the first 20 years, the others being Aberdeen, Celtic and Rangers. Sadly, that record was lost at the end of that season, though membership was immediately regained in 1996.

Including season 1997/98, a total of 21 clubs have been members of the Premier Division (number of seasons in brackets): Aberdeen (23), Airdrie (4), Ayr United (3), Celtic (23), Clydebank (3), Dumbarton (1), Dundee (13), Dundee United (22), Dunfermline Athletic (6), Falkirk (6), Greenock Morton (7), Hamilton Academical (2), Hearts (19), Hibernian (22), Kilmarnock (9), Motherwell (19), Partick Thistle (10), Raith Rovers (3), Rangers (23), St Johnstone (7) and St Mirren (15).

PROGRAMMES

The issuing of match programmes did not become widespread amongst Scottish League clubs until the 1950s, unlike in England where it was common 40 years earlier.

The first season in which Dundee United are known to have issued a regular match programme was 1933/34, and the earliest issue known to remain in existence is that for the visit of Leith Athletic* for a Division Two match on 10 March 1934.

Until the mid-1960s, the content of United programmes was extremely thin, comprising little more than a four-page fold-out. The contents were dominated by the team lists (which were usually less than accurate) and the half-time scores. There was also a half-page of rather bland comment from the manager, but virtually no information on the visitors at all. In total, around 60% was taken up by advertisements.

This was transformed with effect from season 1966/67 when the programmme changed from an A4 to an A5 format; it also became much more detailed, containing some reading material, including comments from players and some statistics. Background on the visiting club and its players was also introduced. The style remained little changed until the early 1980s, when it became more comprehensive and was soon among the best in Scotland.

Awards

The Scottish Programme Club assess the programmes of each Scottish League club, issuing awards on a divisional basis. United's programme has won the following awards: Scottish Programme of the Year, 1983/84, 1996,/97; First Division Programme of the Year, 1995/96.

Q

QUALIFYING CUP

By 1895, 22 years after the Scottish Cup was introduced, the number of entrants had increased to such an extent that not all could be accommodated. So a preliminary competition, known as the Qualifying Cup, was introduced in order to provide 16 qualifiers to join the bigger clubs. Only Division One clubs were exempt from the Qualifying Cup; Division Two sides had to take their chances along with non-League clubs until 1921, when all Scottish League clubs were guaranteed entry.

Action from the Qualifying Cup tie against Dunfermline at Tannadice in 1913

Until the First World War, the Qualifying Cup was a popular competition in its own right, providing an opportunity for smaller clubs to win a national trophy, not to mention much-needed income from ties which often proved attractive to supporters.

This was certainly the case as far as Dundee Hibs were concerned and manager Pat Reilly* used to gain considerable local press coverage in the build-up to home ties. A replay with Inverness Caledonian at Tannadice in November 1912 attracted a crowd of more than 6,000, while the League matches before and after attracted 2,000 and 3,000 respectively, the latter a derby with St Johnstone.

That paled into insignificance, however, when the Hibs drew Forfar Athletic in the quarter-final of the following season's competition. Extra seats were installed and the terracing at Tannadice was specially extended to accommodate a new ground record of 15,000 as Reilly's team won 1–0 and moved a step closer to the final. That attendance was reported at the time to be the highest in the history of the Qualifying Cup; it has certainly not been exceeded since.

Inverness Caledonian returned to Tannadice for the semi-final, this time watched by 8,500; it ended in a draw and the following week two special trains took 800 Hibs supporters to the Highland capital to cheer their team through to the final. They were asked to dig deep for the club's first ever national cup final, because it went to three games before Albion Rovers eventually took the trophy. The first match, held at Tynecastle Park on 13 December 1913, attracted an attendance of 11,000, the highest ever for a Qualifying Cup final.

Unfortunately, that was the only occasion on which Dundee Hibs made an impression on the Qualifying Cup, in which they last competed in 1920. The competition is still in existence today, although since 1931 it has operated in north and south sections, the semi-finalists in each gaining entry to the Scottish Cup.

It's a fact: Dundee Hibs played ten ties in the competition of 1913, including three in the final.

QUEEN OF THE SOUTH FC

United have shared League status with the Dumfries club on only seven occasions since their first meeting in 1927/28, in Division Two. There were three more at the same level before the Second World War, plus two in the 1950s, the last involving United's promotion season of 1959/60, when they finished in second place, a single point ahead of Queens. The only encounters in Division One came in the 1960s, and the last League meeting took place at Tannadice in March 1964.

The playing record against Queen of the South in major competitions is:

Scottish League: P 16 W 7 D 6 L 3 F 36 A 26 (63%)

Scottish Cup: the clubs were drawn together in 1932, 1963, 1978, 1985 and 1990.

Record: P 9 W 5 D 4 L 0 F 19 A 7

League Cup: the clubs were drawn together in 1986 and 1992.

Record: P 2 W 2 D 0 L 0 F 7 A 0

It's a fact: On the first two occasions the clubs met in the Scottish Cup, the tie required a third game to settle it; 31 years apart, each was staged at Ibrox Stadium.

QUEEN'S PARK FC

Queen's Park were the first Division One club to face Dundee Hibs when they met in the Scottish Cup in 1913. That ended in an honourable 2–4 defeat for Pat Reilly's* team in what was also the club's first ever Scottish Cup tie.

The club had become Dundee United when next they met, in Division One in 1925, and Queen's Park were also opponents during the other three seasons which United spent in that division up until 1932. These were their only League encounters at the top level, the remaining ten seasons they spent together being in either B Division or Division Two between 1948 and 1960.

The last time United met the amateurs in a League match was at Tannadice in January 1960.

The playing record against Queen's Park in major competitions is:

Scottish League: P 28 W 12 D 6 L10 F 60 A 47 (54%)

Scottish Cup: the clubs were drawn together in 1913, 1935, 1947, 1963, 1969 and 1978.

Record: P 7 W 4 D 1 L 2 F 16 A 13

Notable transfers to: Bert McCann (1954)

Notable transfers from: Doug Wilkie (1979)

It's a fact: When United beat Queen's Park 6–3 at Tannadice in 1935 it was regarded as a giant-killing, the visitors then being in Division One. The match was watched by 21,263, in a season when United's average home League attendance was 5,600.

League Cup: the clubs were drawn together in 1959 and 1979.

Record: P 3 W 3 D 0 L0 F 9 A 1

It's another fact: There was no question of a Hampden hoodoo* as far as United were concerned in 1959 – they won there twice in a fortnight, scoring 12 goals in the process! On 29 August they beat Queen's Park 4–0 in a League Cup sectional tie, then romped home 8–1 in a Division Two fixture on 12 September.

QUICKEST GOALS

The quickest goal scored by a Dundee United player came just 14 seconds into the Division One match against Hamilton Academical at Tannadice on 16 October 1965. It was scored by Finn Dossing* and United went on to win 7–0.

On 13 August 1996, Robbie Winters scored after only 19 seconds of the Coca-Cola (League) Cup second-round tie with Stirling Albion at Forthbank Stadium; United won 2–1.

On 11 December 1993, Dave Bowman* put United ahead after 24 seconds against Rangers in a Premier Division meeting at Ibrox and they went on to complete a 3–0 victory.

On 23 January 1954 Frank Quinn* scored after 40 seconds against Motherwell in a B Division fixture at Fir Park, but on that occasion it did them little good. The home side replied six times *in each half*, to inflict United's record League defeat.

Frank QUINN (born 1926)

'He delighted to have three or four opponents round him and to beat them with a few deft moves. How he squeezed himself through a group of players and still held the ball, I don't know . . . on his day the most entertaining player in the country.' That was how United's record goalscorer Peter McKay* described Frank Quinn in 1954. He was well qualified to offer an opinion, the two men being members of United's forward line dubbed The Famous Five* between 1948 and 1954.

Quinn was a shipyard welder when he signed for Celtic in 1946. He was unable to command a regular first-team place and joined United during the summer of 1948. At 5ft 10in, Quinn was bigger and heavier than most wingers but he also carried a fair turn of speed and he used these attributes to excellent advantage, becoming one of only seven players to score more than 100 times for the club. After being freed in 1954 he signed for Hamilton Accies, later playing for Cowdenbeath and Stranraer.

Dundee United playing record (1948–54)

	Appearances	Goals
Scottish League	157	90
Scottish Cup	14	5
League Cup	26	13

R

RAITH ROVERS FC

Dundee Hibs had their first encounter with Raith Rovers in the wartime Eastern League* of 1917/18. The Hibs did not play any competitive matches the following season, but when they returned to the Eastern League in 1919 the Kirkcaldy club had been accepted into the Scottish League and fielded their A team against the Hibs.

The next occasion on which Raith Rovers faced the club it was Dundee United, in Division One of 1925/26, but that was the only one of United's four inter-war seasons in that division that the two were together. They did share seven seasons in Division Two during the 1930s, as well as the various leagues in which United played during the Second World War. After the first three which followed it in B Division, the clubs did not meet again until United won promotion in 1960.

Having been in the top division since 1949, Rovers decline coincided with United's ascendancy and since 1960 the clubs have spent only eight League seasons together, two in the Premier Division.

The playing record against Raith Rovers in major competitions is:
Scottish League (total): P 42 W 23 D 8 L 11 F 104 A 74 (64%)
Premier Division: P 8 W 3 D 2 L 3 F 13 A 12 (50%)
Scottish Cup: the clubs have met just once, in 1957, when Raith Rovers won 7–0 at Stark's Park to inflict the club's heaviest-ever defeat in the competition.
League Cup: the clubs were drawn together in 1979, 1982 and 1987.
        Record: P 5 W 4 D 1 L 0 F 11 A 3
Notable transfers to: Willie Ouchterlonie (1934), Gordon Wallace* (as player/manager, 1977), Dave Narey* (1994), Jim McInally* (1995)
Notable transfers from: Bobby Bauld (1923), Craig Brewster* (1993), Jim McInally* (1996)
It's a fact: The two Division One meetings with Raith Rovers in season 1962/63 produced a total of 18 goals, United winning 8-1 at Tannadice and 7-2 at Stark's Park.

RANGERS FC

The clubs met for the first time in December 1925 in a League match at Tannadice, goals by Malcolm Campbell and Tommy Simpson giving United a 2–1 win in their inaugural season in Division One. They had spent three more seasons together by 1932, but did not meet again in the League until 1960. Since then, the only season missed has been United's brief sojourn in the First Division in 1995/96.

United's first victory at Ibrox did not come until March 1962, at the eighth attempt. The club's biggest win over Rangers occurred in April 1942 in the North Eastern League Cup, one of the wartime competitions; they won 8–1 at Tannadice.

In the Premier Division, United's biggest win is 4–1, at Ibrox in April 1981; at Tannadice it is 3–0, in December 1978. Overall, 0–5 represents the heaviest defeat, at Tannadice in March 1932 and at Ibrox in October 1931 and March 1963; all were Division One fixtures.

The playing record against Rangers in the major competitions is:

Scottish League (total): P 122 W 24 D 30 L 68 F 109 A 197 (32%)

Premier Division: P 84 W 17 D 25 L 42 F 74 A 111 (35%)

Scottish Cup: the clubs were drawn together in 1929, 1963 (semi-final), 1965, 1973, 1978 (semi-final), 1980 and 1989. They also contested the finals of 1981 and 1994.

Record: P 11 W 1 D 2 L 8 F 7 A 21

League Cup: the clubs were drawn together in 1947 (in the 1946/47 competition), 1964 (semi-final), 1967, 1984 (semi-final, in the 1983/84 competition), 1986 (semi-final) and 1992. They also contested the finals of 1981 and 1984.

Record: P 11 W 0 D 2 L 9 F 8 A20

Notable transfers to: Jimmy Simpson* (1927), Orjan Persson* (1967), Duncan Ferguson* (1993), Alex Cleland* (1995), Gordan Petric* (1995)

Notable transfers from: Davie Wilson (1967), Alex Reid (1968), Doug Houston (1974), Ian Redford (1985), Iain Ferguson (1986), Ally Maxwell (1995)

It's a fact: Arabs do not relish United being paired with Rangers in cup competitions! The Glasgow club are the only one United has never beaten in the League Cup and, until their 1994 Scottish Cup triumph, the same was true in that competition also.

Willie REID (born 1884; died 1964)

Appointed as United manager in June 1931, Reid had an illustrious playing career as a centre forward with Third Lanark*, Motherwell, Portsmouth and Rangers, winning three League championship badges with the Ibrox club, for whom he netted a total of 220 goals. He also gained nine Scotland caps and was manager of Albion Rovers before coming to Tannadice.

He arrived within weeks of United winning promotion but, starved of the resources necessary to strengthen the team, he was unable to keep them in Division One and the decline continued on their return to the lower division.

His record scarcely justified retaining occupancy of the manager's office, but any such considerations were overtaken by the financial crisis which engulfed the club in the early part of 1934. One of the new owners' first decisions was to dispense with Reid's services and he never again held a post in senior football.

John REILLY (born 1962)

Dundee born and bred, Reilly was often underestimated but was an effective striker during his spell at Tannadice. Though he could never claim a regular first-team place, he did make enough appearances to win a League championship medal in 1983.

Transferred to Motherwell in 1985, he was unfortunate to sustain an achilles tendon injury which seemed to have ended his career prematurely at the age of only 24. Happily, a revolutionary operation enabled him to resume his playing career with Motherwell who transferred him to Dunfermline in 1991, and he later played for East Fife.

In 1993 he went into management, taking over at Cowdenbeath, though that proved a thankless task and he remained for less than two years. He retained his link with the game, coaching youngsters while working as a freelance sports journalist.

Dundee United playing record (1980–85)

	Appearances	Goals
Scottish League	54	18
Scottish Cup	1	
League Cup	11	7
European competitions	6	1
Scotland youth	10	5
Scottish League champion 1982/83		

Pat REILLY (born 1874; died 1937)

The founding father of Dundee Hibernian and therefore, by extension, of Dundee United also. Reilly and his family were immigrants from Ireland who came to Dundee in the late 1870s. His father worked in the jute mills, as did the young Pat from the day on which he left school, though he soon illustrated the independence of thought and determination which would come to characterise his life.

Pat Reilly, pictured in 1910

By the age of 20 he had opened a shop selling

spare parts for bicycles, and he soon developed this into selling the models himself, then taking the logical step of actually manufacturing them. His business expanded rapidly, not least as a result of the upsurge in women taking up cycling around the turn of the century, enabling him to open branches in Edinburgh and Perth.

It seems that, while establishing his business in the capital, he developed an interest in Hibernian FC and, given his active involvement in both the Roman Catholic church and the Irish business community in Dundee, decided that his home city should have a football club with similar links. Although others were involved, Pat Reilly was without doubt the driving force behind the founding and establishment of Dundee Hibernian, his inspiration and determination being primarily responsible for securing Clepington Park* and, a year later, membership of the Scottish League. No other club since the formation of the League had gained admission within a year of being formed; it was an astonishing feat and it ensured that Dundee Hibs had a foundation secure enough to enable it to consolidate both on and off the park.

Reilly became manager/secretary at Tannadice from day one, joint responsibilities he held for more than 13 years, with the exception of Herbert Dainty's* two-year spell as player/manager from 1915 (during which time Reilly remained club secretary).

There is no record of the extent to which Reilly himself financed the new club, but his input must have been substantial. It was only as a result of the protracted absence of League football after World War One that the club got into financial difficulties, and it was typical of Reilly that when an offer was forthcoming to take over the club and pay its debts in December 1922 he did not baulk at the fact that one of the conditions attached was that all of the then committee had to stand down.

Reilly appreciated that ensuring the continued existence of Dundee Hibs was of greater importance than his personal position, though one can but speculate as to what he thought of the new owners' decision to ditch the club's traditional name and colours. This may explain why he became a Dundee United shareholder, though never a member of the board. He also remained a regular visitor to Tannadice, and it was entirely appropriate that the club flag flew at half mast and there was a minute's silence at the ground on 10 April 1937 as a mark of respect following his death.

It would be difficult to exaggerate the contribution made by Pat Reilly to the formation of the club which is now Dundee United; quite simply, without his vision, and the energy to turn it into reality, there would have been no Dundee United.

REPLAYS

United are not known as replay 'specialists' in the Scottish Cup, although they do have a considerably better-than-average record. In all, the club has been involved in 58 replays, including second replays; 31 have been won, nine drawn and 18 lost.

United have a good record in semi-final replays; indeed, it was a 100% record until Kilmarnock spoiled it by winning in 1997. On the previous occasions on which they required a second attempt (1974,1981,1985 and 1994), and in 1988 when they needed a second replay, United had always reached the final. Then the problems usually started . . .

United participated in the last-ever Scottish Cup final replay, losing to Rangers in 1981. Since 1990, extra-time and penalty kicks, if necessary, have been used to decide the winner on Cup final day.

REPUBLIC OF IRELAND
See also Ireland and Northern Ireland
United have met only two clubs from the Republic. In the North American Soccer League* of 1967, they beat Shamrock Rovers 5–1 in Boston, while Bohemians were their opponents in the 1985/86 UEFA Cup first round. United recorded a 5–2 victory in the first leg in Dublin but the Irish side regained some pride in the return, drawing 2–2 at Tannadice.

United have met League of Ireland opposition since then, drawing 0–0 with Derry City in a pre-season friendly in 1992. Although the club is based in Northern Ireland, it does not play in the Irish League; it is a member of the FAI and plays in the Republic's league as a consequence of the political situation in Ireland.

RESERVES
Dundee United had no reserve team until after the Second World War. It was only on the formation of C Division* of the Scottish League that the club responded to the invitation to assist in making up the numbers for the new division. Prior to that, even during the period between 1924 and 1934 (including four seasons in Division One) when the club was full-time, they did not compete in the Scottish Alliance*, the competition for the second teams of the top clubs, or a local league competition, which would not have been much of a drain on resources.

United reserves continued in C Division until 1952, then reverted to running only a first team. A second XI was resurrected when the Scottish Alliance League was formed in 1956; it involved a total of only six clubs, and lasted just one season.

For the following two years there was no formal reserve team at Tannadice, although friendlies against local junior clubs were arranged from time to time. When Jerry Kerr* took over as manager in 1959 he insisted that he needed a reserve team and so United entered the Combined Reserve League*. They remained for only one season, but for the best of reasons: following promotion in 1960, United took their place in the Scottish Reserve League along with other Division One clubs.

The club has won the following reserve honours: Premier Reserve League championship 1988, 1989, 1990; Reserve League East championship 1981, 1983, 1992; Reserve League Cup 1964, 1983, 1991; 2nd XI Cup 1963, 1981, 1988.

Ernest ROBERTSON (born 1892; died 1982)

There cannot be many examples of one person's service on the board of a Scottish football club extending over a period of more than 50 years, but Ernest Robertson is one such.

In 1926, his father, owner of John Robertson and Son, Aerated Water Manufacturers, bought 50 shares in the Dundee United Football Company. Two years later the shares were transferred to Ernest who, in March 1929, became a director of Dundee United, assuming the chairmanship in 1931 at the age of 38.

With the exception of the period between 1936 and 1941 when the club was taken over on two separate occasions, he spent the remainder of his life as a member of the board. He returned as chairman in 1948 for a marathon stint of 15 years, presiding over the barren years of the early and mid-'50s, then the innovation of Taypools* (which he initially funded through a personal loan) to the triumphant return to Division One in 1960.

Happily, Robertson lived to see the club win its first major trophy in 1979 and become established on the European stage. The contrast which that posed with his Tannadice experiences of the 1920s, '30s and '50s must have been breathtaking, but he himself played a telling part in allowing Dundee United to develop to the level where it became first a possibility, then a reality.

Ernest Robertson (extreme right) *pictured with fellow directors in 1979, 50 years after he first joined the Dundee United board. The others are* (left to right) *George Grant, Johnston Grant (receiving a presentation from a whisky company representative), Jimmy Littlejohn and George Fox*

It was fitting that when he died in February 1982 his replacement on the board of directors was the man who translated it into reality, one James Y. McLean*.

ROMANIA

Their European travels have taken United on three journeys to the land of Count Dracula. In the first round of the 1974/75 European Cup Winners' Cup they were drawn against Jiul Petrosani. The star of the first leg at Tannadice was a young Paul Sturrock*, as United built a 3–0 lead. As things turned out they needed it, the Romanians winning the return 2–0 and coming close to taking the tie into extra-time.

By the time the club returned for a UEFA Cup second-round tie 12 years later, they were considerably more accomplished on foreign fields. The first leg again saw United forge ahead by 3–0, and Universitatea Craiova could do no more than pull one back in Romania.

The country's best-known club, Dinamo Bucharest, were United's opponents for a further European Cup Winners' Cup tie in 1988. It was a second-round match and again United had been drawn at home for the first leg. This time there was to be no lead to take to Romania; indeed Dinamo scored the only goal at Tannadice, and although United did well to record a 1–1 draw in Bucharest, it wasn't enough.

S

SCOTTISH ALLIANCE

This competition was introduced in 1919 by the major Scottish League clubs in order to provide competition for their reserve teams. Dundee Hibs were not members and indeed were short by some distance of the standard of the clubs involved, even at reserve-team level. This was evidenced when the Hibs lost their League membership when Division Two was reduced in size at the end of season 1921/22.

There was no obvious choice of another competition to join, but fortunately Celtic had decided to withdraw their second team from the Scottish Alliance and supported the application of Dundee Hibs as their replacement. Welcome though this was at the time, the fact that the Hibs finished third bottom of the Alliance qualifies that season as the club's most forgettable. Thankfully, they were re-elected to the Scottish League for the one which followed, whereupon things quickly improved under the guidance of new manager Jimmy Brownlie*.

SCOTTISH CUP

One of the decisions of the Scottish Football Association at its inaugural meeting in March 1873 was that '. . . the clubs connected with this association subscribe for a challenge cup to be played for annually . . .' The following October the competition began and in the first final Queen's Park beat another Glasgow club, Clydesdale.

Prior to 1921, entry to the Scottish Cup was automatic only for clubs in Division One. Those in Division Two, such as Dundee Hibs, along with non-League clubs, had to enter the Qualifying Cup*, with the last 16 being granted access to the major trophy.

Dundee Hibs never won a Scottish Cup tie. They succeeded in qualifying in their second season as a League club and their first-ever Scottish Cup tie took place, appropriately, at Hampden Park. They lost 2–4 to Queen's Park in a first-round tie on 8 February 1913. The club had become Dundee United before Scottish Cup success was tasted for the first time, in a 5–1 first-round win over the students of Aberdeen University at

Tannadice on 24 January 1925. United did not beat a League club in a Scottish Cup tie until 1928, East Fife being the victims.

The first replay involving United occurred on 27 January 1926, against Hearts at Tynecastle. It ended in a 1–1 draw, with Hearts winning the second replay, having won the toss for home advantage.

The earliest in a season that the club has played a Scottish Cup tie is October, in 1954 and 1955. At that time, the clubs which occupied the bottom eight positions in B Division the previous season were obliged to participate in the first round, along with non-League clubs.

United did not reach the semi-final of the competition until 1963, losing 2–5 to Rangers at Hampden Park. Their first appearance in the final ended in defeat by a similar margin, Celtic scoring three times without reply in 1974.

United have contested seven Scottish Cup finals, with the 1994 victory over Rangers their only triumph. The team which brought the trophy to Tannadice Park for the first time was: van de Kamp, Cleland, Malpas, McInally, Petric, Welsh, Bowman, Hannah, McLaren (sub. Nixon, 83), Brewster, Dailly. Sub. not used: Bollan. Scorer: Craig Brewster (47 minutes). Attendance: 37,450* (at the time, Hampden Park was undergoing re-construction and the capacity was limited to 38,000. All tickets were sold, United's allocation being 12,000, and it seems likely most of the missing 550 would be accounted for from within those allocated to sponsors). Man of the match award: Gordan Petric. Manager: Ivan Golac

It's a fact: Although United failed to win any of their six Scottish Cup finals between 1974 and 1991, this is not a record. Hibernian have lost the last seven finals in which they have appeared, although they are spread over a much longer period (1914–79).

Biggest victories

The 14–0 demolition of hapless Nithsdale Wanderers in 1931 also stands as the club's record win in all competitions. The nearest the club has come to that record was 7–0 against amateurs Arbroath Athletic (h) in 1927. The same scoreline constitutes the record away victory in the Cup, United scoring seven without reply at Arbroath in 1988.

Biggest defeats

Motherwell hold the record for a Scottish Cup win at Tannadice. The Fir Park club were a division higher than United when they triumphed 5–1 in 1939, and the same was the case when Third Lanark* won 4–0 20 years later. But no such excuse could be offered in mitigation of the 0–4 drubbing by Aberdeen in 1972.

Raith Rovers 7 United 0 (1957) and Hearts 6 United 0 (1926) represent the most decisive Cup exits made by the club.

The most Scottish Cup ties played by United in one season was nine, including four replays, in 1988.

United have been drawn against non-League clubs in the Scottish Cup on ten occasions, but only four times since the Second World War. The only defeat by a non-League club in the Cup came in 1953, when Berwick Rangers won 3–2 in a replay at Tannadice. The only other occasion on which United were dismissed from the competition by a club of lesser status occurred when First Division St Mirren won 4–1 at Love Street in 1977.

During their time as a Second Division club, United did have their days as Cup giantkillers. The most famous occasion was in 1949 when Celtic were beaten 4–3 at Tannadice in a first-round tie. In 1929 they defeated city rivals Dundee FC in a replay at Tannadice, and in 1935 they humiliated Queen's Park (then in Division One) 6–3 at Tannadice. Even more notably, two years later Hearts were sent home licking their wounds after a 3–1 upset.

The Edinburgh club was also involved in the most remarkable Scottish Cup tie involving United. It happened in 1968 and Hearts had established a two-goal lead after only 18 minutes; United replied decisively by scoring four times, then Hearts pulled one back – all before half-time. The Norwegian winger Finn Seemann had the opportunity to restore United's two-goal advantage from the penalty spot, but scorned it. Almost immediately, Hearts equalised, only for United to regain the lead four minutes later. A penalty was awarded to the Edinburgh club; they took advantage of it and then, with just five minutes remaining, scored what proved to be the winner in an 11-goal thriller.

The overall record of Dundee Hibs/United in the Scottish Cup, 1913–1997 (70 seasons) is:

P 226 W 98 D 60 L 68 F 402 A 309 (57%)

SCOTTISH FOOTBALL ASSOCIATION

The SFA was formed in March 1873 by eight clubs, all but two of them from Glasgow: Clydesdale, Dumbreck, Eastern, Granville, Kilmarnock, Queen's Park, Third Lanark* Volunteer Reserves and Vale of Leven* (Alexandria, Dunbartonshire). Dundee Hibernian were accepted into membership in May 1909, two months after their formation, allowing them to participate in the Qualifying Cup* which provides access for smaller clubs to the Scottish Cup.

In 1923, when the directors of Dundee Hibs decided to change the name of the club, the permission of the SFA had to be sought. The new name suggested was Dundee City, but because Dundee FC objected, the SFA refused to sanction the change at the monthly meeting of its council in September of that year. The matter was deferred to the following month's meeting and only when Dundee FC accepted the compromise suggestion of Dundee United did the SFA Council agree to ratify it.

It's a fact: In 1963, United were fined £10 by the SFA for not wearing their officially registered colours in the Scottish Cup semi-final with Rangers at Hampden Park. The official colours were white with black hoops, but for most of season 1962/63 United had played in an all-white strip with black edgings, and had received no indication that this was causing the SFA bureaucrats to have sleepless nights. The following season the all-white strip did become United's official colours.

SCOTTISH FOOTBALL LEAGUE

The Scottish League (as it is always known) was formed in April 1890 by the following clubs: Abercorn* (Paisley), Cambuslang (Lanarkshire), Celtic, Cowlairs (Glasgow), Dumbarton, Heart of Midlothian, Renton (Dunbartonshire), St Bernard's* (Edinburgh), St Mirren, Rangers, Third Lanark* (Glasgow), Vale of Leven* (Alexandria, Dunbartonshire).

The first Scottish League matches were played the following August, but St Bernard's could not participate as they had been expelled from the SFA for paying players, professionalism being outlawed at the time. Although Renton began the League programme, they were expelled after only five matches for the same reason, so the first League season had only one division of ten clubs.

Division Two was introduced in 1893, also with ten clubs, but although Division One gradually expanded to include twice that number, admission of new clubs to the League was limited and there were only 12 in Division Two when Dundee Hibs secured election to it in 1910. There was no promotion or relegation between the divisions, clubs in Division One deciding at the AGM whether or not to admit a club from below at the expense of one of their own number; unsurprisingly, this rarely happened.

The same clubs unilaterally decided to suspend Division Two during World War One, reducing the competition to only one division of 20 clubs. Without voting power, there was nothing Division Two clubs could do, though when their division was not reinstated following the return of peacetime, they became increasingly frustrated, their anger eventually leading to their breaking away from the Scottish League in 1921 to form their own competition, which they called the Central League*.

This forced the bigger clubs to capitulate and Division Two was not only reintroduced a year later, but with automatic promotion and relegation for the top and bottom two clubs. However, there was a catch, and it eventually ensnared Dundee Hibs. Twenty clubs had been admitted to form the new Division Two, but the League insisted that this number be reduced to 18 for the following season, the bottom two clubs thus losing their places. After finishing second last, Dundee Hibs were again out of the League, just 12 months after being readmitted.

Such an event could not have come at a worse time for the Hibs and was very nearly the cause of the club going out of business. However, after the first of many takeovers of the club, a new dawn broke at Tannadice and within a further 12 months the Hibs were re-elected to Division Two, reaching Division One for the first time in 1925. Since then the club's participation in the Scottish League has been interrupted only by the suspension of the competition for World War Two.

Scottish League Status
1910 Elected to Division Two; 1910–15 Division Two; (1915–21 Division Two suspended); 1921/22 Division Two; 1923 re-elected to Division Two; 1923–25 Division Two; 1925–27 Division One;1927–29

The first Dundee United team to win a championship, Division Two in season 1924/25. (left to right, standing) *R. Rintoul, J. Osborne, A. Gilmour, D. Richards, F. Bridgeford, J. O'Kane, J. McRoberts, J. Kay, E. Gilfeather, J. Brownlie (manager).* (seated) *W. Hutchison (director), T. Simpson, W. Oswald, J. Smith, R. Bauld, J. Harvey, W. Hogg (director)*

Division Two; 1929/30 Division One; 1930/31 Division Two; 1931/32 Division One; 1932–39 Division Two; (1939–46 Scottish League suspended); 1946–56 B Division; 1956–60 Division Two; 1960–75 Division One; 1975–95 Premier Division; 1995/96 First Division; 1996– Premier Division.

The overall record of Dundee Hibs/United in the Scottish League, 1910–1997 (73 seasons), is:
P 2524 W 1022 D 574 L 928 F 4472 A 4190 (51.9%)

SCOTTISH JUNIOR FA

In 1941, following their closedown as a senior club due to the suspension of the Scottish League, Dundee United were successful in their application to join the SJFA. However, this lasted only a few weeks, as the SFA ruled that it was not possible to hold membership of both associations simultaneously. See United Juniors FC.

THE SHED

The edifice which is the spiritual home of almost every Arab under the age of 50 was erected during 1957. Prior to that, the terracing at the west end of Tannadice Park had always been open and the new enclosure provided some protection from the elements for around 7,000 fans. The Shed was opened for the derby visit of St Johnstone on 21 September 1957 and quickly developed into the place where younger supporters congregated – and generated most noise.

To comply with the demand for all-seated stadiums, the roofing was renewed and seats installed in 1993. With heavy hearts Arabs accepted that progress was inevitable, but few if any can view the new structure without a great sense of longing for just one more chance to do the Shed Boys' dance!

SHIRT SPONSORS

The first occasion on which United's shirts carried sponsorship was in the 1985 Scottish Cup final. VG Foodstores were not put off by the club's failure to bring the Cup home, extending their sponsorship into the season which followed and the one after that.

Belhaven breweries took up the mantle in 1987, and held it for the next six seasons. United had no shirt sponsor during 1993/94, with the exception of the last, and rather important, match. The car manufacturer Rover agreed a two-year sponsorship, starting with the Cup final. When the Rover deal had run its course in 1996, it was replaced by the logo of the telecommunications company Telewest, which also signed a two-year deal.

Dundee United have never revealed how much the club receives in terms of shirt sponsorship; an educated guess might come up with a figure of around £150,000 per season.

Jimmy SIMPSON (born 1908; died 1972)

A Fifer who became one of the real stars of Scottish football in the inter-war period. He was signed by manager Jimmy Brownlie* from Newburgh West End juniors in 1924 and made his debut for United in Division One the following year at the age of 17 as a wing half. Despite his height (six feet) he was both mobile and fast and quickly matured beyond his years. A regular during the club's first two years at the top level, it became inevitable that United could not retain him following relegation in 1927, and he was transferred to Rangers for the then sizeable fee of £1,000.

At Ibrox he was converted into a centre half and became an integral part of the team which dominated the Scottish game during the 1930s. Simpson won five League championships and four Scottish Cups, adding four League caps and 14 full international caps to his collection. For good measure, he also found the time to qualify as an engineer, which became his vocation after he had finished playing.

His son Ronnie's career was, if anything, even more notable, culminating in his arrival at Celtic in time to be part of the team which captured the European Cup in 1967.

Dundee United playing record (1925–27)

	Appearances	Goals
Scottish League	51	6
Scottish Cup	7	

SLOVAKIA
See also Czechoslovakia

Slovakia does not have a distinguished football history. With the exception of Slovan Bratislava, all of the famous Czechoslovak clubs are in what is now the Czech Republic, from which Slovakia split in 1993.

Nonetheless, United's only visit thus far to the new state ended in defeat. Hopes of a run in the European Cup Winners' Cup – which the club entered in their own right for the first time in 1994 – were dashed by the unknowns of Tatran Presov. The damage was really done in the first leg at Tannadice, where the visitors twice led before United restored some respectability with a 3–2 scoreline. A first-minute strike by Jerren Nixon in Presov offered United hope, but some woeful defending allied to inept goalkeeping allowed the Slovaks to score three times for a 4–3 aggregate win.

Doug SMITH (born 1937)

One of the longest-serving employees of the club, having joined from Aberdeen Lads' Club in 1958. A rock-solid centre half, he became a regular only after fellow Aberdonian Ron Yeats* left for Liverpool in 1961. Thereafter he was a permanent fixture in the side until his retirement in 1976, being very unfortunate not to have won any honours from a career of sustained excellence. He made a total of 587 first-team appearances for the club, then a record, and had the almost unbelievable distinction of never once being cautioned! He was captain of United on the occasion of the club's first Scottish Cup final in 1974 and he had also won a runners-up medal in the Summer Cup* in 1965.

During the latter stages of his career he bought the popular Athletic Bar close to Tannadice and devoted himself to running the business following his retirement. He joined the board at Tannadice in November 1983 and was elected vice chairman nine years later. In that role he served on numerous Scottish League and SFA committees and became President of the Scottish League in 1997.

Dundee United playing record (1958–76)

	Appearances	Goals
Scottish League	456	18
Scottish Cup	42	3
League Cup	91	5
Summer Cup	16	
European competitions	15	
Scottish Cup finalist 1974		
Summer Cup finalist 1965		

Reggie SMITH

A former England international and the son of a South African rugby international, he was appointed United manager in September 1954, following the resignation of Willie MacFadyen*.

Reggie Smith, United manager 1954–57

He joined Dundee as a player in 1946 and remained with the club when his playing career was over; he left his post as trainer/coach at Dens Park to join United. Smith resigned to take over as manager of Falkirk (then in Division One) in January 1957 and three months later led his new club to victory in the Scottish Cup final. He later returned to England, managing one of his former clubs, Millwall.

SOUTHERN LEAGUE

The Southern League was established in 1940 and involved only clubs from the central belt, so as to reduce travelling during wartime. Its members also played in a competition called the Southern League Cup, which was the forerunner of the League Cup*, based on sectional format.

United joined the Southern League in 1945, assuming a place in its B Division, along with Dundee FC. Despite its name, the competition embraced those areas of the country where League clubs had been based prior to the war, the Scottish League having resolved not to resume until 1946.

As members of the Southern League, United also participated in the Southern League Cup. They finished level at the top of their section with Ayr United, but lost out in a play-off at Hampden Park.

SOUTH KOREA

When United visited South Korea for a pre-season tour in 1971 it was regarded as missionary work. That said, they found the standard of football higher than had been anticipated, as results of 1–0, 3–3 and 4–3 illustrated. The drawn match was against the South Korean national side which has since made great strides, qualifying for the World Cup finals of 1990 and 1994.

SPAIN

There cannot be a Dundee United supporter who does not know that the club has the unique experience of being drawn against Barcelona twice in Europe and winning all four ties. What made the triumph of 1966 all the more remarkable was that, while the tie represented United's European debut, the wealthy Spanish club had already contested two European Cup finals and were holders of the Fairs Cup trophy – until they met Jerry Kerr's* lads! Fittingly, the second leg at Tannadice attracted a record attendance of 28,000, one which will never be exceeded.

If United were underdogs in 1966, they were even less fancied when the two clubs renewed their acquaintance in the UEFA Cup 20 years on. Barca were managed by Terry Venables and had a galaxy of international stars including Victor, Gary Lineker and Mark Hughes. Nevertheless, within four minutes Kevin Gallacher* had given United a lead which they held without too much trouble. But the fact they could not find a second was held to be their weakness when the cauldron of the Nou Camp had to be endured two weeks later. The Spanish club had levelled the tie before half time, but late strikes by John Clark and Iain Ferguson brought them crashing down as history repeated itself. It is nights like these – inevitably few and far between – which convince football fans that all the bad times are worthwhile!

Nor have United fared too badly in other meetings with Spanish clubs. They did lose 0–2 to Salamanca in a tournament played at Leon in June 1975, but reversed that in beating Espanyol during the Costa Dorada tournament in August 1983. The only other occasion on which Spanish opposition was encountered came in August 1989 when John Toshack brought Real Sociedad to Tannadice for Paul Sturrock's* testimonial match, which United won 1–0.

Derek STARK (born 1958)

A Scotland schoolboy cap at U-18 level, Derek completed his education before pursuing football as his career, joining up at Tannadice in the summer of 1976. Within two years he had won a regular first-team slot and was a member of both League Cup-winning teams as well as making a telling contribution to the 1983 League championship triumph.

A sturdy and aggressive attacking midfielder, he made equally important contributions to some of the club's finest performances in Europe. Sadly, his career was truncated due to a serious knee injury and he retired at the age of 26 in 1985. He was given a testimonial by the club and subsequently took up a career with Fife Police.

Dundee United playing record (1976–85)

	Appearances	Goals
Scottish League	164	7
Scottish Cup	15	
League Cup	41	
European competitions	26	4

Scottish League champion 1982/83
League Cup winner 1979, 1980
Scottish Cup finalist 1981,1985
League Cup finalist 1981

ST BERNARD'S FC

The Edinburgh club joined the Scottish League in 1893 (the year in which they won the Scottish Cup) and remained in membership for the following 40 seasons. The first seven of these were spent in Division One, but the club had settled in Division Two by the time Dundee Hibs were admitted in 1910. St Bernard's won the first Scottish League encounter 4–3 at Logie Green in September of that year.

The clubs spent a total of eighteen seasons together in Division Two between 1910 and 1939. St Bernard's are the ex-League club which Dundee Hibs/United met more often than any other and the Saints had distinctly the better of the exchanges. During that period they had four home grounds : Royal Gymnasium (until 1916), Logie Green (until 1923), Tynecastle Park during 1923/24 while their original ground was being rebuilt, and the Royal Gymnasium Grounds, as it was known, from 1924.

The clubs also met in several other competitions. In the Consolation Cup* of 1911/12; in the Eastern League*, 1915/16 and 1916/17; in the Central League*, 1920/21; in the Eastern Regional League* 1939/40; and in both the North Eastern League* and the North Eastern League Cup in 1941/42.

Dundee United's last Scottish League meeting with Saints was a 5–2 win at Tannadice in November 1938. St Bernard's closed down in 1942 and did not re-form after the war.

The full Scottish League record against St Bernard's was:
P 36 W 12 D 6 L 18 F 64 A 84

It's a fact: The club's first ever match at Tannadice as Dundee United was against St Bernard's on 3 November 1923; it ended with a 3–2 win.

ST JOHNSTONE FC

In addition to being near neighbours, St Johnstone were keen rivals of Dundee Hibs from the very beginning. However, their first contest was fought out not on the pitch, but in a smoke-filled room at the Scottish League's annual general meeting in June 1910 when, contrary to expectations, the Hibs were elected ahead of St Johnstone.

That no ill feeling endured was illustrated by the fact that, two months later, the Perth club accepted an invitation to play a pre-season friendly at Tannadice and no doubt derived considerable satisfaction from their 2–0 win. St Johnstone did join the Hibs in Division Two just a year later and the first League encounter came in September 1911 at the Recreation Grounds, one of three homes the club has had.

They remained together in Division Two until 1915 but St Johnstone decided to close down for the duration of the war, resurfacing in the Eastern League* in 1919, along with Dundee Hibs. They both joined the breakaway Central League* a year later and were accepted into the new Scottish League Division Two in 1921.

St Johnstone's progress outstripped that of their old rivals and they were a Division One club for most of the inter-war years. United met them only in three Division One seasons and one in Division Two during that period.

It was a different story after the war, however. After spending season 1945/46 in Southern League* B Division the clubs shared membership of the Scottish League's lower division from 1946 until they were promoted together in 1960. They continued to meet regularly in Division One, though this has rarely happened in the Premier Division, which the Saints have been members of on only six occasions.

The clubs were involved in the keenly-fought First Division promotion chase in 1995/96. Despite losing at McDiarmid Park in the run-in, it was United who went up with Dunfermline, although Saints joined them a year later after winning that season's championship.

The playing record against St Johnstone in major competitions is:
Scottish League (total): P 104 W 39 D 26 L 39 F 162 A 167 (50%)
Premier Division: P 24 W 11 D 8 L 5 F 40 A 24 (63%)
Scottish Cup: the clubs have been drawn together just twice, in 1933 and 1991 (semi-final).
Record: P 2 W 1 D 0 L 1 F 5 A 5
League Cup: the clubs were drawn together in 1948, 1950, 1958, 1966, 1975 and 1982.
Record: P 12 W 10 D 2 L 0 F 37 A 16
Summer Cup: the clubs met in sectional ties in both 1964 and 1965.
Record: P4 W 4 D 0 L 0 F 11 A 1
Notable transfers to: Bill Taylor (1933), Benny Rooney (1966), George Fleming (1980), Ian Gibson (1983), Paul Hegarty (1990), Paul Sturrock* (as manager, 1993), John O'Neil (1995), Alan Main (1995)
Notable transfers from: Jimmy Howieson (1925), Johnny Hart (1926), Stuart Beedie (1984)
It's a fact: St Johnstone were United's opponents on the inauguration of

the Premier Division in August 1975. The Saints won 1–0 at Muirton Park, but recorded only two further League victories that season, which they finished 21 points adrift at the bottom of the table.

ST MIRREN FC
The clubs did not meet until United made their first appearance in Division One in 1925 and St Mirren were also opponents in the club's three other seasons in that division and also one in Division Two in 1935/36. As that was the Paisley side's only season out of the top division between 1890 (when they were one of the League's founder members) and 1967, United did not meet them on League business until they were promoted in 1960.

League meetings took place on a regular basis between that year and 1992, when St Mirren were relegated, having been members of the Premier Division in all but two out of its first 17 seasons. The club's most recent League encounter was a First Division match at Love Street in March 1996.

The playing record against St Mirren in major competitions is:
Scottish League (total): P 92 W 43 D 19 L 30 F 145 A 116 (55%)
Premier Division: P 60 W 28 D 13 L 19 F 88 A 67 (56%)
Scottish Cup: the clubs were drawn together in 1961, 1964, 1968, 1977, 1979, 1982, 1983 and 1985. They also contested the 1987 final.
        Record: P 10 W 2 D 1 L 7 F 9 A 14
League Cup: the clubs were drawn together in 1963, 1969, 1985, 1988, 1992, 1993 and 1994.
        Record: P 9 W 9 D 0 L 0 F 19 A 7
Notable transfers to: Jimmy Howieson (1925), Jackie Copland (1976)
Notable transfers from: Wilson Humphries (1957), Archie Knox (1972), Billy Thomson (1984)
It's a fact: United's 1-4 Scottish Cup defeat at Love Street in 1977 is one of only two occasions on which they have gone out of the competition to a club from a lower division.

STENHOUSEMUIR FC
Dundee Hibs' first encounter with Stenhousemuir was in the Central League* in 1920 and both clubs proceeded to the resurrected Scottish League Division Two the following season.

Dundee United were in the same division as the Larbert club (always the lower one) in all but four seasons between 1923 and 1960; having met on a total of 68 occasions in all competitions during that period, the clubs have managed just three in the 37 years since.

The last meeting between the clubs was the final of the League Challenge Cup at McDiarmid Park in November 1995. Stenhousemuir were the better team over 120 goalless minutes, so justice was done when they won the penalty shoot-out 5–4.

The playing record against Stenhousemuir in major competitions is:
Scottish League: P 54 W 25 D 5 L 24 F 127 A 109 (51%)
Scottish Cup: the clubs were drawn together in 1929 and 1957.
                Record: P 4 W 2 D 2 L 0 F 8 A 2
League Cup: the clubs were drawn together in 1948, 1950, 1951, 1956, 1960 and 1972.
                Record: P 12 W 4 D 3 L 5 F 28 A 26
It's a fact: United faced Stenhousemuir at Ochilview Park in ten consecutive Scottish League seasons (1932-39 and 1946-49), losing on every occasion.

STIRLING ALBION FC

Albion were admitted to B Division in 1947, two years after their foundation, the town's previous League club King's Park having disbanded during the war.

The new club was characterised over the following two decades by a bizarre snakes and ladders existence, during which time they were promoted on six occasions, but relegated just as often. United's first League meeting with them was in September 1947. Thereafter, becalmed as they were in B Division, they met Albion irregularly, six seasons in total in the lower division and four in Division One.

The clubs have not met in the League since season 1967/68, the last which Albion spent in the top division. The home match that season saw United record their biggest post-war League win, 9–0.

The playing record against Stirling Albion in major competitions is:
Scottish League: P 20 W 7 D 2 L 11 F 41 A 38 (40%)
Scottish Cup: United's 2–0 win at Forthbank Stadium in 1997 was the first occasion on which the clubs had met in the competition.
League Cup: the clubs were drawn together in 1952, 1960 and 1996.
                Record: P 5 W 2 D 0 L 3 F 7 A 17
It's a fact: When the clubs met in sectional ties in 1952, Albion scored six at both Tannadice and Annfield Park.

STRANRAER FC

The clubs met in the Scottish Cup in 1930 (see below), Stranraer gaining full membership of the Scottish League only when B Division was extended in 1955. Prior to that, they met United's reserves in C Division* between 1946 and 1952. Their first League encounter with United came in November and the clubs were together, in what became Division Two, for the following four seasons until United were promoted.

The meeting between the clubs in the League Challenge Cup at Stair Park in August 1995 (which United won 2–0) was their first since the Division Two match at the same ground in January 1960.

The playing record against Stranraer in major competitions is :

Scottish League: P 10 W 4 D 3 L 3 F 15 A 13 (55%)

Scottish Cup: the clubs have been drawn together just once, in 1930 when Stranraer were a non-League club. United won 2–0 at Stair Park.

League Cup: the clubs were drawn together in 1957 and 1959.
Record: P 3 W 3 D 0 L 0 F 9 A 2

Notable transfers from: Jackie Copland (1970), Derek Frye (1978)

It's a fact: Until the League Challenge Cup in 1995, the clubs had not met for 35 years, by far the longest gap involving United and another League club.

STRIPS

The following colours represented the first choice strips worn by Dundee Hibs/United from the club's foundation to the present day:

1909 Green jerseys, white shorts
1913 Green jerseys with a white V, white shorts
1920 Green jerseys, white shorts
1923 White jerseys, black shorts
1928 White jerseys with a black V, black shorts
1930 1" black and white hooped jerseys, white shorts
1933 2" black and white hooped jerseys, white shorts
1937 4" black and white hooped jerseys, white shorts
1959 White jerseys with two black bands, white shorts
1962 White jerseys with black trim, white shorts
1969 Tangerine jerseys with black trim, tangerine shorts
1977 Tangerine jerseys with black trim, black shorts
1993 Tangerine jerseys with thin black stripes, black trim, tangerine shorts
1994 Tangerine jerseys with black sleeves and trim, black shorts

Change strips

It seems unlikely that Dundee Hibs required to have a change strip – at least in League matches – because no other club they met played in green. There are no known photographs of the Hibs playing in a change strip.

Once Dundee United came into being and adopted black and white they would have needed alternative colours, but it is not known what they used. In those days, clubs were not required to register a change strip and it was not uncommon for the smaller clubs to borrow a set of strips if they were meeting a club with the same, or similar, colours to their own. It is known that, on occasion during the 1930s, Dundee United borrowed a set of strips from local junior clubs from time to time. It has always been the responsibility of the visiting club to change.

The earliest that United's change strip can be identified with certainty is the resumption of organised football after the Second World War. From 1946/47, United's official 'away' colours were red shirts and white shorts

↑ While the new Tannadice stand was being built in 1962, the players used the Jute Industries canteen across the road as a dressing room. Pictured wearing United's red and white change strip are (left to right) *Gibby Ormond, Dave Boner, Neil Mochan and Jim Irvine*

and this endured for 14 seasons. Even then, following promotion, there was only a slight modification to Arsenal-style jerseys, red with white sleeves. That remained for two seasons until, in 1962, an all-black strip was introduced and remained in service even when the first choice colours were changed to tangerine in 1969.

Since 1972, United's change strip has been white, although there have, from time to time, been minor alterations. Initially it was all white, although in the late 1970s black trim was added. In the 1980s black shorts were introduced and these have remained.

Today, football strips are as much a fashion accessory as anything else, with the result that financial considerations decide how often they are changed. This now applies also to away strips, as they have come to be known. For that reason, season 1993/94 saw United's traditional white shirt remain, but with a black splash effect which gave it the impression of having been used by a house painter! Nevertheless, for the first time it became a big seller among Arabs*. This led to a different one being brought out for the following season with a throw-back to the promotion side of 1960. The jersey from that era – white with two two-inch black bands, white shorts – was given a 1990s touch with purple trim, and again it proved popular.

That lasted for two years, then was replaced by a return to all-white, but with black sleeves and black shorts, in 1996.

The need to maximise return for the official kit supplier led to the introduction of a third strip in 1995. This, of course, had no practical use and was simply a further means of tempting Arabs keen to identify with the club to part with more of their money. It was basically two shades of grey stripes with black shorts and United played in it only twice during the season. It never became popular with supporters, most of whom preferred to buy either the first or second choice colours. During the following season it was never worn in a first team match.

Nevertheless, the third strip was retained and changed for the start of season 1997/98. It was described thus in *Tangerine and Black*, the club's official monthly magazine: '. . . predominantly ecru in colour with a black collar and number, a tangerine band and black pin on the shoulders and sleeves, black shorts with an ecru flash and tangerine band and ecru socks with an ecru, black and tangerine turnover'.

Ecru is described in Chambers *Twentieth Century Dictionary* as 'like unbleached linen'. Whatever, the club's strip has certainly come a long way since secretary Pat Reilly announced in 1909 that Dundee Hibernian would play in 'emerald green shirts and stockings, with white knickers', anyone wearing that sort of gear 90 years later would probably not have football on their minds!

Paul STURROCK (born 1956)

One of Dundee United's all-time greats, it is no accident that his career (1974–1989) coincided with the most successful period in the club's history, in terms of honours both individually and collectively.

He joined from Luncarty Juniors in 1974 and made his first-team debut later that year at the age of 16 against Jiul Petrosani in a European Cup Winners' Cup tie. With the exception of the Scottish Cup he subsequently won every honour the domestic game has to offer and was named Player of the Year by the Scottish Football Writers Association in 1982. He retired from playing at the end of season 1988/89 and became first team coach at Tannadice. He was appointed manager of St Johnstone in 1993.

His son, Blair, signed apprentice professional forms with United in 1996.

Dundee United playing record (1974–1989)

	Appearances	Goals
Scottish League	385	109
Scottish Cup	48	12
League Cup	79	38
European competitions	60	11
Scotland	20	2
Scotland U-21	9	3
Scotland youth	6	2

Scottish League champion 1982/83
Scottish League Cup winner 1979/80, 1980/81
Uefa Cup finalist 1986/87
Scottish Cup finalist 1981,1985,1987,1988
Scottish League Cup finalist 1981/82, 1984/85
Scottish Football Writers' Player of the Year, 1981/82

SUBSTITUTES

Dundee United's first ever substitute was centre forward Billy Hainey, who was introduced during the second half of the League Cup tie with Dundee at Tannadice on 13 August 1966.

Substitutes often change the course of a match following their introduction, but none in Dundee United's history has done so as dramatically as Owen Coyle in the 1996 play-off second leg. When he came on, the club was trailing 0-1 and heading for a second season in the First Division. A last-minute equaliser sent the match into extra-time, during the second period of which Coyle scored a winner which was worth hundreds of thousands of pounds to Dundee United. Illustrating the vagaries of the game, he was unable to claim a regular place the following season, and eight months later left the club to join Motherwell.

SUMMER CUP

This competition was first played during wartime, but was briefly resurrected in 1964 and 1965. Neither Celtic or Rangers took part, but the remaining 16 Division One clubs were split into sections of four; to maximise interest, this was done on a geographical basis. Thus, on each occasion United's section included Aberdeen, Dundee and St Johnstone. Aberdeen won it in 1964 and went on to the final, where they lost to Hibernian.

United won all six sectional matches the following year and then beat Partick Thistle in the semi-final. Their opponents in the two-legged final were Motherwell and United, with their Scandinavian contingent in top form, were clear favourites despite having only half of their Scandinavian contingent available (Persson* and Wing* were on international duty with Sweden). However, they went down 1–3 in the first leg, though this did not prevent 15,000 turning up at Tannadice, fully expecting United to overturn the deficit. An early goal suggested their optimism was well founded, but in the event Motherwell held out against constant United pressure to take the cup 3–2 on aggregate.

The competition was then laid to rest, its passing mourned by few.

SUNDAY FOOTBALL

The first competitive match played by United on the Sabbath was a Scottish Cup fourth-round tie against Morton at Tannadice on 17 February 1974.

United won 1–0 on the way to the club's first appearance in the final.

Prior to that, the SFA did not allow Sunday football, but the miners' strike during the winter of 1973/74 led the Heath government to introduce a so–called 'three-day week'. To save electricity, factories and offices were instructed to open either from Monday to Wednesday or from Thursday to Saturday. This meant that far fewer people were able to attend football matches, and sanction was given by the SFA for Sunday to be used as an alternative. There was also a ban on the use of floodlights and all matches had to have early kick-offs.

Two weeks after the Morton match, Tannadice again hosted Sunday football with the Division One visit of Aberdeen, and the following Sunday at East End Park United met Dunfermline in the quarter-final of the Cup.

Subsequent Sunday matches involving United have been rare and usually to suit the demands of television:

Motherwell (a) Premier Division 17.4.77
Hearts (h) Premier Division 11.3.84
Rangers (Hampden Park) League Cup final 28.11.84 +
Berwick Rangers (h) Scottish Cup 26.1.92
Aberdeen (a) Scottish Cup 7.2.93 +
Rangers (h) League 4.12.94+
Hearts (a) Scottish Cup 12.3.95 +
Stenhousemuir (McDiarmid Park) League Challenge Cup final 5.11.95
   (fortunately, there is no filmed record of this match)
Celtic (a) Scottish Cup 10.3.96 +
Partick Thistle (a) First Division play-off 16.5.96
Hearts (a) Scottish Cup 16.2.97 +
+ shown live on television

On Sunday, 19 March 1989, United were due to play Rangers in a Scottish Cup quarter-final tie at Ibrox, which was to be shown live on television. However, the match was postponed due to a waterlogged pitch and was played two days later, when only highlights were shown on television.

SUPPLEMENTARY CUP
This competition was introduced in 1946 and was open only to members of the newly-constituted B Division. The aim was to provide extra fixtures due to the fact that the division contained only fourteen clubs, and hence a mere thirteen home League matches.

The Supplementary Cup continued for several years, despite the fact that B Division was increased to sixteen in 1947. It was last competed for in season 1951/52, and its demise was not mourned by United supporters who had seen their team make a first round exit on all but one occasion!

SUPPORTERS & SUPPORTERS CLUBS

See also Arabs

In the years immediately following the formation of Dundee Hibs in 1909, there was a tremendous interest in cup football and it seems that supporters were willing to travel some distance for cup ties. Eight hundred Hibs fans filled a special train - organised by club secretary Pat Reilly - which took them north, along with the players and club officials, for a Qualifying Cup semi-final replay with Inverness Caledonian in 1913. The enthusiasm generated by their club's 2-0 win is illustrated by the fact that 4,000 travelled to Tynecastle Park for the final against Albion Rovers and this time Reilly chartered no less than four trains.

Around this time, supporters of the bigger Scottish clubs had formed what were termed brake clubs to take them to away games, but there is no evidence of any such organisation existing in the name of Dundee Hibs. It seems Pat Reilly's paternalism did not survive the First World War, although by that time interest in the Hibs had flagged to such an extent that few could be tempted to home matches, far less those which involved travelling.

Despite the fact that Dundee United had some success, spending four seasons in Division One between 1925 and 1932, few supporters saw them other than at Tannadice. The poverty and hardship caused by the depression was widespread and very few supporters, even those of Celtic and Rangers, travelled to away games during the inter-war period (the obvious exceptions were derby matches and cup-ties).

Dundee United Supporters Club was formed in 1939 and club rooms were opened in the Murraygate that year. The club seems to have been primarily concerned with arranging social events, with a view to raising money for the football club and there is no evidence of it organising travel to away matches. It continued after the Second World War, though with an extremely low profile, and was effectively absorbed into the Dundee United Sportsmen's Club* when that came into being in 1955.

Despite enjoying a huge boost in attendances at Tannadice in the post-war period, it seems United took few supporters to away matches, other than for derby matches, i.e. St Johnstone and the Angus clubs. Certainly, there was no organised attempt to do so, until the second half of season 1959/60 when it became clear that United had a realistic chance of winning promotion for the first time in 28 years.

That achieved, the following season, in Division One, saw travel clubs established. British Rail also arranged what were termed 'football specials' where the demand justified it (particularly for cup-ties), failing which reduced fares on ordinary services facilitated travel in the days before most football supporters could afford motor cars.

It was only when United, under Jim McLean's guidance, had achieved trophy success that supporters clubs began to mushroom.

The Federation of Dundee United Supporters Clubs was formed in 1991 in response to the array of clubs which sprang up during the second half of the 1980s. United's success saw clubs established all over Scotland and it was felt there was a need to have an umbrella organisation which could co-ordinate the views of supporters and, more importantly, act as a channel of communication with the board at Tannadice. It has been successful in doing so, to the mutual benefit of both parties.

SWEDEN

For most Arabs, mention of Sweden will undoubtedly conjure up visions of IFK Gothenburg and the two unforgettable matches of the UEFA Cup final in 1987 (see UEFA Cup).

Of course, United have links with Sweden going back many years earlier. It was in September 1964 that manager Jerry Kerr* first saw Orjan Persson*, a left winger with the Gothenburg club Orgryte, star against Dunfermline in a Fairs Cup tie at East End Park. It subsequently took him almost three months, but eventually he got his man, and Persson proved his worth many times over during his spell at Tannadice, before leaving for Rangers in 1967.

For most of his time with United the winger was accompanied by Lennart Wing*, an iron-hard wing half who was a resolute servant to the club. Each won several caps while at Tannadice, the first time the club had had a full international.

Surprisingly perhaps, almost 30 years were to elapse before a Swede again donned a United jersey. Tommy McLean* had been in the manager's office only six weeks when striker Kjell Olofsson was signed from the Norwegian League club FC Moss. The following week he was joined by midfielder Lars Zetterlund of Orebro, who had been a member of the IFK Gothenburg team which defeated United in that UEFA Cup final.

Apart from that final, United have faced Swedish opposition in the UEFA Cup on one other occasion. It involved AIK Stockholm in the first round of 1984/85, United progressing after overturning a first-leg deficit of 0–1 by winning 3–0 at Tannadice.

The two subsequent encounters with Swedish clubs resulted in defeats for United. Former European Cup finalists Malmo FF won 3–1 during a pre-season tour of Scandanavia in 1982, while old friends IFK Gothenburg returned to Tannadice in November 1989 for Paul Hegarty's* testimonial match, winning 2–0.

The club's most recent visit to the country came as part of pre-season training in July 1997. Two wins over Third Division Vivalla (by 11–0, the club's biggest victory since 1931) and Second Division Eskilstuna (2–1) were followed by participation in a rather strange tournament in Norrkoping. The other clubs involved were the home club, IFK, and Blackburn Rovers with each match lasting only fifty minutes. Both ended goalless, but United came down to earth in the final match, losing 0–4 to Lars Zetterlund's former colleagues, Orebro.

SWITZERLAND

United's first visit to Switzerland came in the first round of the 1970/71 Fairs Cup. The opposition was provided by Grasshoppers of Zurich and the first leg at Tannadice seemed to herald the end of United's interest as the Swiss took a two-goal lead. However, inspired by midfield dynamo Alex Reid, United stormed back to win the tie 3–2, then held on for a goalless draw in the return.

During a pre-season tour to the German Federal Republic in 1984, the United party made a brief detour to play two matches against non-league opposition in Switzerland, winning one and drawing the other.

The following season, the club returned in more serious vein when the third round of the 1985/86 UEFA Cup paired them with Neuchatel Xamax. In the first leg, which was played in a snowstorm at Tannadice, United won 2–1 after the Swiss team had led. The return was always going to be tricky, but the task seemed to be eased considerably when Eamonn Bannon* gave United an early lead. Sadly, keeper Billy Thomson gifted the Swiss an equaliser and they scored again to take the game into extra-time. A controversial refereeing decision handed the game to Neuchatel, a goal being awarded when television evidence clearly showed the ball not to have crossed the line. The following year Dave Dodds* joined Neuchatel for a reported fee of £200,000.

T

TANNADICE PARK
See also Clepington Park
Development
When the newly formed Dundee Hibs took over the lease of Clepington Park in May 1909, it had been, literally, stripped bare by its disgruntled former occupants, Dundee Wanderers. Even the wooden boundary fence had been dismantled, but the Hibs committee at least had the benefit that they could start from scratch and develop the ground as they wanted it.

Apart from enclosing it, the priority was to provide changing accommodation. In those days, dressing-rooms were not usually built under the grandstand, but were contained in a stand-alone building known as the pavilion. Presumably, this was following the example of cricket grounds, but the pavilion was a common feature at Scottish football grounds, particularly the smaller ones, until well after World War Two (it endured at Tannadice until 1961).

Some indication of the early development of Tannadice can be had from the following report taken from the city's *Evening Telegraph* newspaper of 21 July 1909: 'The pavilion is a splendid two-storey structure built of brick, containing two large dressing-rooms, two committee rooms, press box and referee's room. The pavilion will be lit by electricity. The stand on the road side will be the whole length of the field and will seat about 1,000 people.'

It can be seen that neither time was lost nor money spared in ensuring that the ground would be ready for the club's inaugural match on 18 August. The stand was not completed until midway through the season, but by the time Edinburgh Hibs performed the official opening, earth and ash banking had been built at both ends and the natural slope from Sandeman Street had been similarly consolidated. Added the impressive new pavilion (which was situated at the corner of the ground where the players' tunnel is today) it represented remarkable progress in just three months.

Although the original capacity of Tannadice Park was claimed to be 15,000, this seems to have been a generous estimate. It would probably have held no more than 10,000, a figure which is given credence by the fact that

196

for the Qualifying Cup*-tie against Forfar Athletic in 1913 (see below) the terracings were specially extended and additional temporary seating erected; all of this was necessary to allow a record crowd to be accommodated, and the reported attendance was 15,000.

No further improvements to the ground took place until Dundee United won promotion to Division One for the first time in 1925. The Scottish League Management Committee informed the club that Tannadice would be subject to an inspection during the close season to ensure that it was up to the standard required for the higher level, and this clearly concentrated the directors' minds.

Since 1909, Tannadice had been leased, but the board now decided to buy the ground, paying £2,500. Extensive renovations were then begun, the first to the pitch. There was a steep upwards slope towards the corner where the George Fox and East Stands now meet, and this necessitated solid rock being blasted to enable it to be levelled. For the first time, proper terracings were constructed, using the time-honoured method of disused railway sleepers, while the pavilion was given a facelift and new turnstiles were built.

These improvements made the Scottish League's inspection a formality, but, along with plans for a new 3,000-seat stand, the total cost was reported to be £7,000, a huge sum at the time. The intention was that a share flotation would cover the cost, as well as providing money to improve the playing staff, but it realised only £5,000 when five times that amount had been anticipated. As a result, it was announced that the new stand was to be delayed; in fact, it was 37 years before it materialised!

The various financial crises which beset the club in the 1930s and its general lack of success on the pitch prevented any further ground improvements until 1953. At that time, the north terracing was concreted and four years later the same was done at both ends – the old railway

A view of Tannadice in the mid–1950s, by which time the wooden stand and pavilion were almost fifty years old

197

sleepers from 1925 had given value for money. During the close season of 1957, an important development took place with the construction of the Shed*, which was opened in September of that year.

As in 1925, it required promotion to provide the impetus for the next major development. In August 1962 the new cantilever stand was opened and four months later the floodlights were used for the first time. The stand was only the second in Britain (after Sheffield Wednesday) to offer spectators a view uninterrupted by pillars, and the intention was to extend it to meet the Shed as and when the necessary finance became available. Other priorities were always found, however, that part of the ground being the last to have seating installed, during the summer of 1997. It is worth mentioning that that part of the ground had been designated a parent-and-child enclosure in 1987. At that time it was improved and covered, using the award from UEFA in recognition of the warm reception accorded by United fans to IFK Gothenburg after the UEFA Cup final; in consequence, it was named the Fair Play Enclosure.

Younger supporters may find it difficult to imagine that, apart from the Shed, the terracing at Tannadice had no cover until the north enclosure was built in 1980. That enjoyed but a brief existence, being demolished in 1991 to make way for the George Fox Stand, which opened the following year. The demands of spectator comfort and the requirements of legislation on ground safety fuelled the move to all-seater stadiums, and Dundee United was well to the fore in making the change. The new East Stand, and seats installed in the modernised Shed, were completed in 1994, and in the autumn of 1997 the final piece of the jigsaw was put in place with the construction of the main stand extension.

It is worth noting that, after depreciation charges, Tannadice is now valued at £6.7 million – a far cry from the £2500 which the club paid for the ground in 1925. The re-development during the 1990s has seen more than £6 million spent on the stadium, the majority coming controversially from the sale of players. Although the Football Grounds Improvement Trust made a significant contribution to the cost, unlike most clubs the United board have refused to borrow to finance their share of the improvements, preferring to use cash, either from reserves or revenue.

Tannadice Park is now a first-class stadium, with facilities the equal of any in Scotland. Its new capacity of 14,500 is considerably less than in previous years, but the ground is nonetheless capable – in all respects – of meeting the demands of the modern era.

It's a fact: The first goal at Tannadice Park was scored in the opening match at the ground by John O'Hara of (Edinburgh) Hibernian; to mark the occasion he was presented with a bicycle (Dundee Hibernian's secretary and founding father Pat Reilly* owned a cycle shop). The first goal by Dundee Hibs was scored in the same match by centre forward Jamie Docherty, who received a gold medal to commemorate it.

198

Record Attendances

For the first 50 years or so, attendance figures were very rarely issued by the club and those given in newspaper reports were often no more than inspired guesswork by football writers. With the exception of Scottish Cup ties, it was not until the 1980s that reliable figures became available, unless a match was all-ticket. Nevertheless, the following gives a guide to the records as they were reported as being set.

7,000: this was the attendance at the match which marked the official opening of Tannadice Park on 18 August 1909; it was not threatened by any of Dundee Hibs's League matches before World War One.

15,000: Cup-ties proved much bigger attractions than League matches in the club's early years and this crowd – a huge one for a club of the status of Dundee Hibs – watched a local derby with Forfar Athletic in the Qualifying Cup on 1 November 1913. The ground capacity had to be specially extended for the occasion (see above).

20,000: Following promotion, and major ground improvements, their first-ever meeting with Celtic on 19 September 1925 saw United win 1–0. The match established a new ground record, though not for long.

23,517: Perhaps the most surprising ground record, it was established on 17 April 1926, with St Johnstone the visitors. Despite the local derby aspect to it, with both clubs still fighting relegation, a more modest attendance was anticipated. The match ended 0–0 and both clubs ultimately survived in Division One.

25,000: This remains the largest attendance ever for a League match at Tannadice and was set at the city derby on 3 January 1927. It was also the occasion of United's first League win against Dundee FC.

26,407: It took Aberdeen's visit in a Scottish Cup tie on 23 February 1952 to break the record which had stood for a quarter of a century. United did well to hold their Division One opponents, but narrowly lost the replay at Pittodrie.

28,000: The record which will stand for all time as the biggest crowd to watch a match at Tannadice. It was appropriate to the occasion, too: a Fairs Cup tie in which FC Barcelona were beaten 2–0 on 16 November 1966, to complete a 4–1 aggregate win.

It's another fact: In 1947, United went three months without playing at Tannadice. It was described as the worst winter on record but it seems to have extended into spring as well, because between 11 January and 14 April it was simply impossible to play a home match. As a consequence, the League season continued into May for the first time.

TAYPOOLS

In 1955, Dundee United were a club in debt and going nowhere. Although their existence was not threatened, as it had been 20 years earlier, the post-war boom was almost at an end and crowds at Tannadice were down to around 5,000, only half what they had been at their peak.

George Fox* and Johnston Grant*, who had just joined the board, brought a new sense of purpose and the restructuring of the club's finances was begun. This did not only involve directors, because a number of supporters came together with some of the city's business community to launch the Dundee United Sportsmen's Club* in August 1955.

The aim was to raise desperately needed finance for the football club and they were attracted by a scheme run by Nottingham Forest which raised considerable amounts for that club. A deputation from the Sportsmen's Club, along with United director Jimmy Littlejohn* and assistant manager Ally Gallacher*, visited Nottingham to see at first hand how the English club's pools operated. Obviously impressed, they returned and, within weeks, had launched Taypools, with the assistance of a personal interest-free loan from club chairman Ernest Robertson*.

Tickets were sold for one shilling each, containing numbers which equated to numbers of Scottish and English League matches played each week. The winners were decided by the results of matches, in a variation of ordinary football pools.

Taypools was an immediate success, to such an extent that the first payment of £1,000 to the football club was handed over in early 1957, and formed the first instalment of the cost of erecting the Shed*. Some indication of the numbers participating in Taypools can be gained from the fact that a total of £30,000 was paid out in prize money during season 1957/58, and the following year, with upwards of 50,000 participants, prize money amounted to £1,000 each week. This enabled regular payments to be made to Dundee United and was instrumental in the club attracting Jerry Kerr* as manager and giving him a limited amount to spend on players, both before and after promotion had been gained.

Taypools reached its peak during the 1960s, when over 90,000 tickets were sold weekly, and although other forms of pools arrived on the scene during the '70s and '80s, Taypools continued until 1991 before being wound up. It had been a phenomenally successful venture, without which it is quite possible Dundee United may well have remained languishing in Division Two.

TELEVISION
The first time United appeared on live television was the Scottish Cup final of 1974. Each of the club's subsequent finals in that competition were shown live (with the exception of the 1981 replay), but of the three League Cup finals, only that in 1984, the first to be played on a Sunday, was live on TV.

Live or not, the club's European exploits during the 1980s made great viewing, and still do for many Arabs*. In 1986/87, before the arrival of satellite TV, United created a record by having a total of eight matches – domestic as well as European – transmitted live during a season. The second leg of the UEFA Cup final against IFK Gothenburg was beamed from Tannadice to a television audience reported to be 70 million worldwide.

The city derby Scottish Cup replay in January 1990 was the first live satellite match from Tannadice. Sky viewers saw United win 2–1.

TERRORS

Though referred to less often than was previously the case, The Terrors is the club's official nickname, listed in no less an authority than *Rothman's*, the *Wisden* of football.

It is difficult to identify its origin with accuracy. There is no known reference to it pre-war and the most convincing explanation is that it was earned in the famous Scottish Cup victory over Celtic in January 1949. That was the occasion when United, then a mid-table Division Two club, were given no chance of restraining the Celtic tide, despite the fact the match was at Tannadice. The final score of United 4 Celtic 3 tells less than the full story. United had no fewer than three 'goals' disallowed and simply refused to be disheartened when Celtic cancelled out leads of 2–0 and 3–2. Showing tremendous fighting spirit, Willie MacFadyen's* part-timers ignored the stamina-sapping conditions to score the decisive goal, following which it was Celtic whose demoralisation proved decisive. It was a performance which deserved to have its place permanently enshrined in the club's annals, and the adoption of a nickname which evokes the players responsible for it is indeed apposite.

In 1963, 'The Terrors of Tannadice' was recorded by Scots 'singer' Hector Nicol, and for many years it blared out from the Tannadice loudspeakers as United took the field. A classic of its genre (i.e. a dirge) it has now achieved cult status among Arabs, none of whom will ever admit to actually being old enough to have heard it played – despite knowing every word!

TESTIMONIALS

Today, players become eligible for a testimonial after five years' continuous service. Historically, this involved a single game from which the player received the bulk of the gate money; nowadays the better known players are granted a testimonial year, involving a wide range of fundraising activities, though the major one remains a match against attractive opposition. To respect Inland Revenue guidelines and ensure that the proceeds are not taxed as income, such activities must be organised and run by a testimonial committee and not the player's club.

Whether or not a player receives a testimonial is entirely at the discretion of his club. Throughout the years, these have been granted sparingly by

Dundee United. Dundee Hibs gave one to winger Willie Linn* in 1922, but the only United player to receive one before the Second World War was Jock Kay*, in 1928. With the exception of George Grant* (see below), almost half a century elapsed before Dennis Gillespie's* in 1973, followed four years later by Doug Smith*.

In the modern era, with the club enjoying considerable success and players consequently remaining longer at Tannadice than was hitherto the case, testimonials are more common. Hamish McAlpine* (1983), Dave Narey* (1988), Paul Sturrock* and Paul Hegarty* (both 1989), Maurice Malpas* (1991), John Clark (1994) and Dave Bowman* (1995) have all benefited.

The one United player whose testimonial match did not take place at Tannadice was inside forward George Grant, a stalwart in the decade which followed World War Two. He shared a benefit match with Jimmy Toner of Dundee, the two city clubs meeting at Dens Park in April 1954.

All of the above were in recognition of long service, but there have been two which struck a more poignant chord. Winger Iain McDonald's career was ended at the age of 23 by a knee injury and a benefit match against an invitation XI was held in November 1976. Defender Doug Wilkie joined United from Queen's Park in 1979 but tragically, before having made a first-team appearance, he suffered injuries in a train crash which left him partially paralysed. On his behalf, a testimonial was played in October 1981.

In addition, and unusually for a manager, a testimonial match against Nottingham Forest took place in August 1984. The programme for that match states that it was in tribute to Jim McLean's* decision to turn down the offer to manage Rangers the previous year.

Dundee Hibs/United have also provided the opposition in testimonials for a total of 17 players of other clubs.

TEXACO CUP

This competition was launched in 1970 and ran for the following five seasons. It involved six clubs each from England and Scotland and two each from Northern Ireland and the Republic of Ireland. All ties were decided on a home and away basis.

United participated on three occasions; on the first two, they were eliminated in the first round. In 1971/72 they lost to Derby County and the following season they went out on penalties to Leicester City. However, they did make some progress in 1973/74, beating Sheffield United then gaining revenge on Leicester City before meeting Newcastle United in the semi-final. The first leg at Tannadice saw United build a two-goal lead, but Newcastle pulled it back within 90 minutes at St James' Park, then scored the winner in extra-time.

The competition did not survive the ending of the oil company's sponsorship in 1975; it was replaced the following season by the Anglo-Scottish Cup*.

THIRD LANARK FC

Third Lanark are the most recent club to resign from the Scottish League, and are by some distance the ex-League club which had been the most successful. They were founder members of the League in 1890 and won the championship of Division One in 1904. The following season they won the Scottish Cup for the second time.

One of their most famous internationalists was goalkeeper Jimmy Brownlie*, who later became a legend at Tannadice and managed Dundee United on three separate occasions. Their ground was Cathkin Park, in the Crosshill district of south Glasgow.

United and Third Lanark were League opponents for 13 seasons, almost half of them in Division One, but they first met in Division Two in November 1927, Third winning 5–1 at Cathkin Park. In season 1930/31 the Glasgow club were Division Two champions, with United promoted as runners-up.

The following season was the only one spent together in Division One until 1960/61, the start of a five-year run. By the time the last meeting between the clubs took place in February 1965, Third Lanark were in serious financial difficulties and were relegated at the end of that season. They survived but two more years before going into liquidation in the summer of 1967.

The full playing record against Third Lanark was:

Scottish League: P 26 W 10 D 4 L 12 F 40 A 64

Scottish Cup: the clubs were drawn together twice, both times at Tannadice; United won 5–2 in 1957, but it ended 4–0 for Third Lanark two years later.

League Cup: the clubs met in sectional ties in 1956, with United winning both 2–1.

Notable transfers from: Jimmy Brownlie (as player/manager, 1923), Jock Kay* (1923), Jimmy Walker (1925), Johnny Graham (1964)

TOSS OF THE COIN

Nowadays quite rightly an anachronism, this method was twice used to decide matches involving United. In May 1929, the final of an obscure competition called the Fleming Shield finished in a 2–2 draw at Pittodrie. The low standing of the competition is perhaps illustrated by the fact that it was deemed more appropriate to toss a coin rather than play extra-time to determine the winners. For what it is worth, United won.

The Supplementary Cup* was played for between 1945 and 1950. In the competition's first season, United were drawn against Raith Rovers and their interest seemed to be at an end when they went down 1–4 in the first leg at Tannadice. But they showed considerable resolve in winning 3–0 at Stark's Park and, as the concept of away goals counting as double had yet to be conceived, a play-off was necessary. Dens Park was chosen as the venue, but six goals later the teams still could not be separated, so out came the ubiquitous half-crown. It was the Rovers captain who called correctly, but United were unhappy that extra-time had not been played. They lodged a protest with the SFA, but to no avail.

The most recent occasion involving Dundee United and the toss of a coin was one in which that means of reaching a decision was justified. When the two city clubs reached the final of the League Cup in 1980, the Scottish League – with commendable, if uncharacteristic, wisdom – decided that the match should become the property of the people of Dundee. It was decided that either Dens or Tannadice should stage the final; Dundee won the toss, but United won the cup!

TRANSFER FEES

The history of Dundee Hibs/United as a modest club, playing in the lower divisions and constantly battling against financial difficulties, meant that they were constrained from paying sizeable transfer fees until the1960s. The standard of player the club was able to attract also meant that, during the same period, large transfer fees received were few and far between. The record transfer fee received by the club (based on press reports) has risen as follows:

£1,000 from St Mirren for Jimmy Howieson, 1925; from Hearts for Andy Miller, 1927
£1,250 from Rangers for Jimmy Simpson*, 1927
£4,050 from Newcastle United for Duncan Hutchison*, 1929
£8,000 from Clyde for Johnny Coyle*, 1957
£30,000 from Liverpool for Ron Yeats*, 1961
£50,000 from Newcastle United for Ian Mitchell*, 1970
£110,000 from Aston Villa for Andy Gray*, 1975
£400,000 from West Ham United for Ray Stewart, 1979
£750,000 from Tottenham Hotspur for Richard Gough*, 1986
£950,000 from Coventry City for Kevin Gallacher*, 1990
£4,000,000 from Rangers for Duncan Ferguson*, 1993

The record transfer fee paid by the club (based on press reports) has risen as follows:

£3,000 to Alloa Athletic for Dennis Gillespie*, 1959
£10,000 to Kilmarnock for Kenny Cameron*, 1968
£27,500 to Hamilton Accies for Paul Hegarty*, 1974
£40,000 to Dumbarton for Tom McAdam, 1975
£60,000 to Dumbarton for John Bourke, 1977
£100,000 to Motherwell for Willie Pettigrew*, 1979
£165,000 to Chelsea for Eamonn Bannon*, 1979
£200,000 to Newcastle United for Darren Jackson, 1988; to Red Star Belgrade for Miodrag Krivokapic*, 1988; to Sporting Lisbon for Raphael

Meade, 1988; to BVV Den Bosch for Freddy van der Hoorn, 1989
£350,000 to Newcastle United for Michael O'Neill*, 1989; to San Lorenzo for Victor Ferreyra, 1991
£600,000 to Partizan Belgrade for Gordan Petric*, 1993
£750,000 to Coventry City for Steven Pressley, 1995

TRINIDAD & TOBAGO

Largely as a result of the transfer of Jerren Nixon* in 1993, United undertook a four-match end-of-season tour to his home in the Caribbean islands in May and June of the following year. As it turned out, United's Scottish Cup triumph the week before departure meant the visit was more like a carnival, and the players quite rightly enjoyed themselves.

Three games were played against the Trinidad & Tobago national team, all of which were drawn 1–1. Because a trophy had been put up for competition by the Trinidad & Tobago FA, a winner had to be found and the hosts won it on a penalty shoot-out. A further game was also played against a Tobago XI, which ended 4–2 in United's favour.

TURKEY

The two occasions on which United had contact with Turkish football were not happy ones. The first occurred when they were drawn against Bursaspor in the second round of the 1974/75 European Cup Winners' Cup competition. United could not find a way past the Turks' defence in the goalless first leg at Tannadice, but the visitors had clearly come intent on preventing such a loss. United were subjected to intimidation on their visit to Bursa, including being kept awake by an all-night racket outside their hotel. The atmosphere was no less hostile in the ground and this doubtless contributed to their 0–1 defeat in a match they ought to have won.

The qualifying round of the UEFA Cup in 1997 paired Tommy McLean's team with Trabzonspor. With Turkish football enjoying something of a renaissance following the national side's performance in the Euro96 championship, United were clearly the underdogs. However, a controlled performance in Trabzon restricted the home side to a 1–0 lead and that from a disputed penalty. The return at Tannadice produced a determined attacking display from United which had its reward in a goal after an hour. However, they could not create a second and, as so often happens in Europe, a late defensive lapse allowed the Turks to equalise, rendering the tie irretrievable.

UEFA CUP

This tournament adopted its present name in 1971, hitherto having been known as the Fairs Cup*. United have qualified for the UEFA Cup on 15 occasions, playing a total of 74 ties. The club reached the quarter-finals in both 1981/82 and 1982/83 but, of course, their finest hour came in the 1986/87 competition.

In fact, that great run might have ended almost before it had begun. United's first-round opponents were the French club RC Lens and the hosts had numerous opportunities to put the tie beyond United's reach in the first leg in Picardy. However, a combination of French profligacy and exceptional form from keeper Billy Thomson restricted the score to 0–1, one which was wiped out in the return at Tannadice. There was no such hesitancy in the two rounds which followed, Romanians Universitatea Craiova and Hadjuk Split from Yugoslavia* being comfortably overcome, admitting United to the quarter-finals for the third time in six years.

There was great excitement, matched only by a sense of anticipation, when the draw, in a reprise of the Fairs Cup contest of 1966, brought Barcelona to Tannadice. Before two minutes had been played, a goal from Kevin Gallacher* had United ahead and the Spanish side, which included Gary Lineker and Mark Hughes, could make no impression thereafter. The return at the Nou Camp appeared to be heading for extra-time after Barca scored in the first half, but goals by John Clark and Iain Ferguson in the last five minutes propelled United into the semi-final and brought the club to the attention of Europe, with a vengeance.

Nevertheless, that did not prevent their next opponents, Borussia Moenchengladbach, underestimating Jim McLean's* team, which by now had perfected the art of the counter-attacking game required to succeed in Europe. It might reasonably have been assumed that United's impressive advance to the semi-final, allied to relatively fresh memories of their 5–0 defeat of the Germans in 1981, would have prevented complacency; not so. Borussia clearly believed they had done all that was necessary in drawing 0–0 at Tannadice, the return at the Bokelberg Stadium, in their eyes, assuming an air of formality. In what was arguably their most effective ever away performance in Europe, United swept aside any such notions, goals from Iain Ferguson and Ian Redford landing the prize of a final place which even few Arabs* would have believed possible six months earlier.

It would be difficult, if not impossible, to overestimate the importance to Dundee United of reaching the final of a European competition. A glance at the clubs which had contested previous finals of the UEFA Cup illustrates the point, and their meetings with IFK Gothenburg thrust Dundee United onto centre stage in an unprecedented manner. That point is underlined by the fact that an estimated television audience of 70 million watched live transmission of the second leg from Tannadice Park – a mark of the level to which Jim McLean had raised United in his 14 years as manager.

The record books show that the Swedes won 1–0 in Gothenburg, with the return ending 1–1. So, the UEFA Cup did not come to Tannadice, but there was not a single United supporter at Tannadice on 20 May 1987 who uttered the word 'failure' that evening; how could they? Bringing a European final to Dundee was an astonishing achievement and one of which everyone associated with Dundee United was, and remains, justifiably proud.

UNDERSOIL HEATING

Installed during the close season of 1985 at a reported cost of £100,000, United were the fourth Scottish club to have the facility, following Queen's Park, Rangers and Hibernian. The undersoil heating was first used for the UEFA Cup tie against Neuchatel Xamax on 27 November 1985.

UNEMPLOYED GATE

At the height of the Depression during the 1930s, unemployment was at unprecedented levels throughout the country and was generally accepted as being the main cause of attendances at football matches falling alarmingly. This was hardly surprising, but few Scottish League clubs took advantage of special permission granted by the SFA for an unemployed gate to operate at Scottish Cup ties. It seems that most clubs claimed they could not afford to forego a substantial part of their income, but it is pleasing to note that, despite their own serious financial difficulties, Dundee United were prepared to adopt a more altruistic approach.

The provision was introduced in 1932 and United first put it into practice for a replay with Queen of the South. It attracted a crowd of 11,900, more than 5,000 of whom went through the unemployed gate, paying sixpence instead of the normal admission of one shilling. The replay was drawn and a third match was played, at Ibrox. Although Rangers did not operate an unemployed gate for their home matches, because both United and Queens agreed, it was used for their decider. United won 2–1, watched by 13,000, of whom 6,000 had been admitted for half price. This qualified United for a home tie with Kilmarnock, and again almost half of the crowd entered by the unemployed gate. Just how many extra spectators were attracted by the reduced admission could not be known, but it was clear that the gesture was a costly one to those clubs which chose to operate it.

Because then, as now, Cup gates were shared between the competing clubs, both had to agree to an unemployed gate being provided. The following year, St Johnstone consented for their visit to Tannadice, but in 1935 Hearts refused permission. The Edinburgh club claimed to have based their decision on the spurious grounds that it could lead to overcrowding, a strange concern for a visiting club. There is no evidence of the practice being used the following season and it seems likely it was withdrawn.

UNION OF SOVIET SOCIALIST REPUBLICS
In all United's travels throughout Europe, not once were they drawn against a club from the USSR. They did, however, meet Spartak Moscow in an end-of-season tournament at Leon, Spain in 1975, when the Soviet club won 2–1.

UNITED JUNIORS FC
In July 1940 the Scottish League voted to suspend itself until the conclusion of the Second World War. The larger clubs then formed their own competition, but rejected the approaches of some clubs, including Dundee United, which had been in the Second Division, to be allowed to join.

Despite having no senior options open to them, the United directors declined to follow Dundee FC and close down for the duration of the war. They decided instead to adopt junior status and the club was accepted into membership of the Scottish Junior FA. Eventually this was ruled out by the SFA on the grounds that it was not possible to hold simultaneous membership of the two associations.

Showing considerable ingenuity, a new club was formed and given the name United Juniors. Manager Jimmy Allan* and Sam Irving*, one of the directors, resigned their positions to run the new club and the playing staff showed a remarkable similarity to Dundee United's the previous season; leasing Tannadice Park for the season completed the metamorphosis.

Although Dundee United's period of inactivity lasted just one season, United Juniors continued until 1944. They had to return most of the players, but Allan remained and they continued to use Tannadice as their home.

UNITED STATES OF AMERICA
United's first two visits to the USA to play in the North American Soccer

League* (1967) and the International League* (1969) are documented under these headings. A third visit was made in 1987 to participate in the Los Angeles Gold Cup, where they met Mexico's Guadalajara and San Lorenzo of Argentina.

URUGUAY

United have only once met a club from Uruguay, losing 1–4 to Cerro of Montevideo in New York during the North American Soccer League* in June 1967.

Two players from that country have joined Dundee United. Jose-Luis Pochettino arrived on trial in 1992, making only two substitute appearances before moving on. In January 1995, Juan Ferreri was signed by Ivan Golac*; he also appeared only as a substitute, in his case once. He remained on the club's books during their sojourn in the First Division, though he spent most of the time in his native country. He was freed at the end of that season.

V

VALE OF LEVEN FC

Vale of Leven were one of the giants in the early days of Scottish football, completing a historic hat-trick of Scottish Cup wins between 1877 and 1879.

Not to be confused with the East of Scotland League club Vale of Leithen, this Dunbartonshire club are still in existence today, playing in the Central Junior League at the same ground, Millburn Park, Alexandria, as they did when they were founder members of the Scottish League in 1890.

Vale of Leven were in Division Two when Dundee Hibs joined it in 1910, and their first League meeting came in a 1–1 draw at Tannadice in October of that year. The clubs' paths continued to cross regularly until Vale were relegated to Division Three, but they met only once on League business after Dundee United came into being, a 1–1 draw at Millburn Park in March 1924.

There was one further meeting, however, in the 1927 Scottish Cup, by which time United were in Division One while Vale of Leven had descended to the Scottish Alliance*. Not surprisingly, United won the tie, at Tannadice, 4–1.

The full Scottish League record against Vale of Leven was:
P 14 W 4 D 5 L 5 F 19 A 19

Guido VAN DE KAMP (born 1964)

A member of United's first Scottish Cup-winning squad and a major contributor to that triumph, his safe and often spectacular goalkeeping denying Rangers an equaliser at Hampden Park.

Having joined from Dutch club BVV Den Bosch at the bargain price of only £40,000 in July 1991, he had to await an injury to Alan Main before making his debut. Guido then enjoyed an extensive run during 1992/93, but had reverted to second choice when the following season began. Indeed he had yet to make a first-team appearance that season when Main was again injured in January 1994, but from that point the tall Dutchman never looked back.

Ironically, the Cup final turned out to be his last game for the club. He became embroiled in a dispute with the management over a fee for signing a new contract, and eventually returned to Holland, able only to play amateur football. More than a year later he returned to Scotland, Dunfermline having paid United a nominal fee, and he won a championship medal as his new club edged out his old one in the race for the 1995/96 First Division title. Despite that, he could not command a place on the club's return to the Premier Division and was given a free transfer in June 1997, following which he remained in Fife, joining Raith Rovers.

Dundee United playing record (1991–94)

	Appearances
Scottish League	53
Scottish Cup	10
League Cup	1
Scottish Cup winner 1994	

VICTORY CUP

In 1940, the SFA donated a trophy to be played for by members of the wartime Southern League*. It took the form of a cup competition, and was the forerunner of the Scottish League Cup, which followed it in 1946/47.

The SFA reclaimed the trophy, renamed it the Victory Cup (for obvious reasons), and put it up for a one-off competition. The two-legged first round was as far as United progressed; they were drawn against Queen of the South in April 1946, winning 2–1 at home but losing 1–3 at Palmerston Park.

Rangers won the trophy and were allowed to keep it.

WALES

United's only contact with the Principality was a weekend tour in April 1951, when matches were played against Swansea Town (now City) and Llanelli.

Gordon WALLACE (born 1943)

Currently in his third spell at Tannadice, two of them in a non-playing capacity. A free-scoring centre forward, he had a highly successful playing career, first with Montrose, then Raith Rovers, where he won the Scottish PFA Player of the Year award in 1968, a remarkable achievement for a player with such an unfashionable club. Having joined Dundee FC, he scored the only goal of the 1973 League Cup final to take the trophy to Dens Park.

After a brief taste of football in the USA he signed for United from Seattle Sounders in 1976 and in two seasons at Tannadice played an influential role in helping Jim McLean* develop the fine young squad of home-grown players which brought the club its first trophy in 1979.

By then Gordon had left to become player/manager and then manager at his old stamping ground, Raith Rovers. He spent five years in management at Stark's Park and after leaving was appointed coach at Tannadice in 1983. He left to become manager of Dundee and also spent some time as assistant manager at Dunfermline before returning to Tannadice as a coach under Ivan Golac* in the summer of 1993.

Gordon Wallace holds the distinction of being the oldest player to make a first-team appearance for Dundee United, albeit in an emergency. The coach was aged 50 when he played the full 90 minutes against a Tobago XI on the club's visit to the Caribbean in May 1994.

Dundee United playing record (1976–78)

	Appearances	Goals
Scottish League	39	16
Scottish Cup	1	

League Cup	9	3
European competitions	2	

WARTIME FOOTBALL

During both world wars, government opinion was that senior football in some form should continue, so as to provide a necessary distraction from the austerity and dislocation of the times. Although Britain declared war on Germany and Austria in August 1914, there was no attempt by the football authorities to abandon, or even delay, the Scottish League programme due to begin later that month. The season was played to a conclusion and only then, when it became clear that the conflict would not be short-lived, was any action taken. Even at that, the competition was not suspended, merely restricted to one division.

This left the Division Two clubs out in the cold, but they lost no time in making alternative arrangements, on a geographical basis in order to minimise travel. Dundee Hibs played in the Eastern League*, and remained there between 1915 and 1918.

With the war entering its fifth year, a number of clubs were facing financial difficulties and the Hibs were one of those forced to withdraw from organised football; the following season the club played only friendly and charity matches. With the armistice of November 1918 it was assumed that normal Scottish League arrangements would be resumed for 1919/20. When that did not happen, the Hibs joined a different version of the Eastern League*.

On the outbreak of the Second World War in September 1939, the Scottish League acted much more decisively. The competition was immediately suspended, then, less than a month later, abandoned. The League also convened a meeting at which regional leagues were organised for what it was hoped would be just one season.

Dundee United played in the Eastern Regional League* and had a good season, making full use of the professional players who had returned to the area. This enabled the club to reach its first national cup final, the Emergency War Cup* being the Scottish Cup in all but name.

By the summer of 1940 the conflict was spreading at a rate which suggested it would continue for some considerable time, and the Scottish League decided to suspend all competitions and go into abeyance for the duration of the war. Some clubs followed suit, but others decided to arrange their own competition, again on a regional basis. Dundee United wanted to continue and initially attempted to play as a junior club, but eventually the board conceded that closure would be the best option. So the club did not play a match at all during 1940/41, but did reappear for the following season, being one of eight clubs which formed the North Eastern League*.

In common with most clubs – Rangers were probably the only exception – Dundee United had no signed players between 1941 and 1945. Although clubs did retain the registrations of players who had been on their books when the war started, as with all other men of their age, footballers were called up to one of the armed forces and posted to every theatre of war. However, at any one time there were also a considerable number stationed in Britain, and a fair number of them were in Scotland. Football clubs had to rely on tip-offs as to what former professional players were stationed in their area and then follow these up, negotiating with their commanding officers for their release at weekends. As they were still, notionally at least, registered with their clubs, those clubs had to be contacted and asked to issue clearance for them to play as guests with a club close to where they were stationed. This seems incredibly bureaucratic during a time of national emergency, but it seems it was adhered to nonetheless.

United's secretary manager Arthur Cram* proved adept at obtaining the necessary information on what players were available and travelled widely throughout Scotland and the north of England to arrange their release. Clearly, with a rag-bag of individuals being assembled, rarely the same ones from one match to the next, there was little need for a team manager as such. Presumably, after introducing them to each other, there was little he could utter beyond a cheery 'good luck'.

Dundee United performed modestly during the period 1941–45, but it was thanks very largely to Cram that they performed at all. Dundee FC could not be bothered to make the effort until 1944 and spent the period from 1940 in hibernation.

United remained in the North Eastern League until 1945, when football in Scotland was restructured. Clubs based in the south and west had played in a competition called the Southern League* and it was amalgamated with the North Eastern League to form countrywide A and B divisions. Unsurprisingly, United were in the latter and the following year that was the structure which the Scottish League adopted when it emerged from six years of hibernation.

Brian WELSH (born 1969)

Signed from Tynecastle Boys Club in June 1985, he made his debut two years later, but managed only a further seven appearances over the three seasons which followed and was not a first-team regular until 1993/94, which he ended as a member of United's first Scottish Cup-winning team.

Known for his power in the air, the 6ft 2in central defender used it to excellent effect on two major occasions. In April 1994, Brian scored an 88th-minute equaliser against Aberdeen in the Scottish Cup semi-final at Hampden Park. Two years later he rescued United from a second season in the First Division with a dramatic last-gasp headed goal against Partick Thistle, taking the play-off into extra-time.

Soon afterwards, he became embroiled in a contractual dispute and was transferred to Hibernian for £200,000 in August 1996.

214

Dundee United playing record (1987–96)

	Appearances	Goals
Scottish League	140	10
Scottish Cup	15	3
League Cup	13	1
League Challenge Cup	2	
European competitions	7	
Scotland youth	16	
Scottish Cup winner 1994		

Lennart WING (born 1935)

One of the Scandinavians brought to Tannadice by manager Jerry Kerr*, he arrived in January 1965. There being no professional football in Sweden at the time, Lennart worked as a firefighter and cost Kerr only a signing-on fee when he joined from the Gothenburg club Orgryte, from whom United also signed his colleague, Orjan Persson*.

He shares with Persson the distinction of becoming Dundee United's first full international, when the pair played for Sweden against Cyprus in 1965.

The rugged Swede stayed at Tannadice for just over two years, but his strength and determination made him the commanding figure in defence, which United required at the time.

In 1967 Wing returned to Sweden, where he resumed both his playing career with Orgryte and his firefighting duties.

Dundee United playing record (1965–67)

	Appearances	Goals
Scottish League	68	9
Scottish Cup	7	
League Cup	7	
European competitions	4	
Sweden	7	

WINS
Most in succession

United have twice recorded nine successive victories: between 11 November and 30 December 1950 (all in B Division); and between 24 January and 18 March 1981 (six Premier Division, 3 Scottish Cup).

Curiously, the most successive victories in the Premier Division exceeds that figure. Ten in a row were established, involving the last five matches of season 1982/83 and the first five of the following campaign.

Longest run without a win

After beating Dunfermline Athletic at Tannadice on 5 December 1953, United did not win again until 20 March 1954. In between, they lost eight and drew five B Division matches and also lost a Scottish Cup tie.

The club played 13 matches without a win between 1 November 1975 and 24 January 1975. Twelve of these were in the Premier Division (seven defeats and five draws, a club record for the division), and the other was a drawn UEFA Cup tie.

Most in a League season

United have twice won 24 (66%) of 36 League games during a season, and on each occasion took the championship. Few would argue, however, that the feat was more notable in the Premier Division of 1982/83 than in the Division Two campaign of 1928/29.

Biggest

The 14–0 Scottish Cup victory at the expense of non-League Nithsdale Wanderers on 17 January 1931 will take some displacing as the all-time club record. The 8–0 defeat of Brechin City at Glebe Park on 27 October 1934 in a Division Two fixture stood as the overall away record for more than 60 years but was equalled on 23 July 1997 against CE Principat in the UEFA Cup.

Scottish League

Home 12–1 v East Stirling, Division Two, 13.4.36
9–0 v Stirling Albion, Division One, 30.12.67
8–0 v Stenhousemuir Division Two, 16.3.35
v Dumbarton, Division Two, 28.12.35
v Dumbarton, First Division, 2.12.95
8–1 v King's Park, Division Two, 3.3.34
v Forfar Athletic, B Division, 12.1.52
v Berwick Rangers, B Division, 21.4.56

Away 8–0 v Brechin City, Division Two, 27.10.34
8–1 v Queen's Park, Division Two, 12.9.59
7–0 v Ayr United, Division One, 24.9.66
8–2 v Edinburgh City, Division Two, 15.12.34
6–0 v Berwick Rangers, Division Two, 25.12.56
v Morton, Division One, 14.12.74
7–2 v Raith Rovers, Division One, 2.3.63

Premier Division

Home 7–0 v Kilmarnock, 3.1.81
v Kilmarnock, 11.12.82

v St Johnstone, 12.9.83
v Morton, 17.11.84
Away   5–0 v Kilmarnock, 12.2.83
v Hamilton Acad.,14.1.89

Scottish Cup
Home 14–0 v Nithsdale Wanderers, 17.1.31
Away   7–0 v Arbroath Athletic, 19.1.27
v Arbroath, 30.1.88

League Cup
Home   8–0 v Hamilton Acad., 9.9.64
Away   6–2 v Hamilton Acad., 24.11.79

European competitions
Home   9–0 v CE Principat, UEFA Cup, 30.7.97
Away   8–0 v CE Principat, UEFA Cup, 23.7.97

XENOPHOBIA

Though they might not have used the term, United's (and their fans') fear of strangers must have been at its height when they lost ten out of 19 League games at Tannadice in season 1931/32, the worst home record in their history. The last seven were all lost, with 32 goals conceded in the process.

X-FILES

See Hampden Hoodoo!

XMAS DAY

Until the 1970s, it was commonplace for Xmas Day to feature a full League programme; prior to World War Two, where the day did not fall on a Saturday, clubs often arranged local cup-ties. Since the introduction of the Premier Division in 1975, and taking account of changing social traditions, where Xmas Day falls on a Saturday the League programme is delayed until the following Monday.

Between them, Dundee Hibs and United played on Xmas Day on 13 occasions between 1909 and 1971.

Y

Ron YEATS (born 1937)

A schoolboy international (U-15), he joined up at Tannadice from Aberdeen Lads' Club in 1957 and was a mainstay of the team which secured United's promotion to Division One in 1959/60. A commanding figure at the centre of the defence, very little got past him. The 6ft 2in centre half brought the club its first big transfer fee when he joined Liverpool for £30,000 in 1961.

Ron gained two Scotland caps while with Liverpool, where he also won League championship and FA Cup winners' medals. He later played with, and then managed, Tranmere Rovers, remaining on Merseyside when his career ended. For several years he has been employed as a scout by Liverpool.

Dundee United playing record (1958–61)

	Appearances	Goals
Scottish League	95	1
Scottish Cup	9	
League Cup	14	

YOUNGEST

The youngest first-team player in the club's history was Ian Mitchell*. He was aged 16 years and four months when he made his debut against Hibernian in Division One in September 1962. Sadly, he died in 1996 at the age of only 50.

Both Francis Munro and Christian Dailly* were aged 16 years and ten months when they made their first appearances, with Munro the younger by eleven days. Both scored on their debuts, and both in League Cup ties, Munro against Falkirk in August 1964 and Dailly against Alloa Athletic in August 1990.

Graeme Payne* was the youngest player to appear for United in a Scottish Cup final when he faced Celtic in 1974 aged 18 years and two months.

The youngest player to appear for the club in a European competition was Christian Dailly. He played against the Icelandic club Hafnafjordur the month after making his first-team debut.

YOUTH TEAM

Since Jim McLean* took over as manager in 1971, great importance has been placed on rearing the club's own stars of the future, as an alternative to relying on the transfer market. McLean and his coaches have for many years signed promising young players from various parts of Scotland and offered them regular coaching sessions in their own localities. These 'schools' have been particularly successful in the west of Scotland, producing players who went on to achieve international honours such as Andy Gray* during the 1970s, Kevin Gallacher* in the 1980s and Billy McKinlay* in the 1990s.

However, Dundee itself and the surrounding area has been the most fertile territory for the club, many players gracing the United first team and then going on to win full international honours. Dave Narey*, Paul Sturrock*, Dave Dodds*, Maurice Malpas* and Christian Dailly* span Jim McLean's tenure as manager and they, and others, are a huge tribute to the standards set, and maintained, by Dundee United.

Ralph Milne (third left) *pictured with members of United's youth team, including Dave Dodds* (extreme right). *People did actually dress like this in 1978!*

Over the years, the United youth team has been less successful than might have been expected in the BP Youth Cup, although the greatest prize for the club has always been seen as the progress of a young player into the first team; in that respect, over the past 25 years no other club in Scotland comes close to United's record. In terms of trophies, the youth team won the BP Youth Cup in 1990 and 1991 and won the Premier Youth League (established in 1994) for the first time in season 1996/97. Clearly, the future remains in good hands.

YUGOSLAVIA

The most obvious connection with the country which until 1992 was known as Yugoslavia is Ivan Golac*. His period of a year and eight months as the club's twentieth manager carried a significance out of all proportion to its longevity. Involving the long-awaited Scottish Cup triumph, it also laid the foundations for the club's relegation, two months after his departure, for the first time in 63 years. Nonetheless, his influence on the club and, most importantly, the players was immense and his was a reign which made an indelible mark not just on Dundee United, but on Scottish football.

One of Golac's overseas signings was his fellow Serb, central defender Gordan Petric*, who was a rock at the heart of the United defence during his two years at Tannadice. He created a club record fee of £650,000 when he signed from Partizan Belgrade, and he cost Rangers £1.5m when they took him to Ibrox in August 1995. The other Yugoslav who wore the tangerine was no less accomplished, but stayed considerably longer. Miodrag Krivokapic* arrived from Red Star Belgrade for £200,000 in the summer of 1988. The Yugoslav international defender (he was from Montenegro) was capped four times while with Red Star and he gained one more while with United. In 1990 he played for Yugoslavia B against a Scotland B team which included Billy McKinlay*. Unassuming but unflappable, he quickly settled and became a regular and extremely reliable part of United's team over the following four seasons. A member of the 1991 Cup final side, he was transferred to Motherwell* later that year, and to Raith Rovers in 1996.

Dragutin Ristic, a Croatian, spent just one season at Tannadice after being signed by Ivan Golac from Falkirk during the close season of 1994.

During the 1980s, Yugoslavia was a regular destination for United on their European travels, three visits taking them to various parts of that now fragmented state. The first occurred in 1982, for the UEFA Cup quarter-final. The opponents were Radnicki Nis from Serbia. A semi-final place was there for the taking following a 2–0 first leg gained at Tannadice, but the return in Nis proved disastrous, culminating in a dubious penalty which gave the home side the decisive third goal.

The UEFA Cup of 1985/86 paired United with Vardar Skopje from what is now Macedonia. Again the first leg at home produced a 2–0 lead, but this time United proved better organised and were able to progress to the next round thanks to a 1–1 draw.

The following season, Yugoslavia was again one of United's ports of call, this time literally. The historic Croatian city of Split, which was virtually destroyed in the civil war a few years later, was the destination, the opposition the highly experienced Hajduk. Once more, United built a 2–0 home advantage, evoking memories of Nis. But on this occasion they were composed and confident in the face of fierce pressure in the return, holding out for a goalless draw on their way to that season's final.

Since the break-up of Yugoslavia (which now comprises only Serbia and Montenegro) United have visited the country only once, and it was as a result of Ivan Golac's connections. In December 1994, home and away friendlies were arranged with Partizan Belgrade, the club which Golac had both played for and managed and from which Gordan Petric had been signed. United lost both, 0–3 in the Yugoslav capital and 0–1 at Tannadice.

Z

ZENITH

Such a judgement is necessarily subjective and arguments around such issues are meat and drink to the vast majority of football supporters.

For many Arabs, United winning the League championship in 1983 will be regarded as the club's finest hour, while others may opt for the Scottish Cup triumph in 1994. Either would be understandable and perfectly justifiable, but perhaps the UEFA Cup final in 1987 – despite the outcome – represents the pinnacle of Dundee United's achievements; only by actually winning a European trophy could it be exceeded. There's only one way to find out . . .